THE MUSIC AND WORSHIP PLANNER 1995–1996

David L. Bone
Mary J. Scifres

Abingdon Press
Nashville

THE MUSIC AND WORSHIP PLANNER, 1995–1996

Copyright © 1995 by Abingdon Press

All rights reserved.

No part of this work, with the exception of pages 141-44, may be reproduced or transmitted in any form or by any means, electronic or mechanical, including photocopying and recording, or by any information storage or retrieval system, except as may be expressly permitted by the 1976 Copyright Act or in writing from the publisher. Requests for permission should be addressed in writing to Abingdon Press, 201 Eighth Avenue South, Nashville, TN 37203.

This book is printed on acid-free , recycled paper.

ISBN 0-687-00192-7

Scripture quotations are from the New Revised Standard Version Bible, copyright © 1989 by the Division of Christian Education of the National Council of the Churches of Christ in the USA. Used by permission.

95 96 97 98 99 00 01 02 03 04 — 10 9 8 7 6 5 4 3 2 1

MANUFACTURED IN THE UNITED STATES OF AMERICA

CONTENTS

USING THIS PLANNER

This Planner is designed to give you as many ideas as possible about a given worship service. It is designed to be used along with a worship plan notebook that you create, and a copy of your church's hymnal.

If you are a previous user of this Planner, you will notice several changes in the layout. There have been two major changes.

- The "Hymn and Keyboard Suggestions" now contain a notation as to the copyright status of the hymns. If a hymn is in the public domain, it is marked (PD). This means that you may legally copy this hymn without obtaining further permission. You may find this useful if a hymn is not in your hymnal. Please be advised: The (PD) mark only refers to the hymn that it follows, not all hymns in the listing. Many times an arrangement in one hymnal may be public domain but another arrangement of the same hymn tune in another hymnal may be under copyright.
- The descriptions of the "Hymn Anthem Suggestions" are now found in another resource, *52 Instant Hymn Anthems*. This has created more room for hymn and anthem suggestions in the Planner and allowed the hymn anthem descriptions to be more complete. Information about this collection is found on page 7.

Other features of the Planner remain.
- The suggestions for each week are chosen to suggest a wide variety of styles and to use your hymnal to its fullest.
- Praise hymns and choruses are listed under "Hymn Suggestions," but may also serve as "Calls to Worship" and responses.
- Each item is referenced to scripture or occasion.
- At least one communion hymn is recommended for the first Sunday of each month and liturgical season.
Suggestions for opening (O) and closing (C) hymns are listed each week.

When planning any worship service, it is always best to start with the scripture and let it guide your thoughts and plans. Decide how the other aspects of the service can enhance, augment, and support the proclamation of the Word. If your church is not using the Revised Common Lectionary, but you do know what the scripture will be for a service, look up that scripture in the Index of Scriptures Referenced on page 136. If it is contained in the lectionary during the period covered by this Planner, you can use the suggestions even though you may be using them on a different day.

Read the scripture; study it. Compare it with related or parallel passages. As you do this, keep a list of key phrases, words, and concepts as well as worship ideas, hymns, and anthems that come to mind. Compare your list of ideas with those given in the Planner. Let the ideas in the Planner spark your own creativity.

As you plan, read all of the suggested hymn texts. List other ideas and key words or phrases. The hymns may remind you of anthems, solos, or keyboard selections. It is wise to mark your hymnal with the dates individual hymns are sung to avoid singing some too frequently. The "Hymn Resources" (see p. 6) can enhance congregational singing, but should be used sparingly.

Use a three-ring binder to organize your plans. For each service of worship, include a copy of one of the Worship Planning Sheets found on pages 141-42 (or design your own!) along with blank paper for listing further ideas. Do not simply "fill in the blanks" for each service, but use the Planning Sheet to guide your work.

If the Planner is new to you, you will want to be aware of several other items. The keyboard suggestions are taken from a group of fifteen collections that were chosen for their accessibility and easy to moderate level of difficulty (see p. 6). The suggestions are based on the suggested hymns. Add to this list selections from your own library.

Likewise, the vocal suggestions are also taken from a group of ten collections that range from contemporary settings of hymn texts to spirituals to well-known classics (see p. 6). Augment these suggestions from your own library.

The anthem suggestions include new works as well as generally known works that are already in many church choral libraries. Your study of the scripture and hymn texts will lead you to anthems in your church library that are appropriate. Several anthem suggestions in this year's Planner are taken from the musical *A Season to Celebrate* by Allen Pote. The purchase of this one volume may prove to be a wise use of limited funds.

The other suggestions for each service are varied in their intent and function. Add to this list as you study the scripture and hymn texts.

Use the suggestions in the Planner along with your own page of ideas to begin making decisions about worship. Will the choir sing a "Call to Worship"? Can a hymn verse serve as a prayer response? Can a particular anthem or vocal solo give direction to the sermon? What prayers will be used?

Once your decisions are made, complete the Worship Planning Sheet. Make a separate list of tasks related to that service. Planning worship is an awesome responsibility, but one that can be accomplished with an organized effort along with spiritual guidance.

PLANNING CORPORATE WORSHIP

Planning worship provides an important opportunity for church staff members to work together as a team. Such planning also provides a vehicle in which worship committees can begin to find an important aspect of their ministry. Perhaps the most common worship planning model in churches looks something like this:

1. Preaching pastor picks the scripture readings, often choosing one or more of the common lectionary readings.
2. Preaching pastor chooses a sermon topic to correspond to the reading(s).
3. Preaching pastor chooses hymns to correspond to sermon topic for coming Sunday.
4. Preaching pastor writes or chooses liturgical responses, readings, prayers for bulletin minutes before the last printing deadline.
5. Church secretary or pastor types and prints bulletins.
6. Choir director and/or organist picks up note in mailbox with hymn numbers for coming Sunday. If time permits, choir rehearses hymns during evening rehearsal. Anthem(s) and choral responses for Sunday (which were chosen at least a month ago) are rehearsed as well.
7. Preaching pastor writes sermon.
8. Lay liturgist arrives early on Sunday morning to mark scripture passages and read over bulletin.
9. Worship commences.

Is this how worship most often comes together in your church? If so, you may want to consider other models for planning worship. Many pastors find this model the most convenient because all decisions are made by one person (the preacher) with the exception of the organ prelude/postlude/offertory music and choral anthems. But this model may not be the most efficient, and it is certainly not the most integrated.

With this resource, we hope that many pastors, musicians, and worship leaders will find encouragement and assistance in planning worship in advance and in cooperation with one another. Perhaps the "convenient" model will one day be the exception rather than the rule.

As an alternative, we suggest that all members of the worship planning team meet at last biannually. Some worship teams find weekly, monthly, or seasonal planning meetings helpful, but even two meetings a year can improve communication and coordinate efforts immensely. However often one plans, pastors need to know the time requirements for planning music. Each choir director can communicate to the pastor the average length of time needed to pick an anthem, order the anthem, and rehearse it prior to a Sunday morning performance. Each organist can communicate to the pastor the average length of time needed to pick an organ anthem, order the music, and rehearse it prior to a Sunday morning performance. Likewise, both organist and choir director need to alert the pastor of the time needed to prepare the Sunday morning hymns prior to the Sunday of performance. (Pastors may discover that an organist's playing or a choir's singing improves greatly on hymns rehearsed a few weeks in advance rather than a few days in advance!) Finally, the musicians can communicate with the pastor what their visions are for music ministry as a part of the worship service.

Pastors, likewise, need to inform musicians of special needs for musical support. Some pastors establish cues that alert the musician that light background music is needed during an unexpected situation in worship. A pastor can tell the musicians what expectations are regarding worship leadership roles (i.e., to listen attentively to the sermon, to face the cross during the Doxology, to stand as a hymn introduction begins, to face the congregation during hymn singing). Additionally, the pastor can communicate with the musicians what her or his visions are for music ministry as a part of the worship service.

These initial communications are essential when the worship planners begin to work together and when there are personnel changes in the worship planning team. Many models for the actual planning might be used, but one such model to help a team in starting integrated planning is as follows. In order to use this model, the team needs several copies of this Planner (particularly for use of scripture readings and hymn lists) and a Bible (if lectionary is not being used or for team members who do not have access to a copy of this Planner). Musicians may find it helpful to have copies of each of the music collections suggested in this guide, as well as a single copy file of the anthem collection of your church. Copies of the Worship Planning Sheets from pages 141-42 can be distributed to each team member for each Sunday being discussed.

1. Prior to meeting, the pastor(s) need to have prepared preliminary scripture and sermon outlines; musicians need to have prepared repertoire lists as well as repertoire wish lists.

2. Team meets for a designated time period. (A retreat setting is appropriate, especially if this is to be only a biannual event.)

3. Meeting opens with prayer and discussion of worship and what it means to each team member. There is no need to come up with one particular philosophy or purpose of worship; the diversity in team members' opinions can enhance the planning and implementing processes.

4. Scriptures are read over (perhaps in advance of meeting), and specific scriptures are selected for each Sunday being planned.

5. Sermon topics or emphases are introduced and outlined by the pastor(s).

6. Seasonal needs are discussed and outlined.

7. Hymns are chosen by team, keeping in mind thematic and scriptural emphases; musical abilities; sermon topics; congregational hymn preferences; and desire for introduction of new hymns in a helpful way.

8. Special ideas or plans for specific worship services are introduced and discussed (i.e., Palm Sunday cantata, Christmas Eve candlelight service, scripture drama, children's Sunday, laity Sunday).

9. Liturgy is chosen (by team or part of team, depending on the number of people participating).

10. Vocal, choral, and keyboard music is chosen (by team or part of team, depending on the number of people participating).

11. Services are reviewed for integration and unity as well as diversity.

12. Concerns regarding specific services are discussed.

13. Meeting closes with a brief hymn sing and prayer.

At any one of these steps, all members of the planning team may have valuable input. A pastor may have an idea for a choral anthem to enhance a sermon idea; a musician may have an insight into a sermon topic as it relates to the congregation. At any of these steps, all members of the team will find helpful suggestions in this Planner. The text of each scripture reading is provided, season and color are noted, hymn and music suggestions are offered, liturgical suggestions are provided and other ideas are mentioned that may spark interest in an innovative type of worship service occasionally.

Worship planning need not be a point of departure for a worship staff. Rather, it can be a point of unity and team building. The team that works together models corporate worship for the congregation. If we expect people to walk in the church doors on Sunday morning from their many walks of life to have a corporate experience, we need to review any Lone Ranger approaches with which we have planned worship services previously. In so doing, we may find that the Holy Spirit has found a new freedom in which to work.

RESOURCE KEY

HYMNALS REFERENCED

B   Forbis, Wesley, ed. *The Baptist Hymnal*. Nashville: Convention Press, 1991.

E   *The Hymnal 1982*. New York: The Church Hymnal Corporation, 1985.

F   Bock, Fred, ed. *Hymns for the Family of God*. Nashville: Paragon Associates, Inc., 1976.

L   *Lutheran Book of Worship*. Minneapolis: Augsburg Publishing House, 1978.

P   McKim, LindaJo, ed. *The Presbyterian Hymnal*. Louisville: Westminster/John Knox Press, 1990.

UM   Young, Carlton R., ed. *The United Methodist Hymnal*. Nashville: The United Methodist Publishing House, 1989.

W   Batastini, Robert J., ed. *Worship*. Chicago: GIA Publications, Inc., 1986.

HYMN RESOURCES

H-1   Noble, T. Tertius. *Free Organ Accompaniments to 100 Well-Known Hymn Tunes*. New York: J. Fischer, 1946. Edition #8175.

H-2   Wood, Dale. *New Settings of Twenty Well-Known Hymn Tunes*. Minneapolis: Augsburg Publishing House, 1968. Catalogue #11-9292.

S-1   Smith, Gary Alan, ed. *The United Methodist Hymnal Music Supplement*. Nashville: Abingdon Press, 1991.

S-2   Bennett, Robert C., ed. *The United Methodist Hymnal Music Supplement II*. Nashville: Abingdon Press, 1993.

KEYBOARD SUGGESTION RESOURCES

K-1 (I-IV)   Fleischer, Heinrich, ed. *The Parish Organist (Parts I-IV)*. St. Louis: Concordia Publishing House, 1963. Catalogue #97-1473. Originally published in four volumes. Currently available in one collection, but reference is made to original volumes for those who may own them.

K-2   Peeters, Flor. *Thirty Short Preludes on Well-Known Hymns, Op. 95*. New York: C. F. Peters, 1960. Edition #6195.

K-3   *Preludes and Postludes, vol. 2*. Minneapolis: Augsburg Publishing House, 1973. Catalogue #11-9319. Various composers.

K-4   Pfatteicher, Carl F., and Davison, Archibald T., eds. *The Church Organist's Golden Treasury, vol. 2*. Bryn Mawr, Pa.: Oliver Ditson Company, 1951.

K-5   Pfatteicher, Carl F., and Davison, Archibald T., eds. *The Church Organist's Golden Treasury, vol. 3*. Bryn Mawr, Pa.: Oliver Ditson Company, 1951.

K-6   Lyon, Sharron, ed. *All Hail the Power*. Nashville: Broadman Press, 1976. Catalogue #4570-31.

K-7   Powell, Robert J., arr. *Nine Service Pieces for the Church Year*. Delaware Water Gap, Pa.: Harold Flammer Music, 1992. Catalogue #HF-5194.

K-8   Lyon, Sharron, ed. *Come, All Christians, Be Committed*. Nashville: Genovox, 1989. Catalogue #4570-97.

K-9   *A Galaxy of Hymn-Tune Preludes for Organ*. New York: Galaxy Music Corp., 1966.

K-10   Owen, Barbara, ed. *International Collection of Nineteenth-Century Hymn Tune Preludes*. Melville, N.Y.: McAfee Music, 1982. DM-233.

K-11   Bristol, Lee Hastings, Jr., ed. *The Bristol Collection of Contemporary Hymn Tune Preludes for Organ, vol. 2*. Delaware Water Gap, Pa.: Harold Flammer, 1975. HF-5078.

K-12   Bristol, Lee Hastings, Jr., ed. *The Bristol Collection of Contemporary Hymn Tune Preludes for Organ, vol. 3*. Delaware Water Gap, Pa.: Harold Flammer, 1975. HF-5082.

K-13   Wyrtzen, Don, comp. *Sunday Morning Favorites for Piano, vol. 2*. Nashville: Benson, 1992. Catalogue #25984-0398-7.

K-14   Gerig, Reginald, arr. *Piano Preludes on Hymns and Chorales*. Carol Stream, Ill.: Hope Publishing Company, 1959. Catalogue #251.

K-15   Bock, Fred, arr. *Bock's Best, vol. 4*. Fred Bock Music, 1991. Catalogue #BGO880.

VOCAL SUGGESTION RESOURCES

V-1   Kimbrough, Steven, ed. *Sweet Singer: Hymns of Charles Wesley*. Chapel Hill, N.C.: Hinshaw Music Inc., 1987. Catalogue #CV-1.

V-2   Handel, George Frideric. *Messiah*. Various editions available.

V-3   Courtney, Craig. *Music for the Master*. Columbus, Ohio: Beckenhorst Press, Inc., 1988. Catalogue #VC1.

V-4   Scott, K. Lee, ed. *Sing a Song of Joy*. Minneapolis: Augsburg Fortress, 1989. Catalogue #11-8194.

V-5   Burleigh, Harry T., arr. *The Spirituals of Harry T. Burleigh*. Miami: CPP/Belwin Mills Inc., 1984. Catalogue #EL3151.

V-6   Wolford, Darwin, ed. *Songs of Praise by Contemporary Composers.* Delaware Water Gap, Pa.: Harold Flammer, Inc., 1975. Catalogue #IA-5052.

V-7   Caldwell, Mary Elizabeth. *A Celebration of Melody.* Dayton, Ohio: Lorenz Corp., 1982. Catalogue #TUO 140.

V-8   Pfautsch, Lloyd, ed. *Solos for the Church Year.* New York: Lawson-Gould Music Publishers, Inc., 1957. High and low voice editions available.

V-9   Michaels, Ruth. *The Church Year in Song.* New York: G. Schirmer, 1978. Edition #3104.

V-10   Harrell, Mack, ed. *The Sacred Hour of Song.* New York: Carl Fischer, 1939. Catalogue #278754-62

HYMN ANTHEM RESOURCES

52IHA   Bone, David L. *52 Instant Hymn Anthems.* Nashville: Abingdon Press, 1995.

HA   Morgan, Julia. *Hymnal Anthems for the Church Year.* Nashville: Abingdon Press, 1992.

Jeremiah 2:4-13

⁴Hear the word of the LORD, O house of Jacob, and all the families of the house of Israel. ⁵Thus says the LORD: What wrong did your ancestors find in me that they went far from me, and went after worthless things, and became worthless themselves? ⁶They did not say, "Where is the LORD who brought us up from the land of Egypt, who led us in the wilderness, in a land of deserts and pits, in a land of drought and deep darkness, in a land that no one passes through, where no one lives?" ⁷I brought you into a plentiful land to eat its fruits and its good things. But when you entered you defiled my land, and made my heritage an abomination. ⁸The priests did not say, "Where is the LORD?" Those who handle the law did not know me; the rulers transgressed against me; the prophets prophesied by Baal, and went after things that do not profit. ⁹Therefore once more I accuse you, says the LORD, and I accuse your children's children. ¹⁰Cross to the coasts of Cyprus and look, send to Kedar and examine with care; see if there has ever been such a thing. ¹¹Has a nation changed its gods, even though they are no gods? But my people have changed their glory for something that does not profit. ¹²Be appalled, O heavens, at this, be shocked, be utterly desolate, says the LORD, ¹³for my people have committed two evils: they have forsaken me, the fountain of living water, and dug out cisterns for themselves, cracked cisterns that can hold no water.

Psalm 81:1, 10-16

¹Sing aloud to God our strength; shout for joy to the God of Jacob.
¹⁰I am the LORD your God, who brought you up out of the land of Egypt. Open your mouth wide and I will fill it. ¹¹"But my people did not listen to my voice; Israel would not submit to me. ¹²So I gave them over to their stubborn hearts, to follow their own counsels. ¹³O that my people would listen to me, that Israel would walk in my ways! ¹⁴Then I would quickly subdue their enemies, and turn my hand against their foes. ¹⁵Those who hate the LORD would cringe before him, and their doom would last forever. ¹⁶I would feed you with the finest of the wheat, and with honey from the rock I would satisfy you."

Hebrews 13:1-8, 15-16

¹Let mutual love continue. ²Do not neglect to show hospitality to strangers, for by doing that some have entertained angels without knowing it. ³Remember those who are in prison, as though you were in prison with them; those who are being tortured, as though you yourselves were being tortured. ⁴Let marriage be held in honor by all, and let the marriage bed be kept undefiled; for God will judge fornicators and adulterers. ⁵Keep your lives free from the love of money, and be content with what you have; for he has said, "I will never leave you or forsake you." ⁶So we can say with confidence,
"The Lord is my helper;
I will not be afraid.
What can anyone do to me?"
⁷Remember your leaders, those who spoke the word of God to you; consider the outcome of their way of life, and imitate their faith. ⁸Jesus Christ is the same yesterday and today and forever.
¹⁵Through him, then, let us continually offer a sacrifice of praise to God, that is, the fruit of lips that confess his name. ¹⁶Do not neglect to do good and to share what you have, for such sacrifices are pleasing to God.

Luke 14:1, 7-14

¹On one occasion when Jesus was going to the house of a leader of the Pharisees to eat a meal on the sabbath, they were watching him closely.
⁷When he noticed how the guests chose the places of honor, he told them a parable. ⁸"When you are invited by someone to a wedding banquet, do not sit down at the place of honor, in case someone more distinguished than you has been invited by your host; ⁹and the host who invited both of you may come and say to you, 'Give this person your place,' and then in disgrace you would start to take the lowest place. ¹⁰But when you are invited, go and sit down at the lowest place, so that when your host comes, he may say to you, 'Friend, move up higher'; then you will be honored in the presence of all who sit at the table with you. ¹¹For all who exalt themselves will be humbled, and those who humble themselves will be exalted."
¹²He said also to the one who had invited him, "When you give a luncheon or a dinner, do not invite your friends or your brothers or your relatives or rich neighbors, in case they may invite you in return, and you would be repaid. ¹³But when you give a banquet, invite the poor, the crippled, the lame, and the blind. ¹⁴And you will be blessed, because they cannot repay you, for you will be repaid at the resurrection of the righteous."

Hymn and Keyboard Suggestions
O– "How Firm a Foundation" (Heb.)
    B338, E636, F32, L507, P361, UM529 (PD), W585
    S-1   #133. Harmonization
           #134. Performance note
    K-6   p. 24. Prelude/postlude
    K-11   p. 37. Prelude/meditation
    E637
    H-1   #37. Harmonization
    S-1   #223-26. Various treatments
    K-8   p. 17. Introduction
"We Utter Our Cry" (Jer.)
    UM439
    S-2   #145. Descant
           #146. Harmonization
    B631
    H-1   #37. Harmonization
    S-1   #223-26. Various treatments
    K-8   p. 17. Introduction
"You Satisfy the Hungry Heart" (Ps., Communion)
    P521, UM629, W736
    S-1   #144. Four-part setting of refrain
"Christ Is the King!" (Heb.)
    W500
    H-2   p. 36. Harmonization with descant
    S-1   #137. Descant
    K-11   p. 15. Postlude
    E614, L386
"All My Hope Is Firmly Grounded" (Heb.)
    E665, UM132
"O Jesus, I Have Promised" (Heb.)
    B276, F402, P388, UM396 (PD)
    S-2   #9. Descant
    L503 (PD)
    H-1   #64. Harmonization
    S-1   #243. Harmonization
    K-1(II) #63. Prelude/meditation
    E655, P389
"Saranam, Saranam" ("Refuge") (Heb.)
    UM523
    S-1   #273. Performance note
    S-2   #147. Descant
           #148. Harmonization
"Come, Ye Sinners, Poor and Needy" (Luke)
    B323 (PD), UM340, W756
    S-1   #283. Choral harmonization
           (UM340 only)

C– "Lord, Whose Love Through Humble Service" (Luke)
    L423, UM581
    S-2   #22. Descant
    K-8   p. 2. Prelude
    W630
    H-1   #25. Harmonization
    S-1   #178. Harmonization
           #179. Harmonization
    E610

Vocal Solos
"A Contrite Heart" (Jer.)
V-4   p. 10
"Go Down Moses" (Jer., Ps.)
V-5   p. 42
"Come Sunday" (Heb.)
UM728
"Come, All of You" (Luke)
UM350

Anthems
"Wondrous Love" (Heb.)
arr. Robert A. Boyd
Mark Foster MF265
SATB *a cappella*

"Song of Gentleness" (Heb., Luke)
Douglas Wagner
Beckenhorst Press BP1192
Unison with keyboard or handbells

Hymn Anthem Suggestions
"How Firm a Foundation" (Heb.)
52IHA #23
"What Does the Lord Require" (Jer., Ps.)
52IHA #49
"You Satisfy the Hungry Heart" (Ps., Communion)
52IHA #52
"Come, Ye Sinners, Poor and Needy" (Luke)
52IHA #10

Other Suggestions
Call to Worship: E665, UM132, stanza 1. "All My Hope Is Firmly Grounded"
Psalm Response: E710. "Make a Joyful Noise" (Ps.)
Prayer: UM409. For Grace to Labor (Labor Day)
Prayer: UM423. Finding Rest in God (Labor Day)
Benediction: E665, stanza 5. "All My Hope Is Firmly Grounded"

Jeremiah 18:1-11

[1]The word that came to Jeremiah from the LORD: [2]"Come, go down to the potter's house, and there I will let you hear my words." [3]So I went down to the potter's house, and there he was working at his wheel. [4]The vessel he was making of clay was spoiled in the potter's hand, and he reworked it into another vessel, as seemed good to him.

[5]Then the word of the LORD came to me: [6]Can I not do with you, O house of Israel, just as this potter has done? says the LORD. Just like the clay in the potter's hand, so are you in my hand, O house of Israel. [7]At one moment I may declare concerning a nation or a kingdom, that I will pluck up and break down and destroy it, [8]but if that nation, concerning which I have spoken, turns from its evil, I will change my mind about the disaster that I intended to bring on it. [9]And at another moment I may declare concerning a nation or a kingdom that I will build and plant it, [10]but if it does evil in my sight, not listening to my voice, then I will change my mind about the good that I had intended to do to it. [11]Now, therefore, say to the people of Judah and the inhabitants of Jerusalem: Thus says the LORD: Look, I am a potter shaping evil against you and devising a plan against you. Turn now, all of you from your evil way, and amend your ways and your doings.

Psalm 139:1-6, 13-18

[1]O LORD, you have searched me and known me. [2]You know when I sit down and when I rise up; you discern my thoughts from far away. [3]You search out my path and my lying down, and are acquainted with all my ways. [4]Even before a word is on my tongue, O LORD, you know it completely. [5]You hem me in, behind and before, and lay your hand upon me. [6]Such knowledge is too wonderful for me; it is so high that I cannot attain it.

[13]For it was you who formed my inward parts; you knit me together in my mother's womb. [14]I praise you, for I am fearfully and wonderfully made. Wonderful are your works; that I know very well. [15]My frame was not hidden from you, when I was being made in secret, intricately woven in the depths of the earth. [16]Your eyes beheld my unformed substance. In your book were written all the days that were formed for me, when none of them as yet existed. [17]How weighty to me are your thoughts, O God! How vast is the sum of them! [18]I try to count them—they are more than the sand; I come to the end—I am still with you.

Philemon 1-21

[1]Paul, a prisoner of Christ Jesus, and Timothy our brother,

To Philemon our dear friend and co-worker, [2]to Apphia our sister, to Archippus our fellow soldier, and to the church in your house:

[3]Grace to you and peace from God our Father and the Lord Jesus Christ.

[4]When I remember you in my prayers, I always thank my God [5]because I hear of your love for all the saints and your faith toward the Lord Jesus. [6]I pray that the sharing of your faith may become effective when you perceive all the good that we may do for Christ. [7]I have indeed received much joy and encouragement from your love, because the hearts of the saints have been refreshed through you, my brother.

[8]For this reason, though I am bold enough in Christ to command you to do your duty, [9]yet I would rather appeal to you on the basis of love—and I, Paul, do this as an old man, and now also as a prisoner of Christ Jesus. [10]I am appealing to you for my child, Onesimus, whose father I have become during my imprisonment. [11]Formerly he was useless to you, but now he is indeed useful both to you and to me. [12]I am sending him, that is, my own heart, back to you. [13]I wanted to keep him with me, so that he might be of service to me in your place during my imprisonment for the gospel; [14]but I preferred to do nothing without your consent, in order that your good deed might be voluntary and not something forced. [15]Perhaps this is the reason he was separated from you for a while, so that you might have him back forever, [16]no longer as a slave but more than a slave, a beloved brother—especially to me but how much more to you, both in the flesh and in the Lord.

[17]So if you consider me your partner, welcome him as you would welcome me. [18]If he has wronged you in any way, or owes you anything, charge that to my account. [19]I, Paul, am writing this with my own hand: I will repay it. I say nothing about your owing me even your own self. [20]Yes, brother, let me have this benefit from you in the Lord! Refresh my heart in Christ. [21]Confident of your obedience, I am writing to you, knowing that you will do even more than I say.

Luke 14:25-33

[25]Now large crowds were traveling with him; and he turned and said to them, [26]"Whoever comes to me and does not hate father and mother, wife and children, brothers and sisters, yes, and even life itself, cannot be my disciple. [27]Whoever does not carry the cross and follow me cannot be my disciple. [28]For which of you, intending to build a tower, does not first sit down and estimate the cost, to see whether he has enough to complete it? [29]Otherwise, when he has laid a foundation and is not able to finish, all who see it will begin to ridicule him, [30]saying, 'This fellow began to build and was not able to finish.' [31]Or what king, going out to wage war against another king, will not sit down first and consider whether he is able with ten thousand to oppose the one who comes against him with twenty thousand? [32]If he cannot, then, while the other is still far away, he sends a delegation and asks for the terms of peace. [33]So therefore, none of you can become my disciple if you do not give up all your possessions."

Hymn and Keyboard Suggestions

O– "And Are We Yet Alive" (Luke)
      UM553 (PD)
        H-1   #78. Harmonization

O– "I'll Praise My Maker While I've Breath" (Ps.)
      B35, E429 (PD), P253, UM60
        S-2   #141. Harmonization

"Have Thine Own Way, Lord" (Jer.)
      B294, F400, UM382 (PD)
        S-2   #2. Instrumental descant
        K-13   p. 41. Piano prelude/meditation

"My Lord, What a Morning" (Jer.)
      P449, UM719

"Immortal, Invisible, God Only Wise" (Ps.)
      B6, E423, F319, L526, P263, UM103 (PD), W512
        H-2   p. 28. Harmonization with descant
        S-1   #300. Harmonization

"Creating God, Your Fingers Trace" (Ps.)
      UM109
        S-2   #96. Descant
      E394, P134

"Lord, Thou Hast Searched Me" (Ps.)
      E702

"You Are Before Me, Lord" (Ps.)
      P248

"Tú Has Venido a la Orilla" ("Lord, You Have Come to the Lakeshore") (Ps.)
      P377, UM344

"Dear Lord, Lead Me Day by Day" (Ps.)
      B459, UM411
        S-2   #45. Flute descant

"Help Us Accept Each Other" (Philem.)
      UM560
        S-2   #1. Descant
      P358, W656

"Where He Leads Me" (Luke)
      B288, F607, UM338 (PD)

"This Is a Day of New Beginnings" (Luke)
      B370, UM383, W661

"Must Jesus Bear the Cross Alone" (Luke)
      B475, F504, UM424 (PD)

"Sois la Semilla" ("You Are the Seed") (Luke)
      UM583

"This Little Light of Mine" (Luke)
      UM585

C– "Take Up Thy Cross" (Luke)
      UM415 (PD)
        S-1   #141. Harmonization
                #142-43. Descant and transposition in A major
      B494, E675, L398, P393, W634

Vocal Solos

"My Lord, What a Morning" (Jer.)
V-5   p. 30
"I Know De Lord's Laid His Hands On Me" (Luke)
V-5   p. 90

Anthems

"Galilee Man" in *A Season to Celebrate* (Ps.)
Allen Pote
Hinshaw Music HMB 144
Unison women with keyboard

"Immortal, Invisible, God Only Wise" (Ps.)
Barbara Terry
Chantry Music
Unison with guitar and drums

"The Greeting Song" (Philem.)
Kevin Jeff Herrick
Broadman 4551-82
SATB with keyboard

Hymn Anthem Suggestions

"My Lord, What a Morning" (Jer.)
52IHA   #34
"Tú Has Venido a la Orilla" ("Lord, You Have Come to the Lakeshore") (Ps.)
52IHA   #47
"This Is a Day of New Beginnings" (Luke)
52IHA   #43
"This Little Light of Mine" (Luke)
52IHA   #45

Other Suggestions

Canticle: UM205. Canticle of Light and Darkness (Ps.)
Scripture Response: UM453, stanza 2. "More Love to Thee, O Christ" (Luke)
Benediction: UM256, stanza 5. "We Would See Jesus" (Luke)

Jeremiah 4:11-12, 22-28

[11]At that time it will be said to this people and to Jerusalem: A hot wind comes from me out of the bare heights in the desert toward my poor people, not to winnow or cleanse—[12]a wind too strong for that. Now it is I who speak in judgment against them.

[22]"For my people are foolish, they do not know me; they are stupid children, they have no understanding. They are skilled in doing evil, but do not know how to do good." [23]I looked on the earth, and lo, it was waste and void; and to the heavens, and they had no light. [24]I looked on the mountains, and lo, they were quaking, and all the hills moved to and fro. [25]I looked, and lo, there was no one at all, and all the birds of the air had fled. [26]I looked, and lo, the fruitful land was a desert, and all its cities were laid in ruins before the LORD, before his fierce anger.

[27]For thus says the LORD: The whole land shall be a desolation; yet I will not make a full end. [28]Because of this the earth shall mourn, and the heavens above grow black; for I have spoken, I have purposed; I have not relented nor will I turn back.

Psalm 14

[1]Fools say in their hearts, "There is no God." They are corrupt, they do abominable deeds; there is no one who does good. [2]The LORD looks down from heaven on humankind to see if there are any who are wise, who seek after God. [3]They have all gone astray, they are all alike perverse; there is no one who does good, no, not one. [4]Have they no knowledge, all the evildoers who eat up my people as they eat bread, and do not call upon the LORD? [5]There they shall be in great terror, for God is with the company of the righteous. [6]You would confound the plans of the poor, but the LORD is their refuge. [7]O that deliverance for Israel would come from Zion! When the LORD restores the fortunes of his people, Jacob will rejoice; Israel will be glad.

1 Timothy 1:12-17

[12]I am grateful to Christ Jesus our Lord, who has strengthened me, because he judged me faithful and appointed me to his service, [13]even though I was formerly a blasphemer, a persecutor, and a man of violence. But I received mercy because I had acted ignorantly in unbelief, [14]and the grace of our Lord overflowed for me with the faith and love that are in Christ Jesus. [15]The saying is sure and worthy of full acceptance, that Christ Jesus came into the world to save sinners—of whom I am the foremost. [16]But for that very reason I received mercy, so that in me, as the foremost, Jesus Christ might display the utmost patience, making me an example to those who would come to believe in him for eternal life. [17]To the King of the ages, immortal, invisible, the only God, be honor and glory forever and ever. Amen.

Luke 15:1-10

[1]Now all the tax collectors and sinners were coming near to listen to him. [2]And the Pharisees and the scribes were grumbling and saying, "This fellow welcomes sinners and eats with them."

[3]So he told them this parable: [4]"Which one of you, having a hundred sheep and losing one of them, does not leave the ninety-nine in the wilderness and go after the one that is lost until he finds it? [5]When he has found it, he lays it on his shoulders and rejoices. [6]And when he comes home, he calls together his friends and neighbors, saying to them, 'Rejoice with me, for I have found my sheep that was lost.' [7]Just so, I tell you, there will be more joy in heaven over one sinner who repents than over ninety-nine righteous persons who need no repentance.

[8]"Or what woman having ten silver coins, if she loses one of them, does not light a lamp, sweep the house, and search carefully until she finds it? [9]When she has found it, she calls together her friends and neighbors, saying, 'Rejoice with me, for I have found the coin that I had lost.' [10]Just so, I tell you, there is joy in the presence of the angels of God over one sinner who repents."

Hymn and Keyboard Suggestions
O– "Immortal, Invisible, God Only Wise" (1 Tim.)
        B6, E423, F319, L526, P263, UM103, W512
          H-2   p. 28. Harmonization with descant
          S-1   #300. Harmonization
  "Steal Away to Jesus" (Jer., Ps., Luke)
        UM704
          K-7   p. 6. Prelude
  "My Lord, What a Morning" (Jer., Ps., Luke)
        P449, UM719
  "Out of the Depths I Cry to You" (Ps.)
        L295, P240, UM515
          K-14   p. 18. Piano prelude
  "Saranam, Saranam" ("Refuge") (Ps.)
        UM523
          S-1   #273. Performance note
          S-2   #147. Descant
                    #148. Harmonization
  "Abide with Me" (Ps.)
        B63, E662, F500, L272, P543, UM700
          H-1   #100. Harmonization
          S-2   #58. Harmonization
          K-1(I) #24. Prelude/meditation (may be played manuals only)
  "Depth of Mercy" (1 Tim.)
        UM355
          S-1   #53. Descant
        B306
  "Grace Greater than Our Sin" (1 Tim.)
        B329, F105, UM365
          S-1   #240. Descant idea
          S-2   #124. Harmonization
  "Amazing Grace" (1 Tim.)
        B330, E671, F107, L448, P280, UM378, W583
          S-2   #5. Piano arrangement
                    #6. Descant
                    #7. Harmonization
          K-15   p. 146. Piano prelude/meditation
  "Come, Thou Fount of Every Blessing" (1 Tim., Luke)
        B15, E686, F318, L499, P356, UM400
          S-1   #244. Descant
        B18
  "Source and Sovereign, Rock and Cloud" (Luke)
        UM113
  "How Like a Gentle Spirit" (Luke)
        UM115
  "O God Who Shaped Creation" (Luke)
        UM443
        E392, W552
C– "Marching to Zion" (Luke)
        B524, F550, UM733

C– "Come, We That Love the Lord" (Luke)
        B525
          S-1   #129. Descant
        UM732
          H-1   #3a. Harmonization
          S-1   #311. Descant
                    #312. Harmonization
          K-1(III) #78. Short prelude/postlude (may be played manuals only)
          K-2   p. 29. Short prelude/postlude (manuals only)

Vocal Solos
"Steal Away" (Jer., Ps., Luke)
V-5   p. 14
"My Lord, What a Morning" (Jer., Ps., Luke)
V-5   p. 30
"Amazing Grace" (1 Tim.)
V-3   p. 8

Anthems
"Immortal, Invisible" (1 Tim.)
Ellen Jane Lorenz
Abingdon APM-222
SATB with organ

"In Heavenly Love" (Luke)
John Ness Beck
Choristers Guild
Unison youth or children

"The King of Love My Shepherd Is" (Luke)
Harry Rowe Shelley
Plymouth, no # or G. Schirmer
SATB with alto solo and keyboard

Hymn Anthem Suggestions
"My Lord, What a Morning" (Jer., Ps., Luke)
52IHA   #34
"Out of the Depths I Cry to You" (Ps.)
52IHA   #39
"Come, Thou Fount of Every Blessing" (1 Tim., Luke)
52IHA   #9
"How Like a Gentle Spirit"
52IHA   #24

Other Suggestions
Call to Confession: B306, UM355 (PD), stanza 1. "Depth of Mercy" (1 Tim.)
Response to Confession: B306, UM355 (PD), stanza 4. "Depth of Mercy" (1 Tim.)
Prayer: UM535. A Refuge amid Distraction (Ps.)

Jeremiah 8:18–9:1

[18]My joy is gone, grief is upon me, my heart is sick. [19]Hark, the cry of my poor people from far and wide in the land: "Is the LORD not in Zion? Is her King not in her?" ("Why have they provoked me to anger with their images, with their foreign idols?") [20]"The harvest is past, the summer is ended, and we are not saved." [21]For the hurt of my poor people I am hurt, I mourn, and dismay has taken hold of me. [22]Is there no balm in Gilead? Is there no physician there? Why then has the health of my poor people not been restored?

[1]O that my head were a spring of water, and my eyes a fountain of tears, so that I might weep day and night for the slain of my poor people!

Psalm 79:1-9

[1]O God, the nations have come into your inheritance; they have defiled your holy temple; they have laid Jerusalem in ruins. [2]They have given the bodies of your servants to the birds of the air for food, the flesh of your faithful to the wild animals of the earth. [3]They have poured out their blood like water all around Jerusalem, and there was no one to bury them. [4]We have become a taunt to our neighbors, mocked and derided by those around us. [5]How long, O LORD? Will you be angry forever? Will your jealous wrath burn like fire? [6]Pour out your anger on the nations that do not know you, and on the kingdoms that do not call on your name. [7]For they have devoured Jacob and laid waste his habitation. [8]Do not remember against us the iniquities of our ancestors; let your compassion come speedily to meet us, for we are brought very low. [9]Help us, O God of our salvation, for the glory of your name; deliver us, and forgive our sins, for your name's sake.

1 Timothy 2:1-7

[1]First of all, then, I urge that supplications, prayers, intercessions, and thanksgivings be made for everyone, [2]for kings and all who are in high positions, so that we may lead a quiet and peaceable life in all godliness and dignity. [3]This is right and is acceptable in the sight of God our Savior, [4]who desires everyone to be saved and to come to the knowledge of the truth. [5]For

there is one God;

there is also one mediator

between God and humankind,

Christ Jesus, himself human,

[6]who gave himself a ransom for all

—this was attested at the right time. [7]For this I was appointed a herald and an apostle (I am telling the truth, I am not lying), a teacher of the Gentiles in faith and truth.

Luke 16:1-13

[1]Then Jesus said to the disciples, "There was a rich man who had a manager, and charges were brought to him that this man was squandering his property. [2]So he summoned him and said to him, 'What is this that I hear about you? Give me an accounting of your management, because you cannot be my manager any longer.' [3]Then the manager said to himself, 'What will I do, now that my master is taking the position away from me? I am not strong enough to dig, and I am ashamed to beg. [4]I have decided what to do so that, when I am dismissed as manager, people may welcome me into their homes.' [5]So, summoning his master's debtors one by one, he asked the first, 'How much do you owe my master?' [6]He answered, 'A hundred jugs of olive oil.' He said to him, 'Take your bill, sit down quickly, and make it fifty.' [7]Then he asked another, 'And how much do you owe?' He replied, 'A hundred containers of wheat.' He said to him, 'Take your bill and make it eighty.' [8]And his master commended the dishonest manager because he had acted shrewdly; for the children of this age are more shrewd in dealing with their own generation than are the children of light. [9]And I tell you, make friends for yourselves by means of dishonest wealth so that when it is gone, they may welcome you into the eternal homes.

[10]"Whoever is faithful in a very little is faithful also in much; and whoever is dishonest in a very little is dishonest also in much. [11]If then you have not been faithful with the dishonest wealth, who will entrust to you the true riches? [12]And if you have not been faithful with what belongs to another, who will give you what is your own? [13]No slave can serve two masters; for a slave will either hate the one and love the other, or be devoted to the one and despise the other. You cannot serve God and wealth."

Hymn and Keyboard Suggestions

O– "We Believe in One True God" (1 Tim.)
　　L374
　　　　K-5　　p. 176. Various keyboard treatments,
　　　　　　　　　　through p. 181
　　P137 (PD)
　　　　K-5　　p. 181. Various keyboard treatments,
　　　　　　　　　　through p. 183
　　UM85 (PD)
　　　　H-1　　#29. Harmonization
　　　　S-1　　#278. Harmonization
　　　　　　　#279. Harmonization
"There Is a Balm in Gilead" (Jer.)
　　B269 (PD), E676, F48, P394, UM375, W608
　　　　S-2　　#21. Descant
"Jesus, Lover of My Soul" (Jer.)
　　E699, F222, P303, UM479 (PD)
　　　　S-1　　#6. Descant
　　　　K-9　　p. 10. Prelude/postlude
　　B180 (PD)
"O Love That Wilt Not Let Me Go" (Jer.)
　　B292, F404, L324, P384, UM480 (PD)
"Here, O Lord, Your Servants Gather" (Jer.)
　　B179, P465, UM552
　　　　S-1　　#333. Orff arrangement
　　　　S-2　　#178. Flute descant
"I Want a Principle Within" (Jer., Ps.)
　　UM410 (PD)
"O Thou, in Whose Presence" (Jer., Ps.)
　　UM518
　　　　S-2　　#46. Choral harmonization
　　　　　　　#47. Instrumental arrangement
"God of Many Names" (1 Tim.)
　　UM105
　　　　S-1　　#227. Performance note
"Jesús Es Mi Rey Soberano" ("O Jesus, My King and My
　　Sovereign") (Luke)
　　P157, UM180
"Nothing Between" (Luke)
　　UM373 (PD)
"More Love to Thee, O Christ" (Luke)
　　B473, F476, P359, UM453 (PD)
C– "Dear Lord and Father of Mankind" (Jer., Ps.)
　　B267, E652, F422, L506, P345, UM358 (PD)
　　　　H-1　　#70. Harmonization
　　　　S-2　　#151. Introduction
　　　　　　　#152. Violin descant
　　E653

Vocal Solos

"There Is a Balm in Gilead" (Jer.)
　　V-5　　p. 111
"Jesus, Lover of My Soul" (Jer.)
　　V-1　　p. 37
"O Love, That Wilt Not Let Me Go" (Jer.)
　　V-7　　p. 49
"Serenity" (Jer., Ps.)
　　UMH　　#499

Anthems

"Forgive Us" in *A Season to Celebrate* (Ps.)
Allen Pote
Hinshaw Music HMB 144
SATB with keyboard and optional guitar, bass, and flute

"There Is One God and One Savior" (English/German)
　　(1 Tim.)
Johann Geisler (ed. Nolte)
Boosey & Hawkes 5600
SSAB with organ

"One God" (1 Tim.)
Drake and Shirl (arr. Ringwald)
Shawnee Press A-329
SATB with keyboard

Hymn Anthem Suggestions

"Here, O Lord, Your Servants Gather" (Jer.)
52IHA　　#22
"O Thou, in Whose Presence" (Jer., Ps.)
52IHA　　#38

Other Suggestions

　　Both the opening and closing hymn texts are in the public domain and can be rewritten for more inclusivity.
　　Depending on how strictly you follow the lectionary, you may want to use this week's epistle lesson and corresponding suggestions for a focus on Christian unity on October 1 (World Communion Sunday).
Opening Prayer: UM677. Listen, Lord (Jer., Ps.)
Prayer: UM104. Praising God of Many Names (1 Tim.)
Response: UM471. "Move Me" (Luke)
Affirmation of Faith: UM85. "We Believe in One True
　　God" (1 Tim.)

Jeremiah 32:1-3a, 6-15

[1]The word that came to Jeremiah from the LORD in the tenth year of King Zedekiah of Judah, which was the eighteenth year of Nebuchadrezzar. [2]At that time the army of the king of Babylon was besieging Jerusalem, and the prophet Jeremiah was confined in the court of the guard that was in the palace of the king of Judah, [3]where King Zedekiah of Judah had confined him.

[6]Jeremiah said, The word of the LORD came to me: [7]Hanamel son of your uncle Shallum is going to come to you and say, "Buy my field that is at Anathoth, for the right of redemption by purchase is yours." [8]Then my cousin Hanamel came to me in the court of the guard, in accordance with the word of the LORD, and said to me, "Buy my field that is at Anathoth in the land of Benjamin, for the right of possession and redemption is yours; buy it for yourself." Then I knew that this was the word of the LORD.

[9]And I bought the field at Anathoth from my cousin Hanamel, and weighed out the money to him, seventeen shekels of silver. [10]I signed the deed, sealed it, got witnesses, and weighed the money on scales. [11]Then I took the sealed deed of purchase, containing the terms and conditions, and the open copy; [12]and I gave the deed of purchase to Baruch son of Neriah son of Mahseiah, in the presence of my cousin Hanamel, in the presence of the witnesses who signed the deed of purchase, and in the presence of all the Judeans who were sitting in the court of the guard. [13]In their presence I charged Baruch, saying, [14]Thus says the LORD of hosts, the God of Israel: Take these deeds, both this sealed deed of purchase and this open deed, and put them in an earthenware jar, in order that they may last for a long time. [15]For thus says the LORD of hosts, the God of Israel: Houses and fields and vineyards shall again be bought in this land.

Psalm 91:1-6, 14-16

[1]You who live in the shelter of the Most High, who abide in the shadow of the Almighty, [2]will say to the LORD, "My refuge and my fortress; my God, in whom I trust." [3]For he will deliver you from the snare of the fowler and from the deadly pestilence; [4]he will cover you with his pinions, and under his wings you will find refuge; his faithfulness is a shield and buckler. [5]You will not fear the terror of the night, or the arrow that flies by day, [6]or the pestilence that stalks in darkness, or the destruction that wastes at noonday.

[14]Those who love me, I will deliver; I will protect those who know my name. [15]When they call to me, I will answer them; I will be with them in trouble, I will rescue them and honor them. [16]With long life I will satisfy them, and show them my salvation.

1 Timothy 6:6-19

[6]Of course, there is great gain in godliness combined with contentment; [7]for we brought nothing into the world, so that we can take nothing out of it; [8]but if we have food and clothing, we will be content with these. [9]But those who want to be rich fall into temptation and are trapped by many senseless and harmful desires that plunge people into ruin and destruction. [10]For the love of money is a root of all kinds of evil, and in their eagerness to be rich some have wandered away from the faith and pierced themselves with many pains.

[11]But as for you, man of God, shun all this; pursue righteousness, godliness, faith, love, endurance, gentleness. [12]Fight the good fight of the faith; take hold of the eternal life, to which you were called and for which you made the good confession in the presence of many witnesses. [13]In the presence of God, who gives life to all things, and of Christ Jesus, who in his testimony before Pontius Pilate made the good confession, I charge you [14]to keep the commandment without spot or blame until the manifestation of our Lord Jesus Christ, [15]which he will bring about at the right time—he who is the blessed and only Sovereign, the King of kings and Lord of lords. [16]It is he alone who has immortality and dwells in unapproachable light, whom no one has ever seen or can see; to him be honor and eternal dominion. Amen.

[17]As for those who in the present age are rich, command them not to be haughty, or to set their hopes on the uncertainty of riches, but rather on God who richly provides us with everything for our enjoyment. [18]They are to do good, to be rich in good works, generous, and ready to share, [19]thus storing up for themselves the treasure of a good foundation for the future, so that they may take hold of the life that really is life.

Luke 16:19-31

[19]"There was a rich man who was dressed in purple and fine linen and who feasted sumptuously every day. [20]And at his gate lay a poor man named Lazarus, covered with sores, [21]who longed to satisfy his hunger with what fell from the rich man's table; even the dogs would come and lick his sores. [22]The poor man died and was carried away by the angels to be with Abraham. The rich man also died and was buried. [23]In Hades, where he was being tormented, he looked up and saw Abraham far away with Lazarus by his side. [24]He called out, 'Father Abraham, have mercy on me, and send Lazarus to dip the tip of his finger in water and cool my tongue; for I am in agony in these flames.' [25]But Abraham said, 'Child, remember that during your lifetime you received your good things, and Lazarus in like manner evil things; but now he is comforted here, and you are in agony. [26]Besides all this, between you and us a great chasm has been fixed, so that those who might want to pass from here to you cannot do so, and no one can cross from there to us.' [27]He said, 'Then, father, I beg you to send him to my father's house—[28]for I have five brothers—that he may warn them, so that they will not also come into this place of torment.' [29]Abraham replied, 'They have Moses and the prophets; they should listen to them.' [30]He said, 'No, father Abraham; but if someone goes to them from the dead, they will repent.' [31]He said to him, 'If they do not listen to Moses and the prophets, neither will they be convinced even if someone rises from the dead.' "

Hymn and Keyboard Suggestions

O– "Stand Up, Stand Up for Jesus" (1 Tim.)
      B485, E561, F616, L389, UM514 (PD)
          H-1   #90. Harmonization in A major
          S-2   #192. Introduction
                    #193. Descant
                    #194. Harmonization
          K-1(IV) #92. Prelude/postlude
      B487

O– "Sing Praise to God Who Reigns Above" (Ps.)
      B20, E408, F343, P483, UM126 (PD), W528
          S-1   #237. Descant
  "On Eagle's Wings" (Ps.)
      B71, UM143
          S-2   #143. Stanzas for soloist
  "It Is Well with My Soul" (Ps.)
      B410, F495, L346, UM377 (PD)
          K-13   p. 21. Piano prelude/meditation
          K-15   p. 126. Piano prelude/meditation
  "Within Your Shelter, Loving God" (Ps.)
      P212
  "Creator of the Earth and Skies" (1 Tim.)
      E148, UM450
  "I Sing a Song of the Saints of God" (1 Tim.)
      E293, P364, UM712 (PD)
          S-2   #68. Flute descant
  "Immortal, Invisible, God Only Wise" (1 Tim.)
      B6, E423, F319, L526, P263, UM103 (PD), W512
          H-2   p. 28. Harmonization with descant
          S-1   #300. Harmonization
  "Are Ye Able" (1 Tim., Luke)
      UM530 (PD)
          S-2   #23. Introduction
  "Cuando El Pobre" ("When the Poor Ones") (Luke)
      P407, UM434
  "One Bread, One Body" (World Communion)
      UM620
  "The Voice of God Is Calling" (Luke)
      UM436 (PD)
          S-2   #119. Descant
                    #120. Harmonization

C– "Take My Life, and Let It Be" (1 Tim.)
      B277 (PD), P391
          S-2   #78. Descant
                    #79. Harmonization
                    #80. Introduction
      E707
          H-1   #66. Harmonization
      L406 (PD)
          K-1(II) #71. Prelude/meditation
      B283 (PD), UM399 (PD)

Vocal Solos

"It Is Well with My Soul" (Ps.)
V-3   p. 3
"My Prayer Rises to Heaven" (Ps.)
UM498
"Take My Life" (1 Tim.)
V-3   p. 28

Anthems

"On Eagle's Wings" (Ps.)
Michael Joncas
Oregon Catholic Press
SATB with keyboard

"Be Strong and Courageous" (1 Tim.)
Michael W. Smith
Word Music
Unison with piano

"Poor Man Lazarus" (Luke)
arr. Jester Hairston
Bourne 2653-7
SATB *a cappella* (other voicings available)

"Father Abraham, Have Mercy on Me" (Luke)
H. Schutz
Concordia 97-9348
SSAT with tenor and bass solos and two violins and continuo

"We Sing One Common Lord" (World Communion)
John Carter
Hope Publishing JC307
SATB with keyboard

Hymn Anthem Suggestions

"O Thou, in Whose Presence" (Jer., Ps.)
52IHA   #38
"I Sing A Song of the Saints of God" (1 Tim.)
52IHA   #26
"Cuando El Pobre" ("When the Poor Ones") (Luke)
52IHA   #12

Other Suggestions

If flexibility with the lectionary is a possibility, consider using last week's epistle lesson from 1 Timothy and corresponding Planner suggestions for a World Communion focus on Christian unity.

Prayer: UM412. Prayer of John Chrysostom (World Communion)

Prayer: UM564. For the Unity of Christ's Body (World Communion)

Response: UM471. "Move Me" (Luke)

Response: UM488. "Jesus, Remember Me" (Luke)

Litany: UM556. Litany for Christian Unity (World Communion)

Lamentations 1:1-6

[1]How lonely sits the city that once was full of people! How like a widow she has become, she that was great among the nations! She that was a princess among the provinces has become a vassal. [2]She weeps bitterly in the night, with tears on her cheeks; among all her lovers she has no one to comfort her; all her friends have dealt treacherously with her, they have become her enemies. [3]Judah has gone into exile with suffering and hard servitude; she lives now among the nations, and finds no resting place; her pursuers have all overtaken her in the midst of her distress. [4]The roads to Zion mourn, for no one comes to the festivals; all her gates are desolate, her priests groan; her young girls grieve, and her lot is bitter. [5]Her foes have become the masters, her enemies prosper, because the LORD has made her suffer for the multitude of her transgressions; her children have gone away, captives before the foe. [6]From daughter Zion has departed all her majesty. Her princes have become like stags that find no pasture; they fled without strength before the pursuer.

Psalm 137

[1]By the rivers of Babylon—there we sat down and there we wept when we remembered Zion. [2]On the willows there we hung up our harps. [3]For there our captors asked us for songs, and our tormentors asked for mirth, saying, "Sing us one of the songs of Zion!" [4]How could we sing the LORD's song in a foreign land? [5]If I forget you, O Jerusalem, let my right hand wither! [6]Let my tongue cling to the roof of my mouth, if I do not remember you, if I do not set Jerusalem above my highest joy. [7]Remember, O LORD, against the Edomites the day of Jerusalem's fall, how they said, "Tear it down! Tear it down! Down to its foundations!" [8]O daughter Babylon, you devastator! Happy shall they be who pay you back what you have done to us! [9]Happy shall they be who take your little ones and dash them against the rock!

2 Timothy 1:1-14

[1]Paul, an apostle of Christ Jesus by the will of God, for the sake of the promise of life that is in Christ Jesus,

[2]To Timothy, my beloved child:

Grace, mercy, and peace from God the Father and Christ Jesus our Lord.

[3]I am grateful to God—whom I worship with a clear conscience, as my ancestors did—when I remember you constantly in my prayers night and day. [4]Recalling your tears, I long to see you so that I may be filled with joy. [5]I am reminded of your sincere faith, a faith that lived first in your grandmother Lois and your mother Eunice and now, I am sure, lives in you. [6]For this reason I remind you to rekindle the gift of God that is within you through the laying on of my hands; [7]for God did not give us a spirit of cowardice, but rather a spirit of power and of love and of self-discipline.

[8]Do not be ashamed, then, of the testimony about our Lord or of me his prisoner, but join with me in suffering for the gospel, relying on the power of God, [9]who saved us and called us with a holy calling, not according to our works but according to his own purpose and grace. This grace was given to us in Christ Jesus before the ages began, [10]but it has now been revealed through the appearing of our Savior Christ Jesus, who abolished death and brought life and immortality to light through the gospel. [11]For this gospel I was appointed a herald and an apostle and a teacher, [12]and for this reason I suffer as I do. But I am not ashamed, for I know the one in whom I have put my trust, and I am sure that he is able to guard until that day what I have entrusted to him. [13]Hold to the standard of sound teaching that you have heard from me, in the faith and love that are in Christ Jesus. [14]Guard the good treasure entrusted to you, with the help of the Holy Spirit living in us.

Luke 17:5-10

[5]The apostles said to the Lord, "Increase our faith!" [6]The Lord replied, "If you had faith the size of a mustard seed, you could say to this mulberry tree, 'Be uprooted and planted in the sea,' and it would obey you.

[7]"Who among you would say to your slave who has just come in from plowing or tending sheep in the field, 'Come here at once and take your place at the table'? [8]Would you not rather say to him, 'Prepare supper for me, put on your apron and serve me while I eat and drink; later you may eat and drink'? [9]Do you thank the slave for doing what was commanded? [10]So you also, when you have done all that you were ordered to do, say, 'We are worthless slaves; we have done only what we ought to have done!' "

Hymn and Keyboard Suggestions

O– "I Love Thy Kingdom, Lord" (Ps.)
      B354, E524, F545, L368, UM540 (PD)
         H-1   #3a. Harmonization
         S-1   #311. Descant
                    #312. Harmonization
         K-1(III) #78. Short prelude/postlude (may
                        be played manuals only)
         K-2   p. 29. Short prelude/postlude (man-
                        uals only)

"It's Me, It's Me, O Lord" (Lam.)
      UM352

"Dear Lord, for All in Pain" (Lam.)
      UM458

"O What Their Joy and Their Glory Must Be"
      (Lam., Ps.)
      E623, L337, UM727 (PD)
         H-1   #94. Harmonization
         S-1   #255. Harmonization. A descant may
                        legally be derived from this pub-
                        lic domain setting by adding
                        text to the organ's top line.

"Lonely the Boat" (Lam., 2 Tim.)
      P373, UM476

"Alleluia, Song of Gladness" (Ps.)
      E122 (PD), E123, W413 (PD)

"By the Babylonian Rivers" (Ps.)
      P246, W426

"O Thou Who Camest from Above" (2 Tim.)
      E704, UM501 (PD)

"Standing on the Promises" (2 Tim.)
      B335, UM374 (PD)
      F69

"Holy Spirit, Truth Divine" (2 Tim.)
      L257, P321, UM465 (PD)
         S-1   #53. Descant

"I Know Whom I Have Believed" (2 Tim.)
      B337, F631, UM714 (PD)

"My Faith Looks Up to Thee" (2 Tim., Luke)
      B416, E691, F84, L479, P383, UM452 (PD)
         H-1   #72. Harmonization in D major
         S-2   #142. Flute/violin descant
         K-1(III) #69. Prelude/meditation
         K-14   p. 12. Piano prelude/meditation

"When Our Confidence Is Shaken" (2 Tim., Luke)
      UM505

"The Kingdom of God" (Luke)
      UM275
         S-2   #129. Flute/violin descant

"Let Us Plead for Faith Alone" (Luke)
      UM385 (PD)
         S-2   #165. Descant

"God of Love and God of Power" (Luke)
      UM578 (PD)
         H-2   p. 23. Harmonization with descant
         S-1   #338. Descant
                    #341. Descant

"Give Me the Faith Which Can Remove" (Luke)
      UM650 (PD)
         S-1   #57. Descant
                    #58-60. Harmonizations
                    #61. Choral harmonization

C– "By Gracious Powers" (2 Tim., Luke)
      E695, P342, UM517
      E696, W577

C– "Forth in Thy Name, O Lord" (Luke)
      UM438 (PD)
         K-1(I)   #16. Use as interlude (manuals only)
         H-1   #83. Harmonization
         S-1   #100-103. Various treatments
         K-1(I)   #16. Prelude/postlude
         K-2   p. 8. Short prelude
         K-10   p. 32. Prelude/postlude
      L505 (PD)

Vocal Solo

"Standing in the Need of Prayer" (Lam.)
V-5   p. 201

Anthems

"On the Willows" from *Godspell* (Ps.)
Stephen Schwartz
Valendo/New Cadenza Music
Three-part with piano and/or guitar

"An Anthem of Faith" (2 Tim., Luke)
Carl F. Mueller
G. Schirmer 12029
SATB with keyboard

Hymn Anthem Suggestion

"Out of the Depths I Cry to You" (Lam., Ps., 2 Tim.)
52IHA #39

Other Suggestions

Prayer: UM459. The Serenity Prayer (Lam.)
Prayer Response: UM500, stanza 4. "Spirit of God, Descend
    upon My Heart" (Lam., 2 Tim.)

Jeremiah 29:1, 4-7

[1]These are the words of the letter that the prophet Jeremiah sent from Jerusalem to the remaining elders among the exiles, and to the priests, the prophets, and all the people, whom Nebuchadnezzar had taken into exile from Jerusalem to Babylon.

[4]Thus says the LORD of hosts, the God of Israel, to all the exiles whom I have sent into exile from Jerusalem to Babylon: [5]Build houses and live in them; plant gardens and eat what they produce. [6]Take wives and have sons and daughters; take wives for your sons, and give your daughters in marriage, that they may bear sons and daughters; multiply there, and do not decrease. [7]But seek the welfare of the city where I have sent you into exile, and pray to the LORD on its behalf, for in its welfare you will find your welfare.

Psalm 66:1-12

[1]Make a joyful noise to God, all the earth;
  [2]sing the glory of his name;
  give to him glorious praise.
[3]Say to God, "How awesome are your deeds!
  Because of your great power,
    your enemies cringe before you.
[4]All the earth worships you;
  they sing praises to you,
  sing praises to your name."
[5]Come and see what God has done:
  he is awesome in his deeds among mortals.
[6]He turned the sea into dry land;
  they passed through the river on foot.
There we rejoiced in him,
  [7]who rules by his might forever,
whose eyes keep watch on the nations—
  let the rebellious not exalt themselves.
[8]Bless our God, O peoples,
  let the sound of his praise be heard,
[9]who has kept us among the living,
  and has not let our feet slip.
[10]For you, O God, have tested us;
  you have tried us as silver is tried.
[11]You brought us into the net;
  you laid burdens on our backs;
[12]you let people ride over our heads;
  we went through fire and through water;
yet you have brought us out to a spacious place.

2 Timothy 2:8-15

[8]Remember Jesus Christ, raised from the dead, a descendant of David—that is my gospel, [9]for which I suffer hardship, even to the point of being chained like a criminal. But the word of God is not chained. [10]Therefore I endure everything for the sake of the elect, so that they may also obtain the salvation that is in Christ Jesus, with eternal glory. [11]The saying is sure:
  If we have died with him, we will also live with him;
  [12]if we endure, we will also reign with him;
  if we deny him, he will also deny us;
  [13]if we are faithless, he remains faithful—
  for he cannot deny himself.
[14]Remind them of this, and warn them before God that they are to avoid wrangling over words, which does no good but only ruins those who are listening. [15]Do your best to present yourself to God as one approved by him, a worker who has no need to be ashamed, rightly explaining the word of truth.

Luke 17:11-19

[11]On the way to Jerusalem Jesus was going through the region between Samaria and Galilee. [12]As he entered a village, ten lepers approached him. Keeping their distance, [13]they called out, saying, "Jesus, Master, have mercy on us!" [14]When he saw them, he said to them, "Go and show yourselves to the priests." And as they went, they were made clean. [15]Then one of them, when he saw that he was healed, turned back, praising God with a loud voice. [16]He prostrated himself at Jesus' feet and thanked him. And he was a Samaritan. [17]Then Jesus asked, "Were not ten made clean? But the other nine, where are they? [18]Was none of them found to return and give praise to God except this foreigner?" [19]Then he said to him, "Get up and go on your way; your faith has made you well."

Hymn and Keyboard Suggestions

O– "From All That Dwell Below the Skies" (Ps.)

    B13, UM101 (PD), W521

K-1 (I)	#16.	Use as interlude (manuals only)
H-1	#83.	Harmonization
S-1	#100-103.	Various treatments
K-1 (I)	#16.	Prelude/postlude
K-2	p. 8.	Short prelude
K-10	p. 32.	Prelude/postlude

    E380 (PD), L550

H-1	#24.	Harmonization
S-1	#257-59.	Various treatments
S-2	#140.	Descant
K-1 (III)	#58.	Short prelude/postlude
K-4	p. 12.	Various keyboard treatments, through p. 17

    P229

H-1	#96.	Harmonization
S-1	#198-204.	Various treatments
K-1 (II)	#46.	Prelude/postlude
K-8	p. 29.	Harmonization
K-9	p. 25.	Prelude/postlude
K-13	p. 3.	Piano prelude/meditation
K-15	p. 80.	Piano prelude/postlude

"Lift Every Voice and Sing" (Jer., Ps.)

    B627, E599, L562, P563, UM519, W641

"O God, Our Faithful God" (Jer., Ps., 2 Tim.)

    L504 (PD)

K-14	p. 42.	Prelude/meditation

    P277 (PD)

K-5	p. 33.	Various keyboard treatments, through p. 37

"Praise, My Soul, the King of Heaven" (Ps.)

    B32, E410, F339, L549, P478 or 479, UM66 (PD), W530

S-1	#205.	Harmonization
	#206.	Descant

"Easter People, Raise Your Voices" (2 Tim.)

    B360, UM304

H-1	#7.	Harmonization
S-1	#280.	Descant
	#281.	Harmonization
K-1 (III)	#72.	Short prelude/postlude/interlude
K-2	p. 24.	Short prelude
K-8	p. 28.	Introduction/interlude

"In the Cross of Christ I Glory" (2 Tim.)

    B554, E441, F251, L104, P84, UM295 (PD)

H-1	#51.	Harmonization
S-1	#276-77.	Harmonization with descant
K-2	p. 23.	Short prelude/postlude

    E442

"Jesus, Priceless Treasure" (2 Tim.)

    F277, L457, P365, UM532

K-4	p. 109.	Variations, through p. 119
K-9	p. 33.	Prelude/meditation
K-14	p. 48.	Prelude/meditation/postlude

    L458

"Thine Arm, O Lord" (Luke)

    E567 (PD)

"O Christ, the Healer" (Luke)

    P380, UM265, W747

K-1 (I)	#23.	Short prelude (may be played manuals only)

    L360

"Jesus' Hands Were Kind Hands" (Luke)

    B477, UM273

S-2	#17-19.	Various treatments

C– "I'll Praise My Maker While I've Breath" (Luke)

    B35, E429 (PD), P253, UM60

S-2	#141.	Harmonization

Vocal Solos

"Now Let Us Give Thanks" (Ps., Luke)

V-6	p. 17

"Be Not Proud" (Luke)

V-8	p. 40

Anthems

"A Canon of Praise" (Ps.)
Natalie Sleeth
Choristers Guild A-79
Three-part with organ or handbells

"Ten Lepers" (Luke)
Sister Miriam Therese (arr. Roff)
Vanguard V 516
SATB with piano

"I Will Give Thanks" (Luke)
Michael Jothen
Beckenhorst Press BP1101
Unison with piano and optional flute

Hymn Anthem Suggestions

"O Thou, in Whose Presence" (Jer., Ps.)
52IHA #38
"Easter People, Raise Your Voices" (2 Tim.)
52IHA #13

Other Suggestions

Introit: E710. "Make a Joyful Noise" (Ps.)
Prayers for Healing: UM457. For the Sick (Luke); UM460. In Time of Illness (Luke); UM461. For Those Who Mourn (Luke)

Jeremiah 31:27-34

[27]The days are surely coming, says the LORD, when I will sow the house of Israel and the house of Judah with the seed of humans and the seed of animals. [28]And just as I have watched over them to pluck up and break down, to overthrow, destroy, and bring evil, so I will watch over them to build and to plant, says the LORD. [29]In those days they shall no longer say: "The parents have eaten sour grapes, and the children's teeth are set on edge." [30]But all shall die for their own sins; the teeth of everyone who eats sour grapes shall be set on edge.

[31]The days are surely coming, says the LORD, when I will make a new covenant with the house of Israel and the house of Judah. [32]It will not be like the covenant that I made with their ancestors when I took them by the hand to bring them out of the land of Egypt—a covenant that they broke, though I was their husband, says the LORD. [33]But this is the covenant that I will make with the house of Israel after those days, says the LORD: I will put my law within them, and I will write it on their hearts; and I will be their God, and they shall be my people. [34]No longer shall they teach one another, or say to each other, "Know the LORD," for they shall all know me, from the least of them to the greatest, says the LORD; for I will forgive their iniquity, and remember their sin no more.

Psalm 119:97-104

[97]Oh, how I love your law!
 It is my meditation all day long.
[98]Your commandment makes me
  wiser than my enemies,
 for it is always with me.
[99]I have more understanding than
  all my teachers,
 for your decrees are my meditation.
[100]I understand more than the aged,
 for I keep your precepts.
[101]I hold back my feet from every evil way,
 in order to keep your word.
[102]I do not turn away from your ordinances,
 for you have taught me.
[103]How sweet are your words to my taste,
 sweeter than honey to my mouth!
[104]Through your precepts I get understanding;
 therefore I hate every false way.

2 Timothy 3:14–4:5

[14]But as for you, continue in what you have learned and firmly believed, knowing from whom you learned it, [15]and how from childhood you have known the sacred writings that are able to instruct you for salvation through faith in Christ Jesus. [16]All scripture is inspired by God and is useful for teaching, for reproof, for correction, and for training in righteousness, [17]so that everyone who belongs to God may be proficient, equipped for every good work.

[1]In the presence of God and of Christ Jesus, who is to judge the living and the dead, and in view of his appearing and his kingdom, I solemnly urge you: [2]proclaim the message; be persistent whether the time is favorable or unfavorable; convince, rebuke, and encourage, with the utmost patience in teaching. [3]For the time is coming when people will not put up with sound doctrine, but having itching ears, they will accumulate for themselves teachers to suit their own desires, [4]and will turn away from listening to the truth and wander away to myths. [5]As for you, always be sober, endure suffering, do the work of an evangelist, carry out your ministry fully.

Luke 18:1-8

[1]Then Jesus told them a parable about their need to pray always and not to lose heart. [2]He said, "In a certain city there was a judge who neither feared God nor had respect for people. [3]In that city there was a widow who kept coming to him and saying, 'Grant me justice against my opponent.' [4]For a while he refused; but later he said to himself, 'Though I have no fear of God and no respect for anyone, [5]yet because this widow keeps bothering me, I will grant her justice, so that she may not wear me out by continually coming.' " [6]And the Lord said, "Listen to what the unjust judge says. [7]And will not God grant justice to his chosen ones who cry to him day and night? Will he delay long in helping them? [8]I tell you, he will quickly grant justice to them. And yet, when the Son of Man comes, will he find faith on earth?"

Hymn and Keyboard Suggestions
O– "Come, Let Us Use the Grace Divine" (Jer.)
    UM606 (PD)
      S-2   #100-103. Various treatments
O– "This Is a Day of New Beginnings" (Jer.)
    B370, UM383, W661
O– "O Word of God Incarnate" (2 Tim.)
    E632, L231, P327, UM598 (PD)
      H-1   #64. Harmonization in D major
      S-1   #243. Harmonization
      K-1(II) #63. Prelude/meditation
"Blest Are the Uncorrupt in Heart" (Ps.)
    P233
      S-1   #286. Descant
      K-2   p. 25. Short prelude/postlude
"O Lord, May Church and Home Combine" (Ps.)
    B510, UM695
      S-2   #105. Flute/violin descant
             #106. Harmonization
      K-8   p. 22. Prelude/meditation
"Wonderful Words of Life" (Ps.)
    B261, F29, UM600 (PD)
"Lamp of Our Feet" (Ps., 2 Tim.)
    E627 (PD)
      K-1(II) #55. Prelude/postlude
"Holy Bible, Book Divine" (Ps., 2 Tim.)
    B260 (PD), F34
"Lord, You Give the Great Commission" (2 Tim.)
    P429, UM584, W470
      S-1   #4. Instrumental descant
             #5. Vocal descant
    E528
"I Know Whom I Have Believed" (2 Tim.)
    B337, F631, UM714 (PD)
"Lord, Speak to Me" (2 Tim.)
    B568, F625, L403, P426, UM463 (PD)
      H-1   #74. Harmonization
      S-1   #52. Descant
      K-8   p. 4. Prelude/meditation
"O Master, Let Me Walk with Thee" (2 Tim.)
    B279, E660, F442, L492, P357, UM430 (PD)
      S-2   #118. Descant
    E659
"Thanks to God Whose Word Was Written" (2 Tim.)
    E630, P331, W514
"Thy Word Is a Lamp" (2 Tim.)
    UM601
"Lord, Teach Us How to Pray Aright" (Luke)
    L438
"Not So in Haste, My Heart" (Luke)
    UM455 (PD)
"I Will Trust in the Lord" (Luke)
    B420, UM464

C– "Be Thou My Vision" (Luke)
    B60, E488, F468, P339, UM451
      S-1   #319. Arrangement for organ and
                voices in canon
      K-12   p. 9. Prelude/meditation
C– "Here I Am, Lord" (Jer.)
    P525, UM593

Vocal Solos
"Every Time I Feel The Spirit" (Jer., Luke)
    V-5   p. 5
"Be Thou My Vision" (Luke)
    V-3   p. 13
"Lord, to Thee Do I Lift My Soul" (Luke)
    V-8   p. 38
"Standing in the Need of Prayer" (Luke)
    V-5   p. 201

Anthems
"The New Covenant" (Jer.)
David Stanley York
Theodore Presser 312-40640
SATB with tenor solo and organ

"This Is the New Covenant" (Jer.)
Jean Berger
Augsburg 11-1677
SATB *a cappella*

"Notes from Paul" (2 Tim.)
Eugene Butler
Hinshaw HMC-227
SATB with keyboard

Hymn Anthem Suggestion
"This Is a Day of New Beginnings" (Jer.)
52IHA #43

Other Suggestions
Reading: B259. God's Word (Ps., 2 Tim.)
Prayer of Confession: UM597. For the Spirit of Truth
  (2 Tim.)
Prayer: UM392. Prayer for a New Heart (Jer., Ps.)
Prayer of Preparation: UM602. Concerning the Scriptures
  (2 Tim.)
Prayer Response: P338, UM494. "Kum Ba Yah" (Luke)

Joel 2:23-32

[23]O children of Zion, be glad and rejoice in the LORD your God; for he has given the early rain for your vindication, he has poured down for you abundant rain, the early and the later rain, as before. [24]The threshing floors shall be full of grain, the vats shall overflow with wine and oil. [25]I will repay you for the years that the swarming locust has eaten, the hopper, the destroyer, and the cutter, my great army, which I sent against you. [26]You shall eat in plenty and be satisfied, and praise the name of the LORD your God, who has dealt wondrously with you. And my people shall never again be put to shame. [27]You shall know that I am in the midst of Israel, and that I, the LORD, am your God and there is no other. And my people shall never again be put to shame. [28]Then afterward I will pour out my spirit on all flesh; your sons and your daughters shall prophesy, your old men shall dream dreams, and your young men shall see visions. [29]Even on the male and female slaves, in those days, I will pour out my spirit.

[30]I will show portents in the heavens and on the earth, blood and fire and columns of smoke. [31]The sun shall be turned to darkness, and the moon to blood, before the great and terrible day of the LORD comes. [32]Then everyone who calls on the name of the LORD shall be saved; for in Mount Zion and in Jerusalem there shall be those who escape, as the LORD has said, and among the survivors shall be those whom the LORD calls.

Psalm 65

[1]Praise is due to you, O God, in Zion; and to you shall vows be performed, [2]O you who answer prayer! To you all flesh shall come. [3]When deeds of iniquity overwhelm us, you forgive our transgressions. [4]Happy are those whom you choose and bring near to live in your courts. We shall be satisfied with the goodness of your house, your holy temple. [5]By awesome deeds you answer us with deliverance, O God of our salvation; you are the hope of all the ends of the earth and of the farthest seas. [6]By your strength you established the mountains; you are girded with might. [7]You silence the roaring of the seas, the roaring of their waves, the tumult of the peoples. [8]Those who live at earth's farthest bounds are awed by your signs; you make the gateways of the morning and the evening shout for joy. [9]You visit the earth and water it, you greatly enrich it; the river of God is full of water; you provide the people with grain, for so you have prepared it. [10]You water its furrows abundantly, settling its ridges, softening it with showers, and blessing its growth. [11]You crown the year with your bounty; your wagon tracks overflow with richness. [12]The pastures of the wilderness overflow, the hills gird themselves with joy, [13]the meadows clothe themselves with flocks, the valleys deck themselves with grain, they shout and sing together for joy.

2 Timothy 4:6-8, 16-18

[6]As for me, I am already being poured out as a libation, and the time of my departure has come. [7]I have fought the good fight, I have finished the race, I have kept the faith. [8]From now on there is reserved for me the crown of righteousness, which the Lord, the righteous judge, will give me on that day, and not only to me but also to all who have longed for his appearing.

[16]At my first defense no one came to my support, but all deserted me. May it not be counted against them! [17]But the Lord stood by me and gave me strength, so that through me the message might be fully proclaimed and all the Gentiles might hear it. So I was rescued from the lion's mouth. [18]The Lord will rescue me from every evil attack and save me for his heavenly kingdom. To him be the glory forever and ever. Amen.

Luke 18:9-14

[9]He also told this parable to some who trusted in themselves that they were righteous and regarded others with contempt: [10]"Two men went up to the temple to pray, one a Pharisee and the other a tax collector. [11]The Pharisee, standing by himself, was praying thus, 'God, I thank you that I am not like other people: thieves, rogues, adulterers, or even like this tax collector. [12]I fast twice a week; I give a tenth of all my income.' [13]But the tax collector, standing far off, would not even look up to heaven, but was beating his breast and saying, 'God, be merciful to me, a sinner!' [14]I tell you, this man went down to his home justified rather than the other; for all who exalt themselves will be humbled, but all who humble themselves will be exalted."

Hymn and Keyboard Suggestions

O– "A Mighty Fortress Is Our God" (Reformation, 2 Tim.)
　　B8, E687 or E688, F118, L228 or L229, P259 or
　　P260, UM110 (PD), W575 or W576

H-1	#86.	Harmonization
H-2	p. 10.	Harmonization with descant
S-1	#111-13.	Various treatments
K-1 (I)	#20.	Prelude/postlude/introduction
K-8	p. 13.	Modulation from C major to D major
K-10	p. 22.	Prelude/postlude
K-14	p. 14.	Piano prelude/postlude

O– "Come, Christians, Join to Sing" (Ps.)
　　B231, F342, P150, UM158

S-1	#321.	Descant
K-1 (III)	#82.	Prelude/postlude
K-2	p. 32.	Short prelude

"Come, Holy Ghost, Our Souls Inspire" (Joel)
　　E504, L472 and L473, P125, UM651 (PD)

S-2	#186.	Handbell arrangement
K-4	p. 123.	Prelude/postlude

E503

"O Day of Peace That Dimly Shines" (Joel)
　　E597, P450, UM729, W654

"Sing Praise to God Who Reigns Above" (Ps.)
　　B20, E408, F343, P483, UM126 (PD), W528

S-1	#237.	Descant

"Praise Is Your Right, O God, in Zion" (Ps.)
　　P201

"To Bless the Earth" (Ps.)
　　P200 (PD)

"Abide with Me" (2 Tim.)
　　B63, E662, F500, L272, P543, UM700 (PD)

H-1	#100.	Harmonization
S-2	#58.	Harmonization
K-1 (I)	#24.	Prelude/meditation (may be played manuals only)

"Fight the Good Fight" (2 Tim.)
　　P307 (PD)

K-1 (I)	#16.	Use as interlude (manuals only)
H-1	#83.	Harmonization
S-1	#100-103.	Various treatments
K-1 (I)	#16.	Prelude/postlude
K-2	p. 8.	Short prelude
K-10	p. 32.	Prelude/postlude

E552 (PD), E553, F613, L461

"O Love That Wilt Not Let Me Go" (2 Tim.)
　　B292, F404, L324, P384, UM480 (PD)

"What a Friend We Have in Jesus" (2 Tim.)
　　B182, F466, L439, P403, UM526 (PD)

K-13	p. 56.	Prelude/meditation

"Through It All" (2 Tim.)
　　F43, UM507

"Pass Me Not, O Gentle Savior" (Luke)
　　B308, F416, UM351 (PD)

"Just As I Am, Without One Plea" (Luke)
　　B307, E693, F417, L296, P370, UM357 (PD)

K-15	p. 66.	Piano prelude/meditation

"Lord, I Want to Be a Christian" (Luke)
　　B489, F421, P372 (PD), UM402

K-7	p. 10.	Prelude

"Spirit of God, Descend upon My Heart" (Luke)
　　B245, F147, L486, P326, UM500 (PD)

S-2	#125-28.	Various treatments
K-8	p. 24.	Prelude/meditation

C– "I Am Thine, O Lord" (Luke)
　　B290, F455, UM419 (PD)

C– "Lord, Dismiss Us with Thy Blessing" (Ps.)
　　E344, F520, L259, P538, UM671 (PD)

H-1	#79.	Harmonization

Vocal Solos

"O Love, That Wilt Not Let Me Go" (2 Tim.)
V-7　　p. 49
"Just As I Am" (Luke)
V-3　　p. 23
"Standing in the Need of Prayer" (Luke)
V-5　　p. 201

Anthems

"The Prophecy of Joel" (Joel)
Eugene Butler
Carl Fischer CM7789
SATB with organ

"The Pharisee and the Publican" (Luke)
Warren Martin
Golden Music G-39
SATB with organ

Hymn Anthem Suggestion

"How Firm a Foundation" (2 Tim.)
52IHA　　#23

Other Suggestions

Prayer: UM489. For God's Gifts (Joel, Ps., 2 Tim., Luke)
Prayer: UM574. For Renewal of the Church (Reformation Sunday)

Daniel 7:1-3, 15-18

¹In the first year of King Belshazzar of Babylon, Daniel had a dream and visions of his head as he lay in bed. Then he wrote down the dream: ²I, Daniel, saw in my vision by night the four winds of heaven stirring up the great sea, ³and four great beasts came up out of the sea, different from one another.

¹⁵As for me, Daniel, my spirit was troubled within me, and the visions of my head terrified me. ¹⁶I approached one of the attendants to ask him the truth concerning all this. So he said that he would disclose to me the interpretation of the matter: ¹⁷"As for these four great beasts, four kings shall arise out of the earth. ¹⁸But the holy ones of the Most High shall receive the kingdom and possess the kingdom forever—forever and ever."

Psalm 149

¹Praise the LORD! Sing to the LORD a new song, his praise in the assembly of the faithful. ²Let Israel be glad in its Maker; let the children of Zion rejoice in their King. ³Let them praise his name with dancing, making melody to him with tambourine and lyre. ⁴For the LORD takes pleasure in his people; he adorns the humble with victory. ⁵Let the faithful exult in glory; let them sing for joy on their couches. ⁶Let the high praises of God be in their throats and two-edged swords in their hands, ⁷to execute vengeance on the nations and punishment on the peoples, ⁸to bind their kings with fetters and their nobles with chains of iron, ⁹to execute on them the judgment decreed. This is glory for all his faithful ones. Praise the LORD!

Ephesians 1:11-23

¹¹In Christ we have also obtained an inheritance, having been destined according to the purpose of him who accomplishes all things according to his counsel and will, ¹²so that we, who were the first to set our hope on Christ, might live for the praise of his glory. ¹³In him you also, when you had heard the word of truth, the gospel of your salvation, and had believed in him, were marked with the seal of the promised Holy Spirit; ¹⁴this is the pledge of our inheritance toward redemption as God's own people, to the praise of his glory.

¹⁵I have heard of your faith in the Lord Jesus and your love toward all the saints, and for this reason ¹⁶I do not cease to give thanks for you as I remember you in my prayers. ¹⁷I pray that the God of our Lord Jesus Christ, the Father of glory, may give you a spirit of wisdom and revelation as you come to know him, ¹⁸so that, with the eyes of your heart enlightened, you may know what is the hope to which he has called you, what are the riches of his glorious inheritance among the saints, ¹⁹and what is the immeasurable greatness of his power for us who believe, according to the working of his great power. ²⁰God put this power to work in Christ when he raised him from the dead and seated him at his right hand in the heavenly places, ²¹far above all rule and authority and power and dominion, and above every name that is named, not only in this age but also in the age to come. ²²And he has put all things under his feet and has made him the head over all things for the church, ²³which is his body, the fullness of him who fills all in all.

Luke 6:20-31

²⁰Then he looked up at his disciples and said:
"Blessed are you who are poor,
for yours is the kingdom of God.
²¹"Blessed are you who are hungry now,
for you will be filled.
"Blessed are you who weep now,
for you will laugh.
²²"Blessed are you when people hate you, and when they exclude you, revile you, and defame you on account of the Son of Man. ²³Rejoice in that day and leap for joy, for surely your reward is great in heaven; for that is what their ancestors did to the prophets.
²⁴"But woe to you who are rich,
for you have received your consolation.
²⁵"Woe to you who are full now,
for you will be hungry.
"Woe to you who are laughing now,
for you will mourn and weep.
²⁶"Woe to you when all speak well of you, for that is what their ancestors did to the false prophets.
²⁷"But I say to you that listen, Love your enemies, do good to those who hate you, ²⁸bless those who curse you, pray for those who abuse you. ²⁹If anyone strikes you on the cheek, offer the other also; and from anyone who takes away your coat do not withhold even your shirt. ³⁰Give to everyone who begs from you; and if anyone takes away your goods, do not ask for them again. ³¹Do to others as you would have them do to you."

Hymn and Keyboard Suggestions

O– "Come, Thou Almighty King" (Dan.)
   B247, E365, F341, L522, P139, UM61 (PD), W487
    S-1   #185. Harmonization
         #186. Descant
    K-1(II) #37. Prelude/postlude
    K-2   p. 20. Short prelude/meditation
    K-14 p. 8. Piano prelude/postlude
"For All the Saints" (Dan., Eph.)
   B355, E287, F614, L174, P526, UM711 (PD), W705
    S-1   #314-18. Various treatments
"Give Praise to the Lord" (Ps.)
   P257 (PD)
"Hope of the World" (Eph.)
   UM178
    S-1   #343. Descant
    S-2   #189. Introduction
   E472, L493, P360, W565
"My Hope Is Built" (Eph.)
   B406, F92, L293, P379, UM368 (PD)
    S-2   #171. Trumpet descant
         #172. Descant
   L294 (PD)
    H-1   #80. Harmonization
"Come, Let Us Join Our Friends Above" (Eph.)
   UM709 (PD)
    S-1   #131. Introduction
         #132. Descant
    K-3   p. 25. Short prelude/postlude (manuals only)
    K-6   p. 10. Prelude/postlude
"If Thou But Suffer God to Guide Thee" (Eph., Luke)
   B57, E635, L453, P282, UM142 (PD)
    K-5   p. 141. Harmonization in A minor
    K-1(IV) #94. Prelude/meditation
    K-5   p. 141. Various keyboard treatments, through p. 152
"Faith of Our Fathers" ("Faith of the Martyrs") (Eph., Luke)
   B352, F526, L500, UM710 (PD), W571
    H-1   #60. Harmonization in G major
"How Firm a Foundation" (Luke)
   B338, E636, F32, L507, P361, UM529 (PD), W585
    S-1   #133. Harmonization
         #134. Performance note
    K-6   p. 24. Prelude/postlude
    K-11 p. 37. Prelude/meditation
   E637
    H-1   #37. Harmonization
    S-1   #223-26. Various treatments
    K-8   p. 17. Introduction

"For the Bread Which You Have Broken" (All Saints, Communion)
   P508, UM614
    S-2   #63. Descant
         #64. Harmonization
   E340, UM615
    S-1   #43. Performance note
    S-2   #25. Orff instrument arrangement
   E341, L200, P509
C– "Lift Every Voice and Sing" (Eph., Luke)
   B627, E599, L562, P563, UM519, W641

Vocal Solos

"Come Sunday" (Luke)
UMH   #728
"Nobody Knows the Trouble I've Seen" (Luke)
V-5   p. 119

Anthems

"How Firm a Foundation" (Eph.)
arr. Leonard Van Camp
Carl Fischer CM8003
SATB *a cappella*

"How Firm a Foundation" (Eph.)
arr. Don Whitman
Lillenas AN-236
SATB with optional keyboard

"Blessed Are You" (Luke)
Emma Lou Diemer
Carl Fischer CM 7755
SATB with keyboard

Hymn Anthem Suggestions

"Hail Thee, Festival Day" (Eph.)
HA   p. 48
"How Firm a Foundation" (Luke)
52IHA #23
"This Is the Feast of Victory"
52IHA #44

Other Suggestions

 These scriptures and ideas may also be used on either October 29 or November 5.
Prayer: UM461. For Those Who Mourn (All Saints)
Prayer: UM531. For Overcoming Adversity (Luke)
Prayer: UM713. All Saints (Eph.)
Poem: UM656. If Death My Friend and Me Divide (All Saints)
Canticle: UM652. "Canticle of Remembrance" (Eph.)
Canticle: UM734. "Canticle of Hope" (Isa., Rev.)

Habakkuk 1:1-4; 2:1-4

[1]The oracle that the prophet Habakkuk saw. [2]O LORD, how long shall I cry for help, and you will not listen? Or cry to you "Violence!" and you will not save? [3]Why do you make me see wrongdoing and look at trouble? Destruction and violence are before me; strife and contention arise. [4]So the law becomes slack and justice never prevails. The wicked surround the righteous—therefore judgment comes forth perverted.

[1]I will stand at my watchpost, and station myself on the rampart; I will keep watch to see what he will say to me, and what he will answer concerning my complaint. [2]Then the LORD answered me and said: Write the vision; make it plain on tablets, so that a runner may read it. [3]For there is still a vision for the appointed time; it speaks of the end, and does not lie. If it seems to tarry, wait for it; it will surely come, it will not delay. [4]Look at the proud! Their spirit is not right in them, but the righteous live by their faith.

Psalm 119:137-144

[137]You are righteous, O LORD,
and your judgments are right.
[138]You have appointed your
decrees in righteousness
and in all faithfulness.
[139]My zeal consumes me
because my foes forget your words.
[140]Your promise is well tried,
and your servant loves it.
[141]I am small and despised,
yet I do not forget your precepts.
[142]Your righteousness is an
everlasting righteousness,
and your law is the truth.
[143]Trouble and anguish have come upon me,
but your commandments are my delight.
[144]Your decrees are righteous forever;
give me understanding that I may live.

2 Thessalonians 1:1-4, 11-12

[1]Paul, Silvanus, and Timothy, To the church of the Thessalonians in God our Father and the Lord Jesus Christ:

[2]Grace to you and peace from God our Father and the Lord Jesus Christ.

[3]We must always give thanks to God for you, brothers and sisters, as is right, because your faith is growing abundantly, and the love of everyone of you for one another is increasing. [4]Therefore we ourselves boast of you among the churches of God for your steadfastness and faith during all your persecutions and the afflictions that you are enduring.

[11]To this end we always pray for you, asking that our God will make you worthy of his call and will fulfill by his power every good resolve and work of faith, [12]so that the name of our Lord Jesus may be glorified in you, and you in him, according to the grace of our God and the Lord Jesus Christ.

Luke 19:1-10

[1]He entered Jericho and was passing through it. [2]A man was there named Zacchaeus; he was a chief tax collector and was rich. [3]He was trying to see who Jesus was, but on account of the crowd he could not, because he was short in stature. [4]So he ran ahead and climbed a sycamore tree to see him, because he was going to pass that way. [5]When Jesus came to the place, he looked up and said to him, "Zacchaeus, hurry and come down; for I must stay at your house today." [6]So he hurried down and was happy to welcome him. [7]All who saw it began to grumble and said, "He has gone to be the guest of one who is a sinner." [8]Zacchaeus stood there and said to the Lord, "Look, half of my possessions, Lord, I will give to the poor; and if I have defrauded anyone of anything, I will pay back four times as much." [9]Then Jesus said to him, "Today salvation has come to this house, because he too is a son of Abraham. [10]For the Son of Man came to seek out and to save the lost."

Hymn and Keyboard Suggestions

O– "Stand Up and Bless the Lord" (2 Thess.)
      B30, UM662 (PD)
        S-1   #306. Harmonization
                    #307. Descant
                    #308. Transposition in F major
        K-1(III) #64. Prelude/meditation
      P491
"Be Thou My Vision" (Hab.)
      B60, E488, F468, P339, UM451
        S-1   319. Arrangement for organ and
                      voices in canon
        K-12   p. 9. Prelude/meditation
"Be Still, My Soul" (Hab.)
      F77, UM534
"O Day of God, Draw Nigh" (Hab., 2 Thess.)
      B623, E601, P452, UM730 (PD)
        S-1   #306-8. Various treatments
        K-1(III) #64. Prelude/meditation
"O What Their Joy and Their Glory Must Be" (Hab.)
      E623, L337, UM727 (PD)
        H-1   #94. Harmonization
        S-1   #255. Harmonization. A descant may
                      legally be derived from this
                      public domain setting by
                      adding text to the organ's top
                      line.
"O Lord, May Church and Home Combine" (Ps.)
      B510, UM695
        S-2   #105. Flute/violin descant
                    #106. Harmonization
        K-8   p. 22. Prelude/meditation
"We'll Understand It Better By and By" (Hab.,
   2 Thess.)
      UM525 (PD)
"We Would See Jesus" (Luke)
      UM256 (PD)
"Jesus' Hands Were Kind Hands" (Luke)
      B477, UM273
        S-2   #17-19. Various treatments
"Amazing Grace" (Luke, Communion)
      B330, E671, F107, L448, P280, UM378 (PD),
      W583
        S-2   #5. Piano arrangement
                    #6. Descant
                    #7. Harmonization
        K-15   p. 146. Piano prelude/meditation
"I Am Thine, O Lord" (Luke)
      B290, F455, UM419 (PD)
"Cuando El Pobre" ("When the Poor Ones") (Luke)
      P407, UM434

"Rescue the Perishing" (Luke)
      B559, F661, UM591
        K-8   p. 21. Introduction
"I Come with Joy" (Luke, Communion)
      P607, UM617
        S-2   #52. Choral and keyboard arrange-
                      ment
      B371, E304, W726
        S-2   #105. Flute/violin descant
                    #106. Harmonization
        K-8   p. 22. Prelude/meditation
C– "O Holy City, Seen of John" (Hab.)
      E583, P453, UM726
        S-1   #241. Orff arrangement
                    #242. Descant
        K-3   p. 8. Prelude/postlude
        K-6   p. 39. Prelude/meditation
      E582

Vocal Solos

"Be Thou My Vision" (Hab.)
      V-3   p. 13
"Amazing Grace" (Luke, Communion)
      V-3   p. 8

Anthems

"Righteous, O Lord, Art Thou" (Ps.)
A. Vivaldi
Elkan-Vogel 362-03119
SATB with soprano solo and piano (SAB available)

"Today Is Salvation Come" (Luke)
Raymond Haan
Gregorian Institute of America G-2115
SATB with four handbells

Hymn Anthem Suggestions

"O Holy City, Seen of John" (Hab.)
52IHA #36
"Cuando El Pobre" ("When the Poor Ones") (Luke)
52IHA #12

Other Suggestions

   The scriptures and ideas from November 1 may be used on this day.
Prayer: UM531. For Overcoming Adversity (Hab.)

Haggai 2:1-9

[1]In the second year of King Darius, in the seventh month, on the twenty-first day of the month, the word of the LORD came by the prophet Haggai, saying: [2]Speak now to Zerubbabel son of Shealtiel, governor of Judah, and to Joshua son of Jehozadak, the high priest, and to the remnant of the people, and say, [3]Who is left among you that saw this house in its former glory? How does it look to you now? Is it not in your sight as nothing? [4]Yet now take courage, O Zerubbabel, says the LORD; take courage, O Joshua, son of Jehozadak, the high priest; take courage, all you people of the land, says the LORD; work, for I am with you, says the LORD of hosts, [5]according to the promise that I made you when you came out of Egypt. My spirit abides among you; do not fear. [6]For thus says the LORD of hosts: Once again, in a little while, I will shake the heavens and the earth and the sea and the dry land; [7]and I will shake all the nations, so that the treasure of all nations shall come, and I will fill this house with splendor, says the LORD of hosts. [8]The silver is mine, and the gold is mine, says the LORD of hosts. [9]The latter splendor of this house shall be greater than the former, says the LORD of hosts; and in this place I will give prosperity, says the LORD of hosts.

Psalm 145:1-5, 17-21

[1]I will extol you, my God and King,
  and bless your name forever and ever.
[2]Every day I will bless you,
  and praise your name forever and ever.
[3]Great is the LORD, and greatly to be praised;
  his greatness is unsearchable.
[4]One generation shall laud your
    works to another,
  and shall declare your mighty acts.
[5]On the glorious splendor of your majesty,
  and on your wondrous works, I will meditate.
[17]The LORD is just in all his ways,
  and kind in all his doings.
[18]The LORD is near to all who call on him,
  to all who call on him in truth.
[19]He fulfills the desire of all who fear him;
  he also hears their cry, and saves them.
[20]The LORD watches over all who love him,
  but all the wicked he will destroy.
[21]My mouth will speak the praise
    of the LORD,
  and all flesh will bless his holy
    name forever and ever.

2 Thessalonians 2:1-5, 13-17

[1]As to the coming of our Lord Jesus Christ and our being gathered together to him, we beg you, brothers and sisters, [2]not to be quickly shaken in mind or alarmed, either by spirit or by word or by letter, as though from us, to the effect that the day of the Lord is already here. [3]Let no one deceive you in any way; for that day will not come unless the rebellion comes first and the lawless one is revealed, the one destined for destruction. [4]He opposes and exalts himself above every so-called god or object of worship, so that he takes his seat in the temple of God, declaring himself to be God. [5]Do you not remember that I told you these things when I was still with you?

[13]But we must always give thanks to God for you, brothers and sisters beloved by the Lord, because God chose you as the first fruits for salvation through sanctification by the Spirit and through belief in the truth. [14]For this purpose he called you through our proclamation of the good news, so that you may obtain the glory of our Lord Jesus Christ. [15]So then, brothers and sisters, stand firm and hold fast to the traditions that you were taught by us, either by word of mouth or by our letter.

[16]Now may our Lord Jesus Christ himself and God our Father, who loved us and through grace gave us eternal comfort and good hope, [17]comfort your hearts and strengthen them in every good work and word.

Luke 20:27-38

[27]Some Sadducees, those who say there is no resurrection, came to him [28]and asked him a question, "Teacher, Moses wrote for us that if a man's brother dies, leaving a wife but no children, the man shall marry the widow and raise up children for his brother. [29]Now there were seven brothers; the first married, and died childless; [30]then the second [31]and the third married her, and so in the same way all seven died childless. [32]Finally the woman also died. [33]In the resurrection, therefore, whose wife will the woman be? For the seven had married her."

[34]Jesus said to them, "Those who belong to this age marry and are given in marriage; [35]but those who are considered worthy of a place in that age and in the resurrection from the dead neither marry nor are given in marriage. [36]Indeed they cannot die anymore, because they are like angels and are children of God, being children of the resurrection. [37]And the fact that the dead are raised Moses himself showed, in the story about the bush, where he speaks of the Lord as the God of Abraham, the God of Isaac, and the God of Jacob. [38]Now he is God not of the dead, but of the living; for to him all of them are alive." God of Jacob. Now he is God not of the dead, but of the living; for to him all of them are alive."

Hymn and Keyboard Suggestions

O– "God Is Here" (2 Thess., Luke)
    P461, UM660, W667
        S-1   #4. Instrumental descant
                   #5. Vocal descant

O– "Come, Ye Faithful, Raise the Strain" (2 Thess., Luke)
    E199, P115, UM315 (PD)
        S-2   #161. Descant
        K-9   p. 27. Prelude/meditation/postlude
    E200, L132, P114 (PD), W456
        S-1   #29. Transposition to F major

"Glorious Things of Thee Are Spoken" (Hag.)
    B398, E522 or 523, F376, L358, P446, UM731
    (PD)
        H-1   #59. Harmonization
        S-1   #27. Descant
                   #28. Harmonization in F major
        K-10   p. 6. Variations
        K-14   p. 29. Piano variations

"God of the Ages" (Hag., 2 Thess., Luke)
    B629, E718, F687, L567, P262, UM698 (PD),
    W764
        S-2   #131-32. Harmonization with des-
                       cant

"The Battle Hymn of the Republic" (Hag., 2 Thess.,
   Luke)
    B633, F692, L332, UM717 (PD), W686
        S-1   #40. Refrain descant
        K-15   p. 96. Piano prelude/postlude

"Your Faithfulness, O Lord, Is Sure" (Ps.)
    P251
        H-1   #5. Harmonization
        K-1(I)   #14. Short prelude/postlude
        K-2   p. 35. Short prelude/postlude

"Close to Thee" (2 Thess.)
    B464, F405, UM407 (PD)

"O Love That Wilt Not Let Me Go" (2 Thess.)
    B292, F404, L324, P384, UM480 (PD)

"I Want Jesus to Walk with Me" (2 Thess.)
    B465, P363, UM521

"Children of the Heavenly Father" (Luke)
    B55, F89, L474, UM141
        S-2   #180-85. Various treatments
        K-8   p. 14. Short prelude/meditation

C– "O Master, Let Me Walk with Thee" (2 Thess.)
    B279, E660, F442, L492, P357, UM430 (PD)
        S-2   #118. Descant
    E659

C– "Sent Forth by God's Blessing" (Luke)
    L221, UM664
        S-1   #327. Descant
        K-8   p. 8. Prelude/meditation

Vocal Solos

"Thus Saith the Lord" (Hag.)
V-2
"O Love, That Wilt Not Let Me Go" (2 Thess.)
V-7   p. 49

Anthems

"Gracious Spirit, Dwell with Me" (Hag.)
arr. K. Lee Scott
Augsburg 11-2198
Two-part mixed chorus with keyboard

"Coventry Antiphon" (Hag.)
Herbert Howells
Novello 1420
SATB with organ

"Ain'a That Good News" (Hag.)
arr. William Dawson
KJOS T103A
SATB *a cappella*

"As We Come Together" (2 Thess.)
Stan Pethel
Hope Publishing GC 886
SATB with keyboard

"Blessed Be the King" (Luke)
Harry H. Harter
Harold Flammer 84502
SATB with junior choir and organ

Hymn Anthem Suggestions

"Jesus, Joy of Our Desiring" (Hag.)
52IHA #29
"Children of the Heavenly Father" (Luke)
52IHA #7

Other Suggestions

   Today's Gospel reading is one of the many parables of
Jesus that lends itself well to dramatic reenactment. Ask
eight youth to play the parts of the wife and the seven hus-
bands as one other youth or adult reads the scripture.
Call to Worship: UM211, stanza 7. "O Come, O Come,
   Emmanuel" (Hag.)
Prayer: UM721. Christ the King (Hag., 2 Thess.)

Isaiah 65:17-25

[17]For I am about to create new heavens and a new earth; the former things shall not be remembered or come to mind. [18]But be glad and rejoice forever in what I am creating; for I am about to create Jerusalem as a joy, and its people as a delight. [19]I will rejoice in Jerusalem, and delight in my people; no more shall the sound of weeping be heard in it, or the cry of distress. [20]No more shall there be in it an infant that lives but a few days, or an old person who does not live out a lifetime; for one who dies at a hundred years will be considered a youth, and one who falls short of a hundred will be considered accursed. [21]They shall build houses and inhabit them; they shall plant vineyards and eat their fruit. [22]They shall not build and another inhabit; they shall not plant and another eat; for like the days of a tree shall the days of my people be, and my chosen shall long enjoy the work of their hands. [23]They shall not labor in vain, or bear children for calamity; for they shall be offspring blessed by the LORD—and their descendants as well. [24]Before they call I will answer, while they are yet speaking I will hear. [25]The wolf and the lamb shall feed together, the lion shall eat straw like the ox; but the serpent—its food shall be dust! They shall not hurt or destroy on all my holy mountain, says the LORD.

Isaiah 12

[1]You will say in that day: I will give thanks to you, O LORD, for though you were angry with me, your anger turned away, and you comforted me. [2]Surely God is my salvation; I will trust, and will not be afraid, for the LORD GOD is my strength and my might; he has become my salvation.

[3]With joy you will draw water from the wells of salvation. [4]And you will say in that day: Give thanks to the LORD, call on his name; make known his deeds among the nations; proclaim that his name is exalted. [5]Sing praises to the LORD, for he has done gloriously; let this be known in all the earth. [6]Shout aloud and sing for joy, O royal Zion, for great in your midst is the Holy One of Israel.

2 Thessalonians 3:6-13

[6]Now we command you, beloved, in the name of our Lord Jesus Christ, to keep away from believers who are living in idleness and not according to the tradition that they received from us. [7]For you yourselves know how you ought to imitate us; we were not idle when we were with you, [8]and we did not eat anyone's bread without paying for it; but with toil and labor we worked night and day, so that we might not burden any of you. [9]This was not because we do not have that right, but in order to give you an example to imitate. [10]For even when we were with you, we gave you this command: Anyone unwilling to work should not eat. [11]For we hear that some of you are living in idleness, mere busybodies, not doing any work. [12]Now such persons we command and exhort in the Lord Jesus Christ to do their work quietly and to earn their own living. [13]Brothers and sisters, do not be weary in doing what is right.

Luke 21:5-19

[5]When some were speaking about the temple, how it was adorned with beautiful stones and gifts dedicated to God, he said, [6]"As for these things that you see, the days will come when not one stone will be left upon another; all will be thrown down."

[7]They asked him, "Teacher, when will this be, and what will be the sign that this is about to take place?" [8]And he said, "Beware that you are not led astray; for many will come in my name and say, 'I am he!' and, 'The time is near!' Do not go after them.

[9]"When you hear of wars and insurrections, do not be terrified; for these things must take place first, but the end will not follow immediately." [10]Then he said to them, "Nation will rise against nation, and kingdom against kingdom; [11]there will be great earthquakes, and in various places famines and plagues; and there will be dreadful portents and great signs from heaven.

[12]"But before all this occurs, they will arrest you and persecute you; they will hand you over to synagogues and prisons, and you will be brought before kings and governors because of my name. [13]This will give you an opportunity to testify. [14]So make up your minds not to prepare your defense in advance; [15]for I will give you words and a wisdom that none of your opponents will be able to withstand or contradict. [16]You will be betrayed even by parents and brothers, by relatives and friends; and they will put some of you to death. [17]You will be hated by all because of my name. [18]But not a hair of your head will perish. [19]By your endurance you will gain your souls."

Hymn and Keyboard Suggestions

O– "Marching to Zion" (Isa., Luke)
     B524, F550, UM733 (PD)
 "Jerusalem, My Happy Home" (Isa. 65)
     B517, E620, L331, W690
       S-2   #105. Flute/violin descant
               #106. Harmonization
       K-8   p. 22. Prelude/meditation
 "Jerusalem, the Golden" (Isa. 65)
     B527, E624
       K-2   p. 6. Short prelude/meditation
     L347
 "Soon and Very Soon" (Isa.)
     B192, UM706
       S-2   #187. Piano arrangement
       K-15   p. 68. Piano prelude/postlude
 "O Day of Peace That Dimly Shines" (Isa., Luke)
     E597, P450, UM729, W654
 "Surely It Is God Who Saves Me" (Isa. 12)
     E678, E679, W584
 "Christ, from Whom All Blessings Flow" (2 Thess.)
     UM550 (PD)
       S-1   #53. Descant
 "All Who Love and Serve Your City" (2 Thess., Luke)
     E571, P413, UM433
       S-1   #62. Descant
     E570, L436, W621
 "Where Cross the Crowded Ways of Life" (Luke)
     E609, F665, L429, P408, UM427 (PD)
       S-1   #141. Harmonization
               #142-43. Descant and transposition
                     in A major
 "Lord Christ, When First You Came to Earth" (Luke)
     E598, L421, P7, W438
       S-1   #237. Descant
 "Lord, Speak to Me" (Luke)
     B568, F625, L403, P426, UM463 (PD)
       H-1   #74. Harmonization
       S-1   #52. Descant
       K-8   p. 4. Prelude/meditation
 "Once He Came in Blessing" (Luke)
     E53 (PD), L312
       K-4   p. 8. Various keyboard treatments,
                  through p. 11
C– "O Day of God, Draw Nigh" (Luke)
     B623, E601, P452, UM730 (PD)
       S-1   #306. Harmonization
               #307. Descant
               #308. Transposition in F major
       K-1(III)   #64. Prelude/meditation

C– "Forth in Thy Name, O Lord" (2 Thess.)
     UM438 (PD)
       K-1(I)   #16. Use as interlude (manuals only)
       H-1   #83. Harmonization
       S-1   #100-103. Various treatments
       K-1(I)   #16. Prelude/postlude
       K-2   p. 8. Short prelude
       K-10   p. 32. Prelude/postlude
     L505 (PD)

Vocal Solos
"We Walk with God" (Isa. 12)
     V-7   p. 42
"My Lord, What a Morning" (Luke)
     V-5   p. 30

Anthems
"Prayer for Peace" (Isa. 65)
Dale Wood
Sacred Music Press S-535
SATB with keyboard

"Promised Land" (Isa. 65)
Natalie Sleeth
Sacred Music Press S-5775
Two-part with keyboard

"The First Song of Isaiah" (Isa. 12)
Jack Noble White
Belwin-Mills CMR 3347
SATB with keyboard and optional youth choir, dance,
    guitar, handbells, and percussion

"The Great Day of the Lord" (Luke)
Alan Stout
C. F. Peters 6883
SATB with keyboard

Hymn Anthem Suggestions
"This Is a Day of New Beginnings" (Isa. 65)
52IHA #43
"Let All the World in Every Corner Sing" (Isa. 12)
52IHA #30
"All Who Love and Serve Your City" (2 Thess., Luke)
52IHA #1
"How Firm a Foundation" (Luke)
52IHA #23

Other Suggestions
Introit: B13, UM101 (PD), W521, E380 (PD), L550, P229,
    stanza 1. "From All That Dwell Below the Skies" (Isa. 12)
Prayer: UM409. For Grace to Labor (2 Thess.)
Prayer: UM705. For Direction (2 Thess.)

Deuteronomy 26:1-11

[1]When you have come into the land that the LORD your God is giving you as an inheritance to possess, and you possess it, and settle in it, [2]you shall take some of the first of all the fruit of the ground, which you harvest from the land that the LORD your God is giving you, and you shall put it in a basket and go to the place that the LORD your God will choose as a dwelling for his name. [3]You shall go to the priest who is in office at that time, and say to him, "Today I declare to the LORD your God that I have come into the land that the LORD swore to our ancestors to give us." [4]When the priest takes the basket from your hand and sets it down before the altar of the LORD your God, [5]you shall make this response before the LORD your God: "A wandering Aramean was my ancestor; he went down into Egypt and lived there as an alien, few in number, and there he became a great nation, mighty and populous. [6]When the Egyptians treated us harshly and afflicted us, by imposing hard labor on us, [7]we cried to the LORD, the God of our ancestors; the LORD heard our voice and saw our affliction, our toil, and our oppression. [8]The LORD brought us out of Egypt with a mighty hand and an outstretched arm, with a terrifying display of power, and with signs and wonders; [9]and he brought us into this place and gave us this land, a land flowing with milk and honey. [10]So now I bring the first of the fruit of the ground that you, O LORD, have given me." You shall set it down before the LORD your God and bow down before the LORD your God. [11]Then you, together with the Levites and the aliens who reside among you, shall celebrate with all the bounty that the LORD your God has given to you and to your house.

Psalm 100

[1]Make a joyful noise to the LORD, all the earth.
  [2]Worship the LORD with gladness;
  come into his presence with singing.
[3]Know that the LORD is God.
  It is he that made us, and we are his;
  we are his people, and the sheep of his pasture.
[4]Enter his gates with thanksgiving,
  and his courts with praise.
  Give thanks to him, bless his name.
[5]For the LORD is good;
  his steadfast love endures forever,
  and his faithfulness to all generations.

Philippians 4:4-9

[4]Rejoice in the Lord always; again I will say, Rejoice. [5]Let your gentleness be known to everyone. The Lord is near. [6]Do not worry about anything, but in everything by prayer and supplication with thanksgiving let your requests be made known to God. [7]And the peace of God, which surpasses all understanding, will guard your hearts and your minds in Christ Jesus.

[8]Finally, beloved, whatever is true, whatever is honorable, whatever is just, whatever is pure, whatever is pleasing, whatever is commendable, if there is any excellence and if there is anything worthy of praise, think about these things. [9]Keep on doing the things that you have learned and received and heard and seen in me, and the God of peace will be with you.

John 6:25-35

[25]When they found him on the other side of the sea, they said to him, "Rabbi, when did you come here?" [26]Jesus answered them, "Very truly, I tell you, you are looking for me, not because you saw signs, but because you ate your fill of the loaves. [27]Do not work for the food that perishes, but for the food that endures for eternal life, which the Son of Man will give you. For it is on him that God the Father has set his seal." [28]Then they said to him, "What must we do to perform the works of God?" [29]Jesus answered them, "This is the work of God, that you believe in him whom he has sent." [30]So they said to him, "What sign are you going to give us then, so that we may see it and believe you? What work are you performing? [31]Our ancestors ate the manna in the wilderness; as it is written, 'He gave them bread from heaven to eat.' " [32]Then Jesus said to them, "Very truly, I tell you, it was not Moses who gave you the bread from heaven, but it is my Father who gives you the true bread from heaven. [33]For the bread of God is that which comes down from heaven and gives life to the world." [34]They said to him, "Sir, give us this bread always."

[35]Jesus said to them, "I am the bread of life. Whoever comes to me will never be hungry, and whoever believes in me will never be thirsty."

Hymn and Keyboard Suggestions

O– "The God of Abraham Praise" (Deut.)
      B34, E401, L544, P488, UM116 (PD), W537
      H-1   #44. Harmonization
      S-1   #211. Harmonization

"All People That on Earth Do Dwell" (Ps.)
      B5, E377 and 378, F381, L245, P220, UM75 (PD), W669
      H-1   #24. Harmonization
      S-1   #257-59. Various treatments
      S-2   #140. Descant
      K-1(III)   #58. Short prelude/postlude
      K-4   p. 12. Various keyboard treatments, through p. 17
      W670

"Now Thank We All Our God" (Ps.)
      B638, E396 or E397, F525, L533 or L534, P555, UM102 (PD), W560
      H-1   #27. Harmonization
      H-2   p. 26. Harmonization with descant
      S-1   #252-54. Various treatments
      K-1(II)   #56. Prelude/postlude (manuals only)
      K-11   p. 42. Prelude/meditation

"Rejoice, Ye Pure in Heart" (Phil.)
      B39, E556, F394, P145, UM160 (PD)
      H-1   #92. Harmonization in G major
      S-1   #228. Descant
      E557, P146, UM161

"Rejoice, the Lord Is King" (Phil.)
      B197, F374, P155, UM715 (PD), W493
      S-1   #78-80. Various treatments
      K-1(I)   #13. Prelude/postlude
      E481, UM716
      S-1   #147. Arrangement for two trumpets
      L171 (PD)

"Guide Me, O Thou Great Jehovah" (John)
      B56, E690, F608, L343, P281, UM127 (PD)
      S-1   #76. Descant
               #77. Harmonization
      K-6   p. 30. Prelude/postlude

"Deck Thyself, My Soul, with Gladness" (John)
      E339, L224, P506, UM612 (PD)
      K-1(III)   #80. Prelude/meditation (manuals only)
      K-5   p. 55. Various keyboard treatments, through p. 64

"Eat This Bread" (John, Communion)
      UM628, W734

"You Satisfy the Hungry Heart" (John, Communion)
      P521, UM629, W736
      S-1   #144. Four-part setting of refrain

"O Food to Pilgrims Given" (John, Communion)
      E309, UM631
      K-1(III)   #67. Prelude/postlude
      K-5   p. 51. Various keyboard treatments, through p. 53
      K-10   p. 18. Variations
      E308

"Fill My Cup, Lord" (John, Communion)
      F481, UM641
      S-2   #62. Stanzas for soloist

C– "Sing Praise to God Who Reigns Above" (Ps.)
      B20, E408, F343, P483, UM126 (PD), W528
      S-1   #237. Descant

Vocal Solos

"But the Lord Is Mindful of His Own" (Phil.)
V-10   p. 32
"Now Let Us Give Thanks" (Thanksgiving)
V-6   p. 17
"The Goodness of God" (Thanksgiving)
V-8   p. 49

Anthems

"Sing to the Lord of Harvest" (Deut.)
David Penninger
Hinshaw Music HMC 364
SATB with keyboard

"Let All Things Now Living" (Ps.)
arr. Katherine Davis
E. C. Schirmer 1770
SATB with keyboard

"Rejoice in the Lord Always" (Phil.)
Daniel Moe
Abingdon APM-131
SATB with keyboard

"Thank You, Thank You" (Thanksgiving)
Avery and Marsh (arr. Hustad)
Agape AG 7123
Children or youth mixed choir with keyboard

Hymn Anthem Suggestion

"You Satisfy the Hungry Heart" (Ps., Communion)
52IHA   #52

Other Suggestions

Introit: B253, F382, L564, P591, UM95 (PD). "Praise God, from Whom All Blessings Flow" (Ps.)
Canticle: UM74. "Canticle of Thanksgiving" (Ps.)
Prayer Response: UM630. "Become to Us the Living Bread" (John, Communion)
Prayer: UM489. For God's Gifts (Thanksgiving)

Jeremiah 23:1-6

[1]Woe to the shepherds who destroy and scatter the sheep of my pasture! says the LORD. [2]Therefore thus says the LORD, the God of Israel, concerning the shepherds who shepherd my people: It is you who have scattered my flock, and have driven them away, and you have not attended to them. So I will attend to you for your evil doings, says the LORD. [3]Then I myself will gather the remnant of my flock out of all the lands where I have driven them, and I will bring them back to their fold, and they shall be fruitful and multiply. [4]I will raise up shepherds over them who will shepherd them, and they shall not fear any longer, or be dismayed, nor shall any be missing, says the LORD.

[5]The days are surely coming, says the LORD, when I will raise up for David a righteous Branch, and he shall reign as king and deal wisely, and shall execute justice and righteousness in the land. [6]In his days Judah will be saved and Israel will live in safety. And this is the name by which he will be called: "The LORD is our righteousness."

Luke 1:68-79

[68]"Blessed be the Lord God of Israel,
  for he has looked favorably on
    his people and redeemed them.
[69]He has raised up a mighty savior for us
  in the house of his servant David,
[70]as he spoke through the mouth
  of his holy prophets from of old,
[71]that we would be saved from
  our enemies and from the
  hand of all who hate us.
[72]Thus he has shown the mercy
  promised to our ancestors,
  and has remembered his holy covenant,
[73]the oath that he swore to our
  ancestor Abraham,
  to grant us [74]that we, being
  rescued from the hands of our enemies,
  might serve him without fear,
[75]in holiness and righteousness
  before him all our days.
[76]And you, child, will be called the
  prophet of the Most High;
  for you will go before the Lord
  to prepare his ways,
[77]to give knowledge of salvation to his people
  by the forgiveness of their sins.
[78]By the tender mercy of our God,
  the dawn from on high will
  break upon us,
[79]to give light to those who sit in
  darkness and in the shadow of death,
  to guide our feet into the way of peace."

Colossians 1:11-20

[11]May you be made strong with all the strength that comes from his glorious power, and may you be prepared to endure everything with patience, while joyfully [12]giving thanks to the Father, who has enabled you to share in the inheritance of the saints in the light. [13]He has rescued us from the power of darkness and transferred us into the kingdom of his beloved Son, [14]in whom we have redemption, the forgiveness of sins.

[15]He is the image of the invisible God, the firstborn of all creation; [16]for in him all things in heaven and on earth were created, things visible and invisible, whether thrones or dominions or rulers or powers—all things have been created through him and for him. [17]He himself is before all things, and in him all things hold together. [18]He is the head of the body, the church; he is the beginning, the firstborn from the dead, so that he might come to have first place in everything. [19]For in him all the fullness of God was pleased to dwell, [20]and through him God was pleased to reconcile to himself all things, whether on earth or in heaven, by making peace through the blood of his cross.

Luke 23:33-43

[33]When they came to the place that is called The Skull, they crucified Jesus there with the criminals, one on his right and one on his left. [34]Then Jesus said, "Father, forgive them; for they do not know what they are doing." And they cast lots to divide his clothing. [35]And the people stood by, watching; but the leaders scoffed at him, saying, "He saved others; let him save himself if he is the Messiah of God, his chosen one!" [36]The soldiers also mocked him, coming up and offering him sour wine, [37]and saying, "If you are the King of the Jews, save yourself!" [38]There was also an inscription over him, "This is the King of the Jews."

[39]One of the criminals who were hanged there kept deriding him and saying, "Are you not the Messiah? Save yourself and us!" [40]But the other rebuked him, saying, "Do you not fear God, since you are under the same sentence of condemnation? [41]And we indeed have been condemned justly, for we are getting what we deserve for our deeds, but this man has done nothing wrong." [42]Then he said, "Jesus, remember me when you come into your kingdom." [43]He replied, "Truly I tell you, today you will be with me in Paradise."

Hymn and Keyboard Suggestions

O– "Hail, Thou Once Despised Jesus" (Luke 23)
      E495, UM325 (PD)
          H-1   #25. Harmonization
          S-1   #178. Harmonization
                   #179. Harmonization

O– "Jesus Shall Reign" (Jer.)
      B587, E544, F238, L530, P423, UM157 (PD),
      W492
          K-1(I) #16. Use as interlude (manuals only)
          H-1   #83. Harmonization
          S-1   #100-103. Various treatments
          K-1(I) #16. Prelude/postlude
          K-2   p. 8. Short prelude
          K-10   p. 32. Prelude/postlude
      "Blessed Be the God of Israel" (Luke 1)
      E444, P602, UM209
      "Christ Is the World's Light" (Luke 1, Col.,)
      UM188, W543
          S-1   #64. Descant
      "I Want to Walk as a Child of the Light" (Luke 1, Col.)
      E490, UM206, W510
          S-2   #91. Descant
      "Beneath the Cross of Jesus" (Col., Luke 23)
      B291, E498, F253, L107, P92, UM297 (PD)
          H-1   #52. Harmonization
      "Jesus, Keep Me Near the Cross" (Col., Luke 23)
      B280, UM301 (PD)
          S-2   #133. Descant
                   #134. Harmonization
      "Alas! and Did My Savior Bleed" (Col., Luke 23)
      B145, F274, L98, P78, UM294 (PD)
          S-2   #116-17. Harmonizations
          K-6   p. 12. Prelude/meditation/postlude
      B139, UM359 (PD)
      "Victory in Jesus" (Col., Luke 23)
      B426, F82, UM370
          S-2   #75. Piano arrangement
      "Jesus, Remember Me" (Luke 23)
      P599, UM488, W423

C– "It Is Well with My Soul" (Col.)
      B410, F495, L346, UM377 (PD)
          K-13   p. 21. Piano prelude/meditation
          K-15   p. 126. Piano prelude/meditation

Vocal Solos

"It Is Well with My Soul" (Col.)
V-3   p. 3
"Of the Father's Love Begotten" (Col.)
V-3   p. 17

Anthems

"There Shall a Star Come Out of Jacob" (Jer.)
Felix Mendelssohn
Schmitt, Hall, & McCreary SCHCH 1903
SATB with keyboard

"Victory in Jesus" (Col., Luke 23)
Buryl Red
TUO 108
SATB with keyboard

"Thy Throne, O God Is Forever and Ever" (Col.)
Christian Latrobe (ed. Kroeger)
Boosey & Hawkes 6051
SATB with SATB solos and keyboard

"Prepare a Royal Highway" in *A Season to Celebrate* (Christ the King)
Allen Pote
Hinshaw Music HMB 144
SATB with keyboard, optional guitar, flute, and tambourine

Hymn Anthem Suggestions

"Blessed Be the God of Israel" (Luke 1)
52IHA   #3
"I Want to Walk as a Child of the Light" (Luke 1, Col.)
52IHA   #27

Other Suggestions

Call to Worship: B88, E87, F184, L60, P31, UM240 (PD), W387, stanza 2. "Hark! the Herald Angels Sing" (Col.)
Canticle: UM208. "Canticle of Zechariah" (Luke 1)
Prayer: UM360. Freedom in Christ (Luke 23)
Prayer: UM466. An Invitation to Christ (Luke 1, Christ the King)
Prayer: UM489. For God's Gifts (Luke 1)
Prayer: UM721. Christ the King

Isaiah 2:1-5

[1]The word that Isaiah son of Amoz saw concerning Judah and Jerusalem. [2]In days to come the mountain of the LORD's house shall be established as the highest of the mountains, and shall be raised above the hills; all the nations shall stream to it. [3]Many peoples shall come and say, "Come, let us go up to the mountain of the LORD, to the house of the God of Jacob; that he may teach us his ways and that we may walk in his paths." For out of Zion shall go forth instruction, and the word of the LORD from Jerusalem. [4]He shall judge between the nations, and shall arbitrate for many peoples; they shall beat their swords into plowshares, and their spears into pruning hooks; nation shall not lift up sword against nation, neither shall they learn war any more. [5]O house of Jacob, come, let us walk in the light of the LORD!

Psalm 122

[1]I was glad when they said to me,
  "Let us go to the house of the
    LORD!"
[2]Our feet are standing
  within your gates,
    O Jerusalem.
[3]Jerusalem—built as a city
  that is bound firmly together.
[4]To it the tribes go up,
  the tribes of the LORD,
    as was decreed for Israel,
  to give thanks to the name of
    the LORD.
[5]For there the thrones for
    judgment were set up,
  the thrones of the house of
    David.
[6]Pray for the peace of Jerusalem:
  "May they prosper who love
    you.
[7]Peace be within your walls,
  and security within your
    towers."
[8]For the sake of my relatives and
    friends
  I will say, "Peace be within you."
[9]For the sake of the house of the
    LORD our God,
  I will seek your good.

Romans 13:11-14

[11]Besides this, you know what time it is, how it is now the moment for you to wake from sleep. For salvation is nearer to us now than when we became believers; [12]the night is far gone, the day is near. Let us then lay aside the works of darkness and put on the armor of light; [13]let us live honorably as in the day, not in reveling and drunkenness, not in debauchery and licentiousness, not in quarreling and jealousy. [14]Instead, put on the Lord Jesus Christ, and make no provision for the flesh, to gratify its desires.

Matthew 24:36-44

[36]"But about that day and hour no one knows, neither the angels of heaven, nor the Son, but only the Father. [37]For as the days of Noah were, so will be the coming of the Son of Man. [38]For as in those days before the flood they were eating and drinking, marrying and giving in marriage, until the day Noah entered the ark, [39]and they knew nothing until the flood came and swept them all away, so too will be the coming of the Son of Man. [40]Then two will be in the field; one will be taken and one will be left. [41]Two women will be grinding meal together; one will be taken and one will be left. [42]Keep awake therefore, for you do not know on what day your Lord is coming. [43]But understand this: if the owner of the house had known in what part of the night the thief was coming, he would have stayed awake and would not have let his house be broken into. [44]Therefore you also must be ready, for the Son of Man is coming at an unexpected hour."

Hymn and Keyboard Suggestions
O– "We've a Story to Tell to the Nations" (Isa.)
    B586, F659, UM569 (PD)
      K-8   p. 26. Introduction
O– "Wake, Awake, for Night Is Flying" (Rom.)
    E61, L31, P17, UM720 (PD), W371
      K-1(IV) #90. Prelude/postlude (may be played manuals only)
      K-5 p. 105. Prelude/postlude. Simple, three-part writing. May be played by piano with a solo instrument (cello, flute, oboe) playing melody, which is found in the bass clef beginning in measure 13. Effectively followed by choir singing chorale as introit.
      K-15 p. 30. Piano prelude
"Let There Be Light" (Isa.)
    UM440, W653
"O Day of Peace That Dimly Shines" (Isa.)
    E597, P450, UM729, W654
"With Joy I Heard My Friends Exclaim" (Ps.)
    P235
"Awake, O Sleeper" (Rom.)
    E547, UM551
      S-2 #115. Descant
    W586
      S-1 #33-38. Various treatments
"My Lord, What Morning" (Rom.)
    P449, UM719
"Now Let Us from This Table Rise" (Rom., Communion)
    UM634, W625
      S-2 #48. Descant
        #49. Harmonization
"Come, Thou Long-Expected Jesus" (Matt., Rom.)
    B77, F168, P2, UM196 (PD)
      S-1 #168-71. Various treatments
      K-2 p. 12. Short prelude
      K-9 p. 7. Prelude/postlude
    E66, P1 (PD), W364
      H-1 #1. Harmonization
      H-2 p. 34. Harmonization with descant
    L30
      K-3 p. 4. Prelude/meditation
"People, Look East" (Matt., Rom.)
    P12, UM202, W359
      S-2 #26. Flute descant
"Let All Mortal Flesh Keep Silence" (Advent, Communion)
    B80, E324, F166, L198, P5, UM626 (PD), W523
      H-1 #33. Harmonization
      S-1 #268. Handbell part
        #269. Descant
      K-3 p. 14. Prelude/meditation

C– "O God of Every Nation" (Isa.)
    E607, P289, UM435
      S-1 #215. Harmonization
    L416, W650

Vocal Solos
"Come, Thou Long-Expected Jesus" (Matt., Rom.)
V-1 p. 5
V-8 p. 4
"For Behold, Darkness Shall Cover the Earth" and "The People That Walked in Darkness"
"Rejoice Greatly, O Daughter of Zion" (Isa.)
V-2
"My Lord, What a Morning" (Rom.)
V-5 p. 30

Anthems
"Hurry Lord! Come Quickly!" (Isa., Matt.)
Lloyd Pfautsch
Agape AG 7169
SATB with keyboard and optional string or electric bass

"Star of the East" (Isa., Matt.)
Amanda Kennedy (arr. Roger Wilson)
Lorenz B36
SATB with keyboard and junior choir or solo

"Hosanna" in *A Season to Celebrate* (Advent)
Allen Pote
Hinshaw Music HMB 144
SATB with keyboard

Hymn Anthem Suggestions
"Hail to the Lord's Anointed" (Ps.)
52IHA #20
"Wake, Awake, O Sleeper" (Rom.)
52IHA #48
"My Lord, What a Morning" (Rom.)
52IHA #34
"People, Look East" (Matt., Rom.)
HA p. 1

Other Suggestions
Response: E490, UM206, W510, refrain. "I Want to Walk as a Child of the Light" (Advent)
Response: B76, E56, F169, L34, P9, UM211, W357, stanza 1. "O Come, O Come Emmanuel" (Advent)
Benediction Response: B660, UM665. "Go Now in Peace." See S-1, #146 for Orff accompaniment (Isa.).

Isaiah 11:1-10

[1]A shoot shall come out from the stump of Jesse, and a branch shall grow out of his roots. [2]The spirit of the LORD shall rest on him, the spirit of wisdom and understanding, the spirit of counsel and might, the spirit of knowledge and the fear of the LORD. [3]His delight shall be in the fear of the LORD. He shall not judge by what his eyes see, or decide by what his ears hear; [4]but with righteousness he shall judge the poor, and decide with equity for the meek of the earth; he shall strike the earth with the rod of his mouth, and with the breath of his lips he shall kill the wicked. [5]Righteousness shall be the belt around his waist, and faithfulness the belt around his loins. [6]The wolf shall live with the lamb, the leopard shall lie down with the kid, the calf and the lion and the fatling together, and a little child shall lead them. [7]The cow and the bear shall graze, their young shall lie down together; and the lion shall eat straw like the ox. [8]The nursing child shall play over the hole of the asp, and the weaned child shall put its hand on the adder's den. [9]They will not hurt or destroy on all my holy mountain; for the earth will be full of the knowledge of the LORD as the waters cover the sea.

[10]On that day the root of Jesse shall stand as a signal to the peoples; the nations shall inquire of him, and his dwelling shall be glorious.

Psalm 72:1-7, 18-19

[1]Give the king your justice, O God,
 and your righteousness to a king's son.
[2]May he judge your people with righteousness,
 and your poor with justice.
[3]May the mountains yield prosperity for the people,
 and the hills, in righteousness.
[4]May he defend the cause of the poor of the people,
 give deliverance to the needy,
 and crush the oppressor.
[5]May he live while the sun endures,
 and as long as the moon, throughout all generations.
[6]May he be like rain that falls on the mown grass,
 like showers that water the earth.
[7]In his days may righteousness flourish
 and peace abound, until the moon is no more.
[18]Blessed be the LORD, the God of Israel,
 who alone does wondrous things.
[19]Blessed be his glorious name forever;
 may his glory fill the whole earth.
  Amen and Amen.

Romans 15:4-13

[4]For whatever was written in former days was written for our instruction, so that by steadfastness and by the encouragement of the scriptures we might have hope. [5]May the God of steadfastness and encouragement grant you to live in harmony with one another, in accordance with Christ Jesus, [6]so that together you may with one voice glorify the God and Father of our Lord Jesus Christ.

[7]Welcome one another, therefore, just as Christ has welcomed you, for the glory of God. [8]For I tell you that Christ has become a servant of the circumcised on behalf of the truth of God in order that he might confirm the promises given to the patriarchs, [9]and in order that the Gentiles might glorify God for his mercy. As it is written, "Therefore I will confess you among the Gentiles, and sing praises to your name"; [10]and again he says, "Rejoice, O Gentiles, with his people"; [11]and again, "Praise the Lord, all you Gentiles, and let all the peoples praise him"; [12]and again Isaiah says, "The root of Jesse shall come, the one who rises to rule the Gentiles; in him the Gentiles shall hope." [13]May the God of hope fill you with all joy and peace in believing, so that you may abound in hope by the power of the Holy Spirit.

Matthew 3:1-12

[1]In those days John the Baptist appeared in the wilderness of Judea, proclaiming, [2]"Repent, for the kingdom of heaven has come near." [3]This is the one of whom the prophet Isaiah spoke when he said, "The voice of one crying out in the wilderness: 'Prepare the way of the Lord, make his paths straight.' " [4]Now John wore clothing of camel's hair with a leather belt around his waist, and his food was locusts and wild honey. [5]Then the people of Jerusalem and all Judea were going out to him, and all the region along the Jordan, [6]and they were baptized by him in the river Jordan, confessing their sins.

[7]But when he saw many Pharisees and Sadducees coming for baptism, he said to them, "You brood of vipers! Who warned you to flee from the wrath to come? [8]Bear fruit worthy of repentance. [9]Do not presume to say to yourselves, 'We have Abraham as our ancestor'; for I tell you, God is able from these stones to raise up children to Abraham. [10]Even now the ax is lying at the root of the trees; every tree therefore that does not bear good fruit is cut down and thrown into the fire.

[11]"I baptize you with water for repentance, but one who is more powerful than I is coming after me; I am not worthy to carry his sandals. He will baptize you with the Holy Spirit and fire. [12]His winnowing fork is in his hand, and he will clear his threshing floor and will gather his wheat into the granary; but the chaff he will burn with unquenchable fire."

Hymn and Keyboard Suggestions

O– "Hail to the Lord's Anointed" (Ps.)
      UM203 (PD)
          S-1   #114. Descant
                     #115. Harmonization
      E616 (PD), L87, P205
"Savior of the Nations, Come" (Isa.)
      E54, P14 (PD), UM214, W372
          K-1(III) #59. Short prelude/meditation
                     (manuals only)
          K-5   p. 11. Various keyboard treatments,
                     through p. 17
"Isaiah the Prophet Has Written of Old" (Isa.)
      P337
"Lo, How a Rose E'er Blooming" (Isa.)
      B78, E81, F174, L58, P48 (PD), UM216, W374
          S-2   #56. Male chorus arrangement
                     #57. Two-octave handbell arrange-
                     ment
          K-1(I)   #21. Short prelude
          K-14   p. 40. Short prelude (manuals only)
"O Day of Peace That Dimly Shines" (Isa.)
      E597, P450, UM729, W654
"O Day of God, Draw Nigh" (Isa.)
      B623, E601, P452, UM730 (PD)
          S-1   #306-8. Various treatments
          K-1(III) #64. Prelude/meditation
"Blessed Be the Name" (Ps.)
      B206, UM63
"Help Us Accept Each Other" (Rom.)
      UM560
          S-2   #1. Descant
      P358, W656
"On Jordan's Bank the Baptist's Cry" (Matt.)
      E76, P10 (PD), W356
          H-1   #5. Harmonization
          K-1(I)   #14. Short prelude/postlude
          K-2   p. 35. Short prelude/postlude
      L36
C– "Heralds of Christ" (Matt.)
      UM567 (PD)
          S-2   #131-32. Harmonization with des-
                     cant
C– "Jesus Shall Reign" (Ps.)
      B587, E544, F238, L530, P423, UM157 (PD),
      W492
          K-1(I)   #16. Use as interlude (manuals only)
          H-1   #83. Harmonization
          S-1   #100-103. Various treatments
          K-1(I)   #16. Prelude/postlude
          K-2   p. 8. Short prelude
          K-10   p. 32. Prelude/postlude

Vocal Solos

"Come, Thou Long-Expected Jesus" (Rom.)
    V-1   p. 5
    V-8   p. 4 (text adapted)
"Standing in the Need of Prayer" (Matt.)
    V-5   p. 201
"A Carol for Advent"
    V-7   p. 7

Anthems

"Prepare a Royal Highway" in *A Season to Celebrate* (Isa.,
    Matt.)
Allen Pote
Hinshaw Music HMB 144
SATB with keyboard, optional guitar, flute, and tam-
    bourine

"O Hearken Ye" in *The Alfred Burt Carols, Set 2* (Isa., Rom.)
Alfred Burt
Shawnee Press A-450
SATB *a cappella*

"I Wonder as I Wander" (Ps.)
arr. John Rutter
Hinshaw HMC-673
SATB *a cappella*

Hymn Anthem Suggestion

"Hail to the Lord's Anointed"
52IHA   #20

Other Suggestions

    This would be an excellent Sunday to schedule baptisms.
Introit: UM207, W369. "Prepare the Way of the Lord"
    (Matt.)
Greeting: Isaiah 35:3-4. Be strong; do not fear (Isa.)
Prayer: UM201. Advent (Isa., Matt.)
Prayer: UM602. Concerning the Scriptures (Rom.)
Psalm: P204. Psalm 72 (Ps.)
Response: E490, UM206, W510, refrain. "I Want to Walk as
    a Child of the Light"
Response: B76, E56, F169, L34, P9, UM211, W357, stanza
    2. "O Come, O Come Emmanuel" (Advent)

Isaiah 35:1-10

[1]The wilderness and the dry land shall be glad, the desert shall rejoice and blossom; like the crocus [2]it shall blossom abundantly, and rejoice with joy and singing. The glory of Lebanon shall be given to it, the majesty of Carmel and Sharon. They shall see the glory of the Lord, the majesty of our God. [3]Strengthen the weak hands, and make firm the feeble knees. [4]Say to those who are of a fearful heart, "Be strong, do not fear! Here is your God. He will come with vengeance, with terrible recompense. He will come and save you." [5]Then the eyes of the blind shall be opened, and the ears of the deaf unstopped; [6]then the lame shall leap like a deer, and the tongue of the speechless sing for joy. For waters shall break forth in the wilderness, and streams in the desert; [7]the burning sand shall become a pool, and the thirsty ground springs of water; the haunt of jackals shall become a swamp, the grass shall become reeds and rushes. [8]A highway shall be there, and it shall be called the Holy Way; the unclean shall not travel on it, but it shall be for God's people; no traveler, not even fools, shall go astray. [9]No lion shall be there, nor shall any ravenous beast come up on it; they shall not be found there, but the redeemed shall walk there. [10]And the ransomed of the Lord shall return, and come to Zion with singing; everlasting joy shall be upon their heads; they shall obtain joy and gladness, and sorrow and sighing shall flee away.

Luke 1:47-55

[47]"My soul magnifies the Lord,
and my spirit rejoices in God
my Savior,
[48]for he has looked with favor on
the lowliness of his
servant.
Surely, from now on all
generations will call me
blessed;
[49]for the Mighty One has done
great things for me,
and holy is his name.
[50]His mercy is for those who fear
him
from generation to generation.
[51]He has shown strength with his
arm;
he has scattered the proud in
the thoughts of their
hearts.
[52]He has brought down the
powerful from their
thrones,
and lifted up the lowly;
[53]he has filled the hungry with
good things,
and sent the rich away empty.
[54]He has helped his servant Israel,
in remembrance of his mercy,
[55]according to the promise he
made to our ancestors,
to Abraham and to his
descendants forever."

James 5:7-10

[7]Be patient, therefore, beloved, until the coming of the Lord. The farmer waits for the precious crop from the earth, being patient with it until it receives the early and the late rains. [8]You also must be patient. Strengthen your hearts, for the coming of the Lord is near. [9]Beloved, do not grumble against one another, so that you may not be judged. See, the Judge is standing at the doors! [10]As an example of suffering and patience, beloved, take the prophets who spoke in the name of the Lord.

Matthew 11:2-11

[2]When John heard in prison what the Messiah was doing, he sent word by his disciples [3]and said to him, "Are you the one who is to come, or are we to wait for another?" [4]Jesus answered them, "Go and tell John what you hear and see: [5]the blind receive their sight, the lame walk, the lepers are cleansed, the deaf hear, the dead are raised, and the poor have good news brought to them. [6]And blessed is anyone who takes no offense at me."

[7]As they went away, Jesus began to speak to the crowds about John: "What did you go out into the wilderness to look at? A reed shaken by the wind? [8]What then did you go out to see? Someone dressed in soft robes? Look, those who wear soft robes are in royal palaces. [9]What then did you go out to see? A prophet? Yes, I tell you, and more than a prophet. [10]This is the one about whom it is written, 'See, I am sending my messenger ahead of you, who will prepare your way before you.' [11]Truly I tell you, among those born of women no one has arisen greater than John the Baptist; yet the least in the kingdom of heaven is greater than he."

Hymn and Keyboard Suggestions
O– "Lift Up Your Heads, Ye Mighty Gates" (Isa.)
  B128, E436, F239, P8, UM213 (PD), W363
    S-1   #334. Descant
          #335. Harmonization
  "Lo, How a Rose E'er Blooming" (Isa.)
  B78, E81, F174, L58, P48 (PD), UM216, W374
    S-2   #56. Male chorus arrangement
          #57. Two-octave handbell arrange-
            ment
    K-1(I) #21. Short prelude
    K-14   p. 40. Short prelude (manuals only)
  "En el Frío Invernal" ("Cold December Flies Away")
    (Isa.)
    L53, UM233
    S-1   #216. Introduction/harmonization
          #217. Flute descant
  "It Came upon the Midnight Clear" (Isa., James, Matt.)
  B93, E89, F197, L54, P38, UM218 (PD), W400
    S-2   #39. Descant
  E90
  "Ye Who Claim the Faith of Jesus" (Luke)
  E268, UM197
    S-1   #191. Descant
  E269
  "My Soul Gives Glory to My God" (Luke)
  P600, UM198
    S-1   #241. Orff arrangement
          #242. Descant
    K-3   p. 8. Prelude/postlude
    K-6   p. 39. Prelude/meditation
  "Tell Out, My Soul" (Luke)
  B81, E438, UM200, W534
    S-2   #201. Descant
  E437
  "O For a Thousand Tongues to Sing" (Matt.)
  B216, E493, F349, L559, P466, UM57 and 59
  (PD)
    S-1   #33-38. Various treatments
  "O That I Had a Thousand Voices" (Matt.)
  L560, P475, W546
    K-1(II) #61. Prelude/postlude
C– "I Want to Walk as a Child of the Light" (James)
  E490, UM206, W510
    S-2   #91. Descant
C– "Blessed Be the God of Israel" (Luke, Matt.)
  E444, P602, UM209

Vocal Solos
"My Soul Doth Magnify the Lord" (Luke)
V-6   p. 28
"Patiently Have I Waited for the Lord" (James)
V-4   p. 24
"O For a Thousand Tongues to Sing" (Matt.)
V-1   p. 32

Anthems
"O Come, O Come Emmanuel" (Isa.)
arr. Alice Parker and Robert Shaw
Lawson-Gould 727
SATB *a cappella*

"Go and Tell John" (Matt.)
Lloyd Pfautsch
Hope Publishing CY 3334
SATB *a cappella*

Hymn Anthem Suggestions
"En el Frío Invernal" ("Cold December Flies Away") (Isa.)
52IHA   #14
"I Want to Walk as a Child of the Light" (James)
52IHA   #27
"Blessed Be the God of Israel" (Luke, Matt.)
52IHA   #3

Other Suggestions
Introit: UM207, W369. "Prepare the Way of the Lord"
  (Matt.)
Canticle: F176, L180, UM199, W553. Various settings of
  the "Canticle of Mary" (Luke)
Response: E490, UM206, W510, refrain. "I Want to Walk as
  a Child of the Light" (James)
Response: B76, E56, F169, L34, P9, UM211, W357, stanza
  6. "O Come, O Come Emmanuel" (Advent)
Prayer: UM201. Advent (Isa., Matt.)
Interpretive movement would greatly enhance the singing
  or reading of the Luke passage.

Isaiah 7:10-16

[10]Again the LORD spoke to Ahaz, saying, [11]Ask a sign of the LORD your God; let it be deep as Sheol or high as heaven. [12]But Ahaz said, I will not ask, and I will not put the LORD to the test. [13]Then Isaiah said: "Hear then, O house of David! Is it too little for you to weary mortals, that you weary my God also? [14]Therefore the Lord himself will give you a sign. Look, the young woman is with child and shall bear a son, and shall name him Immanuel. [15]He shall eat curds and honey by the time he knows how to refuse the evil and choose the good. [16]For before the child knows how to refuse the evil and choose the good, the land before whose two kings you are in dread will be deserted."

Psalm 80:1-7, 17-19

[1]Give ear, O Shepherd of Israel,
    you who lead Joseph like a flock!
You who are enthroned upon the
      cherubim, shine forth
  [2]before Ephraim and
    Benjamin and Manasseh.
Stir up your might,
    and come to save us!
[3]Restore us, O God;
    let your face shine, that we may be saved.
[4]O LORD God of hosts,
    how long will you be angry
      with your people's prayers?
[5]You have fed them with the
      bread of tears,
    and given them tears to drink
      in full measure.
[6]You make us the scorn of our neighbors;
    our enemies laugh among themselves.
[7]Restore us, O God of hosts;
    let your face shine, that we may be saved.
[17]But let your hand be upon the
      one at your right hand,
    the one whom you made
      strong for yourself.
[18]Then we will never turn back from you;
    give us life, and we will call on your name.
[19]Restore us, O LORD God of hosts;
    let your face shine, that we may be saved.

Romans 1:1-7

[1]Paul, a servant of Jesus Christ, called to be an apostle, set apart for the gospel of God, [2]which he promised beforehand through his prophets in the holy scriptures, [3]the gospel concerning his Son, who was descended from David according to the flesh [4]and was declared to be Son of God with power according to the spirit of holiness by resurrection from the dead, Jesus Christ our Lord, [5]through whom we have received grace and apostleship to bring about the obedience of faith among all the Gentiles for the sake of his name, [6]including yourselves who are called to belong to Jesus Christ,

[7]To all God's beloved in Rome, who are called to be saints:

Grace to you and peace from God our Father and the Lord Jesus Christ.

Matthew 1:18-25

[18]Now the birth of Jesus the Messiah took place in this way. When his mother Mary had been engaged to Joseph, but before they lived together, she was found to be with child from the Holy Spirit. [19]Her husband Joseph, being a righteous man and unwilling to expose her to public disgrace, planned to dismiss her quietly. [20]But just when he had resolved to do this, an angel of the Lord appeared to him in a dream and said, "Joseph, son of David, do not be afraid to take Mary as your wife, for the child conceived in her is from the Holy Spirit. [21]She will bear a son, and you are to name him Jesus, for he will save his people from their sins." [22]All this took place to fulfill what had been spoken by the Lord through the prophet: [23]"Look, the virgin shall conceive and bear a son, and they shall name him Emmanuel," which means, "God is with us." [24]When Joseph awoke from sleep, he did as the angel of the Lord commanded him; he took her as his wife, [25]but had no marital relations with her until she had borne a son; and he named him Jesus.

Hymn and Keyboard Suggestions

O– "O Come, O Come, Emmanuel" (Isa., Matt.)
      B76, E56, F169, L34 (PD), P9, UM211, W357
        S-1   #342. Handbell accompaniment
        K-1(IV) #87. Prelude (manuals only)

O– "Angels from the Realms of Glory" (Matt.)
      B94, E93, F190, L50, P22, UM220, W377
        H-1   #7. Harmonization
        S-1   #280. Descant
                  #281. Harmonization
        K-1(III) #72. Short prelude/postlude/interlude
        K-2   p. 24. Short prelude
        K-8   p. 28. Introduction/interlude

"The King of Glory Comes" (Isa.)
      B127, W501

"Emmanuel, Emmanuel" (Isa., Matt.)
      B82, UM204

"Hark! the Herald Angels Sing" (Isa., Matt.)
      B88, E87, F184, L60, P31, UM240 (PD), W387
        H-1   #9. Harmonization
        S-1   #234. Harmonization
                  #235-36. Harmonization with descant
        K-1(II) #50. Prelude/meditation

"O Hear Our Cry, O Lord" (Ps.)
      P206

"O Come, All Ye Faithful" (Rom., Matt.)
      B89, E83, F193, L45, P41, UM234 (PD), W392
        H-1   #8. Harmonization
        H-2   p. 2. Harmonization with descant
        S-1   #7-13. Various treatments
        K-8   p. 28. Introduction
        K-1(I)   #3. Short prelude or postlude
        K-10   p. 16. Prelude/meditation

"Praise We the Lord This Day" (Matt.)
      E267 (PD), W696

"Ye Who Claim the Faith of Jesus" (Matt.)
      E268, UM197
        S-1   #191. Descant
      E269

"To a Maid Engaged to Joseph" (Matt.)
      P19, UM215
        S-2   #12-13. Descants

"He Is Born" ("Il Est Né") (Matt.)
      B112, UM228
        S-1   #177. Orff instrument arrangement

C– "O Little Town of Bethlehem" (Matt.)
      B86, E79, F178, L41, P44, UM230, W386
        H-1   #14. Harmonization
        S-1   #304. Harmonization
        K-3   p. 24. Prelude/meditation (manuals only)

      E78, P43
        S-1   #131. Introduction
                  #132. Descant
        K-3   p. 25. Short prelude/postlude (manuals only)
        K-6   p. 10. Prelude/postlude

Vocal Solos

"Behold! A Virgin Shall Conceive" and
"O Thou That Tellest Good Tidings to Zion" (Isa., Matt.)
V-2

"Hark! the Herald Angels Sing" (Matt.)
V-1   p. 13

"Let Us Turn to Bethlehem" (General)
V-6   p. 54

Anthems

"Advent Song" in *A Season to Celebrate* (Isa., Matt.)
Allen Pote
Hinshaw Music HMB 144
SATB with keyboard, optional guitar

"The Child of Promise" (Isa.)
Michael Richardson
Mark Foster MF 548
SATB with keyboard and optional flute, guitar and string bass

"Jesus Is Love with Us" (Matt.)
John Shepherd
Choristers Guild CGA-365
Unison or two-part with keyboard

Hymn Anthem Suggestion

"To a Maid Engaged to Joseph" (Matt.)
52IHA   #46

Other Suggestions

   See UM211 for the spoken antiphons that accompany the hymn. If you use a processional, stop each time an antiphon is read, and then move during the singing of the next stanza.

Introit: B76, E56, F169, L34 (PD), P9, UM211, W357, stanza 1. "O Come, O Come, Emmanuel." Handbell part, S-1, #342. (Isa., Matt.)

Response: E490, UM206, W510, refrain. "I Want to Walk as a Child of the Light"

Response: B76, E56, F169, L34 (PD), P9, UM211, W357, stanza 7. "O Come, O Come Emmanuel" (Advent)

Isaiah 9:2-7

²The people who walked in darkness have seen a great light; those who lived in a land of deep darkness—on them light has shined. ³You have multiplied the nation, you have increased its joy; they rejoice before you as with joy at the harvest, as people exult when dividing plunder. ⁴For the yoke of their burden, and the bar across their shoulders, the rod of their oppressor, you have broken as on the day of Midian. ⁵For all the boots of the tramping warriors and all the garments rolled in blood shall be burned as fuel for the fire. ⁶For a child has been born for us, a son given to us; authority rests upon his shoulders; and he is named Wonderful Counselor, Mighty God, Everlasting Father, Prince of Peace. ⁷His authority shall grow continually, and there shall be endless peace for the throne of David and his kingdom. He will establish and uphold it with justice and with righteousness from this time onward and forevermore. The zeal of the LORD of hosts will do this.

Psalm 96

¹O sing to the LORD a new song; sing to the LORD, all the earth. ²Sing to the LORD, bless his name; tell of his salvation from day to day. ³Declare his glory among the nations, his marvelous works among all the peoples. ⁴For great is the LORD, and greatly to be praised; he is to be revered above all gods. ⁵For all the gods of the peoples are idols, but the LORD made the heavens. ⁶Honor and majesty are before him; strength and beauty are in his sanctuary. ⁷Ascribe to the LORD, O families of the peoples, ascribe to the LORD glory and strength. ⁸Ascribe to the LORD the glory due his name; bring an offering, and come into his courts. ⁹Worship the LORD in holy splendor; tremble before him, all the earth. ¹⁰Say among the nations, "The LORD is king! The world is firmly established; it shall never be moved. He will judge the peoples with equity." ¹¹Let the heavens be glad, and let the earth rejoice; let the sea roar, and all that fills it; ¹²let the field exult, and everything in it. Then shall all the trees of the forest sing for joy ¹³before the LORD; for he is coming, for he is coming to judge the earth. He will judge the world with righteousness, and the peoples with his truth.

Titus 2:11-14

¹¹For the grace of God has appeared, bringing salvation to all, ¹²training us to renounce impiety and worldly passions, and in the present age to live lives that are self-controlled, upright, and godly, ¹³while we wait for the blessed hope and the manifestation of the glory of our great God and Savior, Jesus Christ. ¹⁴He it is who gave himself for us that he might redeem us from all iniquity and purify for himself a people of his own who are zealous for good deeds.

Luke 2:1-20

¹In those days a decree went out from Emperor Augustus that all the world should be registered. ²This was the first registration and was taken while Quirinius was governor of Syria. ³All went to their own towns to be registered. ⁴Joseph also went from the town of Nazareth in Galilee to Judea, to the city of David called Bethlehem, because he was descended from the house and family of David. ⁵He went to be registered with Mary, to whom he was engaged and who was expecting a child. ⁶While they were there, the time came for her to deliver her child. ⁷And she gave birth to her firstborn son and wrapped him in bands of cloth, and laid him in a manger, because there was no place for them in the inn.

⁸In that region there were shepherds living in the fields, keeping watch over their flock by night. ⁹Then an angel of the Lord stood before them, and the glory of the Lord shone around them, and they were terrified. ¹⁰But the angel said to them, "Do not be afraid; for see—I am bringing you good news of great joy for all the people: ¹¹to you is born this day in the city of David a Savior, who is the Messiah, the Lord. ¹²This will be a sign for you: you will find a child wrapped in bands of cloth and lying in a manger." ¹³And suddenly there was with the angel a multitude of the heavenly host, praising God and saying,

¹⁴"Glory to God in the highest heaven,
and on earth peace among those whom he favors!"

¹⁵When the angels had left them and gone into heaven, the shepherds said to one another, "Let us go now to Bethlehem and see this thing that has taken place, which the Lord has made known to us." ¹⁶So they went with haste and found Mary and Joseph, and the child lying in the manger. ¹⁷When they saw this, they made known what had been told them about this child; ¹⁸and all who heard it were amazed at what the shepherds told them. ¹⁹But Mary treasured all these words and pondered them in her heart. ²⁰The shepherds returned, glorifying and praising God for all they had heard and seen, as it had been told them.

Hymn and Keyboard Suggestions

O– "Hark! the Herald Angels Sing" (Luke)
    B88, E87, F184, L60, P31, UM240 (PD), W387
    H-1   #9. Harmonization
    S-1   #234. Harmonization
             #235-36. Harmonization with descant
    K-1(II) #50. Prelude/meditation

O– "On This Day Earth Shall Ring" (Ps., Titus, Luke)
    E92, P46, UM248 (PD)
    S-1   #267. Handbell part

"Break Forth, O Beauteous Heavenly Light" (Isa.)
    B114 (PD), E91, F207, P26, UM223

"In the Bleak Midwinter" (Ps., Titus, Luke)
    E112, P36, UM221 (PD)

"What Child Is This" (Luke)
    B118, E115, F180, L40, P53, UM219 (PD), W411
    S-1   p. 150. Guitar chords
    K-3   p. 30. Prelude/meditation
    K-9   p. 21. Prelude/meditation

"Angels from the Realms of Glory" (Luke)
    B94, E93, F190, L50, P22, UM220 (PD), W377
    H-1   #7. Harmonization
    S-1   #280. Descant
             #281. Harmonization
    K-1(III) #72. Short prelude/postlude/interlude
    K-2   p. 24. Short prelude
    K-8   p. 28. Introduction/interlude

"Infant Holy, Infant Lowly" (Luke)
    B106, F194, L44, P37, UM229, W393
    S-1   #345. Handbell/keyboard arrangement

"O Little Town of Bethlehem" (Luke)
    B86, E79, F178, L41, P44, UM230, W386
    H-1   #14. Harmonization
    S-1   #304. Harmonization
    K-3   p. 24. Prelude/meditation (manuals only)
    E78, P43
    S-1   #131. Introduction
             #132. Descant
    K-3   p. 25. Short prelude/postlude (manuals only)
    K-6   p. 10. Prelude/postlude

"When Christmas Morn Is Dawning" (Luke)
    L59, UM232
    S-2   #199. Descant

"Once in Royal David's City" (Luke)
    E102, P49, UM250 (PD), W402
    S-1   #182. Descant
             #183-84. Harmonization with descant
    K-2   p. 15. Short prelude

"Let All Mortal Flesh Keep Silence" (Communion)
    B80, E324, F166, L198, P5, UM626 (PD), W523
    H-1   #33. Harmonization
    S-1   #268. Handbell part
             #269. Descant
    K-3   p. 14. Prelude/meditation

C– "Go, Tell It on the Mountain" (Luke)
    B95, E99, F205, L70, P29, UM251, W397

C– "Joy to the World" (Luke)
    B87, E100, F171, L39, P40, UM246 (PD), W399
    S-1   #19-20. Trumpet descants
    K-1(I) #6. Postlude

Vocal Solos

"Hark! the Herald Angels Sing" (Luke)
V-1   p. 13
"Go Tell It on the Mountain" (Luke)
V-5   p. 152
"O Holy Night"
V-3   p. 39
"The Virgin's Slumber Song"
V-4   p. 28

Anthems

"Bethlehem Baby" in *A Season to Celebrate* (Luke)
Allen Pote
Hinshaw Music HMB 144
SATB with keyboard, optional guitar and flute

"A Baby in the Cradle" (Luke)
Barbara Kinyon
Beckenhorst BP 1348
Two-part with keyboard and optional handbells

Hymn Anthem Suggestions

"Go, Tell It on the Mountain" (Luke)
52IHA #17
"Carol Medley"
52IHA #6

Other Suggestions

You may wish to begin the service in quiet darkness, gradually increasing the light throughout the service, ending in a festive manner, perhaps with "Joy to the World."
Greeting: Isaiah 9:6. A child has been born (Isa.)
Greeting: Luke 2:10-14. Good news of great joy (Luke)
Canticle: UM91. "Canticle of Praise to God" (Ps.)
Prayer: UM231. Christmas (Luke)
See 1994-95 volume of this Planner for suggestions related to a family-oriented or children's service.

Isaiah 63:7-9

[7]I will recount the gracious deeds of the LORD, the praiseworthy acts of the LORD, because of all that the LORD has done for us, and the great favor to the house of Israel that he has shown them according to his mercy, according to the abundance of his steadfast love. [8]For he said, "Surely they are my people, children who will not deal falsely"; and he became their savior [9]in all their distress. It was no messenger or angel but his presence that saved them; in his love and in his pity he redeemed them; he lifted them up and carried them all the days of old.

Psalm 148

[1]Praise the LORD! Praise the LORD from the heavens; praise him in the heights! [2]Praise him, all his angels; praise him, all his host! [3]Praise him, sun and moon; praise him, all you shining stars! [4]Praise him, you highest heavens, and you waters above the heavens! [5]Let them praise the name of the LORD, for he commanded and they were created. [6]He established them forever and ever; he fixed their bounds, which cannot be passed. [7]Praise the LORD from the earth, you sea monsters and all deeps, [8]fire and hail, snow and frost, stormy wind fulfilling his command! [9]Mountains and all hills, fruit trees and all cedars! [10]Wild animals and all cattle, creeping things and flying birds! [11]Kings of the earth and all peoples, princes and all rulers of the earth! [12]Young men and women alike, old and young together! [13]Let them praise the name of the LORD, for his name alone is exalted; his glory is above earth and heaven. [14]He has raised up a horn for his people, praise for all his faithful, for the people of Israel who are close to him. Praise the LORD!

Hebrews 2:10-18

[10]It was fitting that God, for whom and through whom all things exist, in bringing many children to glory, should make the pioneer of their salvation perfect through sufferings. [11]For the one who sanctifies and those who are sanctified all have one Father. For this reason Jesus is not ashamed to call them brothers and sisters, [12]saying,

"I will proclaim your name to
my brothers and sisters,
in the midst of the
congregation I will praise you."
[13]And again,
"I will put my trust in him."
And again,
"Here am I and the children
whom God has given me."

[14]Since, therefore, the children share flesh and blood, he himself likewise shared the same things, so that through death he might destroy the one who has the power of death, that is, the devil, [15]and free those who all their lives were held in slavery by the fear of death. [16]For it is clear that he did not come to help angels, but the descendants of Abraham. [17]Therefore he had to become like his brothers and sisters in every respect, so that he might be a merciful and faithful high priest in the service of God, to make a sacrifice of atonement for the sins of the people. [18]Because he himself was tested by what he suffered, he is able to help those who are being tested.

Matthew 2:13-23

[13]Now after they had left, an angel of the Lord appeared to Joseph in a dream and said, "Get up, take the child and his mother, and flee to Egypt, and remain there until I tell you; for Herod is about to search for the child, to destroy him." [14]Then Joseph got up, took the child and his mother by night, and went to Egypt, [15]and remained there until the death of Herod. This was to fulfill what had been spoken by the Lord through the prophet, "Out of Egypt I have called my son."

[16]When Herod saw that he had been tricked by the wise men, he was infuriated, and he sent and killed all the children in and around Bethlehem who were two years old or under, according to the time that he had learned from the wise men. [17]Then was fulfilled what had been spoken through the prophet Jeremiah:

[18]"A voice was heard in Ramah,
wailing and loud lamentation,
Rachel weeping for her children;
she refused to be consoled,
because they are no more."

[19]When Herod died, an angel of the Lord suddenly appeared in a dream to Joseph in Egypt and said, [20]"Get up, take the child and his mother, and go to the land of Israel, for those who were seeking the child's life are dead." [21]Then Joseph got up, took the child and his mother, and went to the land of Israel. [22]But when he heard that Archelaus was ruling over Judea in place of his father Herod, he was afraid to go there. And after being warned in a dream, he went away to the district of Galilee. [23]There he made his home in a town called Nazareth, so that what had been spoken through the prophets might be fulfilled, "He will be called a Nazorean."

Hymn and Keyboard Suggestions
O– "Good Christian Friends, Rejoice" (Ps., Luke)
        B96, E107 (PD), F177, L55, P28, UM224, W391
    H-2   p. 14. Harmonization with descant
    S-1   #180. Rhythm instrument accompaniment
    K-3   p. 26. Three-section prelude (manuals only)
    K-4   p. 97. Various keyboard treatments, through p. 104
    K-10   p. 25. Prelude/meditation
    K-14   p. 26. Piano prelude
"Ye Who Claim the Faith of Jesus" (Isa.)
        E268, UM197
    S-1   #191. Descant
        E269
"In Thee Is Gladness" (Isa., Heb.)
        L552, UM169
    K-4   p. 93. Various keyboard treatments, through p. 96
"O Sing a Song of Bethlehem" (Isa., Heb., Matt.)
        B120, F208, P308, UM179 (PD)
    S-2   #100-103. Various treatments
"En el Frío Invernal" ("Cold December Flies Away") (Isa., Heb., Matt.)
        L53, UM233
    S-1   #216. Introduction/harmonization
              #217. Flute descant
"Joy to the World" (Matt.)
        B87, E100, F171, L39, P40, UM246 (PD), W399
    S-1   #19-20. Trumpet descants
    K-1(I)   #6. Postlude
"Hark! the Herald Angels Sing" (Isa., Matt.)
        B88, E87, F184, L60, P31, UM240 (PD), W387
    H-1   #9. Harmonization
    S-1   #234. Harmonization
              #235-36. Harmonization with descant
    K-1(II) #50. Prelude/meditation
"Let the Whole Creation Cry" (Ps.)
        L242, P256 (PD)
"The Head That Once Was Crowned" (Heb.)
        E483, L173, P149, UM326 (PD), W464
    S-1   #305. Descant
"Break Forth, O Beauteous Heavenly Light" (Heb., Matt.)
        B114 (PD), E91, F207, P26, UM223
"A La Ru" ("O Sleep, Dear Holy Baby")
        E113, P45
"Our Parent, by Whose Name" (Matt.)
        E587, L357, UM447, W570
    S-1   #284. Descant
              #285. Harmonization

"What Child Is This" (Matt.)
        B118, E115, F180, L40, P53, UM219 (PD), W411
    S-1   #150. Guitar chords
    K-3   p. 30. Prelude/meditation
    K-9   p. 21. Prelude/meditation
C– "Love Came Down at Christmas" (Isa., Matt.)
        B109, E84, UM242
C– "Sing We Now of Christmas" (Luke)
        B111, UM237
    S-1   #136. Orff instrument arrangement

Vocal Solos
"Gentle Jesus, Meek and Mild" (Matt.)
V-1   p. 11
"Scottish Christmas Song" (Matt.)
V-4   p. 4
"Sweet, Holy Child" (Matt.)
V-7   p. 10

Anthems
"Nazareth Boy" in *A Season to Celebrate* (Matt.)
Allen Pote
Hinshaw Music HMB 144
SATB with piano and optional Orff instruments

"Angels' Carol" (Matt.)
John Rutter
Hinshaw HMC-1002
SATB with piano or harp

Hymn Anthem Suggestions
"Cantemos al Señor" ("Let's Sing Unto the Lord") (Isa.)
52IHA #5
"En el Frío Invernal" ("Cold December Flies Away") (Isa., Heb., Matt.)
52IHA #14
"That Boy-Child of Mary" (Matt.)
52IHA #42

Other Suggestions
The lections and suggestions for December 31/January 1 (Watch Night/New Year) or January 6 (Epiphany) may also be used on this day.
Introit: B114 (PD), E91, F207, P26, UM223, stanza 1. "Break Forth, O Beauteous Heavenly Light" (Heb.)
Response: B54, F98, P276, UM140. "Great Is Thy Faithfulness" (Isa.)
For children: UM227. "The Friendly Beasts" (Heb. 2:10). Accompany a soloist with guitar or piano. This tune is also recommended for the Watch Night service (Dec. 31/Jan. 1).

Ecclesiastes 3:1-13

[1]For everything there is a season, and a time for every matter under heaven: [2]a time to be born, and a time to die; a time to plant, and a time to pluck up what is planted; [3]a time to kill, and a time to heal; a time to break down, and a time to build up; [4]a time to weep, and a time to laugh; a time to mourn, and a time to dance; [5]a time to throw away stones, and a time to gather stones together; a time to embrace, and a time to refrain from embracing; [6]a time to seek, and a time to lose; a time to keep, and a time to throw away; [7]a time to tear, and a time to sew; a time to keep silence, and a time to speak; [8]a time to love, and a time to hate; a time for war, and a time for peace.

[9]What gain have the workers from their toil? [10]I have seen the business that God has given to everyone to be busy with. [11]He has made everything suitable for its time; moreover he has put a sense of past and future into their minds, yet they cannot find out what God has done from the beginning to the end. [12]I know that there is nothing better for them than to be happy and enjoy themselves as long as they live; [13]moreover, it is God's gift that all should eat and drink and take pleasure in all their toil.

Psalm 8

[1]LORD, our Sovereign,
　how majestic is your name in all the earth!
You have set your glory above the heavens.
　[2]Out of the mouths of babes and infants
you have founded a bulwark because of your foes,
　to silence the enemy and the avenger.
[3]When I look at your heavens, the work of your fingers,
　the moon and the stars that you have established;
[4]what are human beings that you are mindful of them,
　mortals that you care for them?
[5]Yet you have made them a little lower than God,
　and crowned them with glory and honor.
[6]You have given them dominion
　　over the works of your hands;
　you have put all things under their feet,
[7]all sheep and oxen,
　and also the beasts of the field,
[8]the birds of the air, and the fish of the sea,
　whatever passes along the paths of the seas.
[9]O LORD, our Sovereign,
　how majestic is your name in all the earth!

Revelation 21:1-6a

[1]Then I saw a new heaven and a new earth; for the first heaven and the first earth had passed away, and the sea was no more. [2]And I saw the holy city, the new Jerusalem, coming down out of heaven from God, prepared as a bride adorned for her husband. [3]And I heard a loud voice from the throne saying, "See, the home of God is among mortals. He will dwell with them as their God; they will be his peoples, and God himself will be with them; [4]he will wipe every tear from their eyes. Death will be no more; mourning and crying and pain will be no more, for the first things have passed away."

[5]And the one who was seated on the throne said, "See, I am making all things new." Also he said, "Write this, for these words are trustworthy and true." [6a]Then he said to me, "It is done! I am the Alpha and the Omega, the beginning and the end."

Matthew 25:31-46

[31]"When the Son of Man comes in his glory, and all the angels with him, then he will sit on the throne of his glory. [32]All the nations will be gathered before him, and he will separate people one from another as a shepherd separates the sheep from the goats, [33]and he will put the sheep at his right hand and the goats at the left. [34]Then the king will say to those at his right hand, 'Come, you that are blessed by my Father, inherit the kingdom prepared for you from the foundation of the world; [35]for I was hungry and you gave me food, I was thirsty and you gave me something to drink, I was a stranger and you welcomed me, [36]I was naked and you gave me clothing, I was sick and you took care of me, I was in prison and you visited me.' [37]Then the righteous will answer him, 'Lord, when was it that we saw you hungry and gave you food, or thirsty and gave you something to drink? [38]And when was it that we saw you a stranger and welcomed you, or naked and gave you clothing? [39]And when was it that we saw you sick or in prison and visited you?' [40]And the king will answer them, 'Truly I tell you, just as you did it to one of the least of these who are members of my family, you did it to me.' [41]Then he will say to those at his left hand, 'You that are accursed, depart from me into the eternal fire prepared for the devil and his angels; [42]for I was hungry and you gave me no food, I was thirsty and you gave me nothing to drink, [43]I was a stranger and you did not welcome me, naked and you did not give me clothing, sick and in prison and you did not visit me.' [44]Then they also will answer, 'Lord, when was it that we saw you hungry or thirsty or a stranger or naked or sick or in prison, and did not take care of you?' [45]Then he will answer them, 'Truly I tell you, just as you did not do it to one of the least of these, you did not do it to me.' [46]And these will go away into eternal punishment, but the righteous into eternal life."

Hymn and Keyboard Suggestions

O– "For the Fruits of This Creation" (Ps.)
    B643
        S-2   #14. Descant
    E424, L563, P553, UM97, W562

O– "O God, Our Help in Ages Past" (Ps., Rev., Matt.)
    B74, E680, F370, L320, P210, UM117 (PD), W579
        H-1   #46. Harmonization
        S-1   #293-96. Various treatments
        K-1(III)   #74. Short prelude/postlude
        K-14   p. 34. Piano variations

"By Gracious Powers" (Eccles.)
    E695 and E696, P342, UM517, W577

"Sing Praise to God Who Reigns Above" (Eccles., Ps.)
    B20, E408, F343, P483, UM126 (PD), W528
        S-1   #237. Descant

"Children of the Heavenly Father" (Ps.)
    B55, F89, L474, UM141
        S-2   #180-85. Various treatments
        K-8   p. 14. Short prelude/meditation

"How Great Thou Art" (Ps.)
    B10, F2, L532, P467, UM77
        S-1   #163. Harmonization
        K-15   p. 134. Piano prelude/meditation

"Lord, Our Lord, Thy Glorious Name" (Ps.)
    P163 (PD)
        K-1(I)   #26. Prelude/postlude

"O Holy City, Seen of John" (Rev.)
    E583, P453, UM726
        S-1   #241. Orff arrangement
                   #242. Descant
        K-3   p. 8. Prelude/postlude
        K-6   p. 39. Prelude/meditation
    E582

"This Is a Day of New Beginnings" (Rev., Communion)
    B370, UM383, W661

"O What Their Joy and Their Glory Must Be" (Rev.)
    E623, L337, UM727 (PD)
        H-1   #94. Harmonization
        S-1   #255. Harmonization. A descant may
                   legally be derived from this
                   public domain setting by
                   adding text to the organ's top
                   line.

"Come, Ye Disconsolate" (Rev., Matt.)
    B67, UM510 (PD)
        S-2   #42. Harmonization

"Cuando El Pobre" ("When the Poor Ones") (Matt.)
    P407, UM434

"Rescue the Perishing" (Matt.)
    B559, F661, UM591 (PD)
        K-8   p. 21. Introduction

C– "There's a Spirit in the Air" (Matt.)
    UM192
        S-1   #261. Instructions for children's
                   drama (UM227 only)
        S-2   #144. Orff instrument arrangement
        K-1(III)   #70. Prelude/postlude
        K-12   p. 6. Prelude/meditation
        K-12   p. 18. Postlude
    B393, P433, W531

Vocal Solos

"Every Time I Feel the Spirit" (Eccles.)
V-5   p. 5
"I Want to Be Ready" (Rev.)
V-5   p. 195

Anthems

"How Great Thou Art" (Ps.)
Stuart Hine (arr. Meier)
Manna Music MCC-0
SATB with organ

"I Have Felt the Touch of God" (Matt.)
Lloyd Larson
Shawnee Press A-6218
SATB with keyboard

Hymn Anthem Suggestions

"Children of the Heavenly Father" (Ps.)
52IHA   #7
"This Is a Day of New Beginnings" (Rev.)
52IHA   #43
"O Holy City, Seen of John" (Rev.)
52IHA   #36
"This Is the Feast of Victory" (Rev., Communion)
52IHA   #44
"Cuando El Pobre" ("When the Poor Ones") (Matt.)
52IHA   #12

Other Suggestions

These lections and ideas may be used for the First Sunday After Christmas Day (December 31, morning) service. Covenant Services are commonly associated with this night.
Prayer: UM607. A Covenant Prayer in the Wesleyan Tradition
Canticle: UM734. "Canticle of Hope" (Rev.)
Response: B215, UM176. "Majesty, Worship His Majesty" (Ps., Rev.)
Response: B177, F227, UM171. "There's Something About That Name" (Rev.)

Isaiah 60:1-6

[1]Arise, shine; for your light has come, and the glory of the LORD has risen upon you. [2]For darkness shall cover the earth, and thick darkness the peoples; but the LORD will arise upon you, and his glory will appear over you. [3]Nations shall come to your light, and kings to the brightness of your dawn. [4]Lift up your eyes and look around; they all gather together, they come to you; your sons shall come from far away, and your daughters shall be carried on their nurses' arms. [5]Then you shall see and be radiant; your heart shall thrill and rejoice, because the abundance of the sea shall be brought to you, the wealth of the nations shall come to you. [6]A multitude of camels shall cover you, the young camels of Midian and Ephah; all those from Sheba shall come. They shall bring gold and frankincense, and shall proclaim the praise of the LORD.

Psalm 72:1-7, 10-14

[1]Give the king your justice, O God, and your righteousness to a king's son. [2]May he judge your people with righteousness, and your poor with justice. [3]May the mountains yield prosperity for the people, and the hills, in righteousness. [4]May he defend the cause of the poor of the people, give deliverance to the needy, and crush the oppressor. [5]May he live while the sun endures, and as long as the moon, throughout all generations. [6]May he be like rain that falls on the mown grass, like showers that water the earth. [7]In his days may righteousness flourish and peace abound, until the moon is no more.

[10]May the kings of Tarshish and of the isles render him tribute, may the kings of Sheba and Seba bring gifts. [11]May all kings fall down before him, all nations give him service. [12]For he delivers the needy when they call, the poor and those who have no helper. [13]He has pity on the weak and the needy, and saves the lives of the needy. [14]From oppression and violence he redeems their life; and precious is their blood in his sight.

Ephesians 3:1-12

[1]This is the reason that I Paul am a prisoner for Christ Jesus for the sake of you Gentiles—[2]for surely you have already heard of the commission of God's grace that was given me for you, [3]and how the mystery was made known to me by revelation, as I wrote above in a few words, [4]a reading of which will enable you to perceive my understanding of the mystery of Christ. [5]In former generations this mystery was not made known to humankind, as it has now been revealed to his holy apostles and prophets by the Spirit: [6]that is, the Gentiles have become fellow heirs, members of the same body, and sharers in the promise in Christ Jesus through the gospel.

[7]Of this gospel I have become a servant according to the gift of God's grace that was given me by the working of his power. [8]Although I am the very least of all the saints, this grace was given to me to bring to the Gentiles the news of the boundless riches of Christ, [9]and to make everyone see what is the plan of the mystery hidden for ages in God who created all things; [10]so that through the church the wisdom of God in its rich variety might now be made known to the rulers and authorities in the heavenly places. [11]This was in accordance with the eternal purpose that he has carried out in Christ Jesus our Lord, [12]in whom we have access to God in boldness and confidence through faith in him.

Matthew 2:1-12

[1]In the time of King Herod, after Jesus was born in Bethlehem of Judea, wise men from the East came to Jerusalem, [2]asking, "Where is the child who has been born king of the Jews? For we observed his star at its rising, and have come to pay him homage." [3]When King Herod heard this, he was frightened, and all Jerusalem with him; [4]and calling together all the chief priests and scribes of the people, he inquired of them where the Messiah was to be born. [5]They told him, "In Bethlehem of Judea; for so it has been written by the prophet: [6]'And you, Bethlehem, in the land of Judah, are by no means least among the rulers of Judah; for from you shall come a ruler who is to shepherd my people Israel.'"

[7]Then Herod secretly called for the wise men and learned from them the exact time when the star had appeared. [8]Then he sent them to Bethlehem, saying, "Go and search diligently for the child; and when you have found him, bring me word so that I may also go and pay him homage." [9]When they had heard the king, they set out; and there, ahead of them, went the star that they had seen at its rising, until it stopped over the place where the child was. [10]When they saw that the star had stopped, they were overwhelmed with joy. [11]On entering the house, they saw the child with Mary his mother; and they knelt down and paid him homage. Then, opening their treasure chests, they offered him gifts of gold, frankincense, and myrrh. [12]And having been warned in a dream not to return to Herod, they left for their own country by another road.

Hymn and Keyboard Suggestions

O– "Hail to the Lord's Anointed" (Ps.)
    UM203 (PD)
        S-1   #114. Descant
                  #115. Harmonization
    E616 (PD), L87, P205
"Rise, Shine, You People" (Isa.)
    L393, UM187
"O Morning Star, How Fair and Bright" (Isa., Ps., Matt.)
    E497, L76, P69, UM247, W390
        K-1(IV) #97. Prelude
        K-3   p. 32. Short postlude
        K-5   p. 159. Various keyboard treatments,
                         through p. 173
"There's a Song in the Air" (Isa., Ps., Matt.)
    UM249 (PD)
        S-2   #40. Descant
"Angels from the Realms of Glory" (Matt.)
    B94, E93, F190, L50, P22, UM220 (PD), W377
        H-1   #7. Harmonization
        S-1   #280. Descant
                  #281. Harmonization
        K-1(III) #72. Short prelude/postlude/inter-
                     lude
        K-2   p. 24. Short prelude
        K-8   p. 28. Introduction/interlude
"Brightest and Best of the Stars of the Morning" (Matt.)
    E117 and E118 (PD), L84, P67 (PD)
"De Tierra Lejana Venimos" ("From a Distant Home")
    (Matt.)
    P64, UM243
        S-2   #94. Performance note
"The First Noel" (Matt.)
    B85, E109, F179, L56, P56, UM245 (PD), W408
        H-1   #11. Harmonization
        S-1   #328-30. Various treatments
"On This Day Earth Shall Ring" (Matt.)
    E92, P46, UM248 (PD)
        S-1   #267. Handbell part
"We Three Kings" (Matt.)
    B113, E128, F206, L66, UM254 (PD), W406
        S-2   #97-98. Introduction/interlude/
                     harmonization
"What Star Is This, with Beams So Bright" (Matt.)
    E124, P68, W407
"When Christ's Appearing Was Made Known" (Matt.)
    L85
        K-1(IV) #98. Prelude/meditation/postlude
    E131 and E132
C– "As with Gladness Men of Old" (Matt.)
    B117, E119, F202, L82, P63 (PD), W409
        H-1   #16. Harmonization
        S-1   #93-96. Various treatments

        K-1(I)   #15. Short prelude/postlude
        K-3   p. 31. Postlude

Vocal Solos
"O Thou That Tellest Good Tidings to Zion" (Isa.)
V-2
"Go Tell It on the Mountain" (Eph., Matt.)
V-5   p. 152

Anthems
"One Little Candle" (Isa.)
Mysels and Roach (arr. Naylor)
Shawnee Press A-212
SATB with keyboard

"We Must Be on Our Journey" in *A Season to Celebrate*
    (Matt.)
Allen Pote
Hinshaw Music HMB 144
SATB with piano and men's trio, optional instruments

"All Was Calm, All Was Bright" (Matt.)
Cynthia Gray
Heritage Music H 385
SATB with keyboard

"Videntes Stellam" from *Four Christmas Motets* (Matt.)
F. Poulenc
Salabert SAL.14
SATB *a cappella*

Hymn Anthem Suggestions
"This Little Light of Mine" (Isa.)
52IHA   #45
"Hail to the Lord's Anointed" (Ps.)
52IHA   #20
"Go, Tell It on the Mountain" (Eph., Matt.)
52IHA   #17
"We Three Kings" (Matt.)
HA   p. 14

Other Suggestions
    If there is no service on January 6, these lections may be used on Sunday, December 31. Consider keeping the Christ candle from the Advent wreath in the sanctuary and lit during the season of Epiphany.
Canticle: UM225. "Canticle of Simeon" (Ps., Matt.)
Response: UM585. "This Little Light of Mine" (Isa.)
Prayer: UM255. Epiphany (Isa., Eph.)
Benediction: B95, E99, F205, L70, P29, UM251, W397, refrain and stanza 3. "Go, Tell It on the Mountain" (Eph.)
The Shakespearean text "When mercy seasons justice" (V-6, p. 50) might be used with the Psalm reading.

Isaiah 42:1-9

[1]Here is my servant, whom I uphold, my chosen, in whom my soul delights; I have put my spirit upon him; he will bring forth justice to the nations. [2]He will not cry or lift up his voice, or make it heard in the street; [3]a bruised reed he will not break, and a dimly burning wick he will not quench; he will faithfully bring forth justice. [4]He will not grow faint or be crushed until he has established justice in the earth; and the coastlands wait for his teaching. [5]Thus says God, the LORD, who created the heavens and stretched them out, who spread out the earth and what comes from it, who gives breath to the people upon it and spirit to those who walk in it: [6]I am the LORD, I have called you in righteousness, I have taken you by the hand and kept you; I have given you as a covenant to the people, a light to the nations, [7]to open the eyes that are blind, to bring out the prisoners from the dungeon, from the prison those who sit in darkness. [8]I am the LORD, that is my name; my glory I give to no other, nor my praise to idols. [9]See, the former things have come to pass, and new things I now declare; before they spring forth, I tell you of them.

Psalm 29

[1]Ascribe to the LORD, O heavenly beings,
    ascribe to the LORD glory and strength.
[2]Ascribe to the LORD the glory of his name;
    worship the LORD in holy splendor.
[3]The voice of the LORD is over the waters;
    the God of glory thunders,
    the LORD, over mighty waters.
[4]The voice of the LORD is powerful;
    the voice of the LORD is full of majesty.
[5]The voice of the LORD breaks the cedars;
    the LORD breaks the cedars of Lebanon.
[6]He makes Lebanon skip like a calf,
    and Sirion like a young wild ox.
[7]The voice of the LORD flashes
      forth flames of fire.
[8]The voice of the LORD shakes
    the wilderness;
  the LORD shakes the
    wilderness of Kadesh.
[9]The voice of the LORD causes the oaks to whirl,
    and strips the forest bare;
and in his temple all say, "Glory!"
[10]The LORD sits enthroned over the flood;
    the LORD sits enthroned as king forever.
[11]May the LORD give strength to his people!
    May the LORD bless his people with peace!

Acts 10:34-43

[34]Then Peter began to speak to them: "I truly understand that God shows no partiality, [35]but in every nation anyone who fears him and does what is right is acceptable to him. [36]You know the message he sent to the people of Israel, preaching peace by Jesus Christ—he is Lord of all. [37]That message spread throughout Judea, beginning in Galilee after the baptism that John announced: [38]how God anointed Jesus of Nazareth with the Holy Spirit and with power; how he went about doing good and healing all who were oppressed by the devil, for God was with him. [39]We are witnesses to all that he did both in Judea and in Jerusalem. They put him to death by hanging him on a tree; [40]but God raised him on the third day and allowed him to appear, [41]not to all the people but to us who were chosen by God as witnesses, and who ate and drank with him after he rose from the dead. [42]He commanded us to preach to the people and to testify that he is the one ordained by God as judge of the living and the dead. [43]All the prophets testify about him that everyone who believes in him receives forgiveness of sins through his name."

Matthew 3:13-17

[13]Then Jesus came from Galilee to John at the Jordan, to be baptized by him. [14]John would have prevented him, saying, "I need to be baptized by you, and do you come to me?" [15]But Jesus answered him, "Let it be so now; for it is proper for us in this way to fulfill all righteousness." Then he consented. [16]And when Jesus had been baptized, just as he came up from the water, suddenly the heavens were opened to him and he saw the Spirit of God descending like a dove and alighting on him. [17]And a voice from heaven said, "This is my Son, the Beloved, with whom I am well pleased."

Hymn and Keyboard Suggestions

O– "I'll Praise My Maker While I've Breath" (Ps.)
    B35, E429 (PD), P253, UM60
        S-2   #141. Harmonization

"Jesus Shall Reign" (Isa.)
    B587, E544, F238, L530, P423, UM157 (PD),
    W492
        H-1   #83. Harmonization
        S-1   #100-103. Various treatments
        K-1(I)   #16. Prelude/postlude/interlude
                        (manuals only)
        K-2   p. 8. Short prelude
        K-10   p. 32. Prelude/postlude

"Where Cross the Crowded Ways of Life" (Isa.)
    E609, F665, L429, P408, UM427 (PD)
        S-1   #141. Harmonization
                       #142-43. Descant and transposition
                           in A major

"Word of God, Come Down on Earth" (Isa.)
    UM182, W513
        S-2   #112-14. Various treatments
        K-1(II)   #51. Prelude/postlude/meditation
        K-4   p. 135. Various keyboard treatments,
                           through p. 139

"For the Healing of the Nations" (Isa., Acts)
    UM428
        S-1   #76. Descant
                       #77. Harmonization
        K-6   p. 30. Prelude/postlude
    W643
        S-1   #346. Descant

"We've a Story to Tell to the Nations" (Isa., Acts)
    B586, F659, UM569 (PD)
        K-8   p. 26. Introduction

"Praise and Thanksgiving Be to God" (Ps., Baptism)
    L191, UM604
        S-1   #64. Descant

"The God of Heaven" (Ps.)
    P180

"We Meet You, O Christ" (Acts)
    UM257
        S-2   #166. Descant
    P311

"I Come with Joy" (Acts, Communion)
    B371, E304, W726
        S-2   #105. Flute/violin descant
                       #106. Harmonization
        K-8   p. 22. Prelude/meditation
    P607, UM617
        S-2   #52. Choral and keyboard arrange-
                       ment

"Christ, When for Us You Were Baptized" (Matt.)
    E121 (PD), P70

"When Jesus Came to Jordan" (Matt.)
    UM252, P72, W697

"Songs of Thankfulness and Praise" (Matt.)
    E135 (PD), L90, W410

"This Is the Spirit's Entry Now" (Matt., Communion)
    UM608
        S-1   #33-38. Various treatments
    L195, W722

C– "Fairest Lord Jesus" (Isa., Matt.)
    B176, E383, F240, P306, UM189 (PD)
        H-1   #54. Harmonization
        S-1   #301. Descant
        S-2   #158. Choral harmonization
        K-1(III)   #79. Short prelude or meditation
        K-2   p. 4. Prelude/postlude
        K-15   p. 11. Piano prelude/meditation

Vocal Solos

"Spirit of Faith, Come Down" (Matt.)
V-1   p. 43
"The Call"
V-4   p. 31
"I Know De Lord's Laid His Hands on Me"
V-5   p. 90

Anthems

"The God of Glory Thundereth" (Ps.)
Alan Hovhaness
C. F. Peters 6440
SATB with organ

"Beautiful Savior" (Isa., Matt.)
arr. Robert Thygerson
Richmond Music Press MI-229
SATB with keyboard

"The Baptism of Jesus" (Matt.)
Henry Hallstrom
Abingdon APM-581
SATB with organ

Hymn Anthem Suggestion

"God of the Sparrow God of the Whale" (Ps.)
52IHA   #19

Other Suggestions

   Today is an excellent day to schedule baptisms—infant, youth, or adult. Be sure the celebration is joyous. You may also schedule a congregational reaffirmation of the baptismal covenant.
Prayer: UM253. Baptism of the Lord.
Prayer: UM607. A Covenant Prayer in the Wesleyan Tradition (Baptism)
Prayer: UM429. For Our Country (Isa., Acts)

Isaiah 49:1-7

[1]Listen to me, O coastlands, pay attention, you peoples from far away! The LORD called me before I was born, while I was in my mother's womb he named me. [2]He made my mouth like a sharp sword, in the shadow of his hand he hid me; he made me a polished arrow, in his quiver he hid me away. [3]And he said to me, "You are my servant, Israel, in whom I will be glorified." [4]But I said, "I have labored in vain, I have spent my strength for nothing and vanity; yet surely my cause is with the LORD, and my reward with my God." [5]And now the LORD says, who formed me in the womb to be his servant, to bring Jacob back to him, and that Israel might be gathered to him, for I am honored in the sight of the LORD, and my God has become my strength—[6]he says, "It is too light a thing that you should be my servant to raise up the tribes of Jacob and to restore the survivors of Israel; I will give you as a light to the nations, that my salvation may reach to the end of the earth." [7]Thus says the LORD, the Redeemer of Israel and his Holy One, to one deeply despised, abhorred by the nations, the slave of rulers, "Kings shall see and stand up, princes, and they shall prostrate themselves, because of the LORD, who is faithful, the Holy One of Israel, who has chosen you."

Psalm 40:1-11

[1]I waited patiently for the LORD; he inclined to me and heard my cry. [2]He drew me up from the desolate pit, out of the miry bog, and set my feet upon a rock, making my steps secure. [3]He put a new song in my mouth, a song of praise to our God. Many will see and fear, and put their trust in the LORD. [4]Happy are those who make the LORD their trust, who do not turn to the proud, to those who go astray after false gods. [5]You have multiplied, O LORD my God, your wondrous deeds and your thoughts toward us; none can compare with you. Were I to proclaim and tell of them, they would be more than can be counted. [6]Sacrifice and offering you do not desire, but you have given me an open ear. Burnt offering and sin offering you have not required. [7]Then I said, "Here I am; in the scroll of the book it is written of me. [8]I delight to do your will, O my God; your law is within my heart." [9]I have told the glad news of deliverance in the great congregation; see, I have not restrained my lips, as you know, O LORD. [10]I have not hidden your saving help within my heart, I have spoken of your faithfulness and your salvation; I have not concealed your steadfast love and your faithfulness from the great congregation. [11]Do not, O LORD, withhold your mercy from me; let your steadfast love and your faithfulness keep me safe forever.

1 Corinthians 1:1-9

[1]Paul, called to be an apostle of Christ Jesus by the will of God, and our brother Sosthenes,

[2]To the church of God that is in Corinth, to those who are sanctified in Christ Jesus, called to be saints, together with all those who in every place call on the name of our Lord Jesus Christ, both their Lord and ours:

[3]Grace to you and peace from God our Father and the Lord Jesus Christ.

[4]I give thanks to my God always for you because of the grace of God that has been given you in Christ Jesus, [5]for in every way you have been enriched in him, in speech and knowledge of every kind—[6]just as the testimony of Christ has been strengthened among you—[7]so that you are not lacking in any spiritual gift as you wait for the revealing of our Lord Jesus Christ. [8]He will also strengthen you to the end, so that you may be blameless on the day of our Lord Jesus Christ. [9]God is faithful; by him you were called into the fellowship of his Son, Jesus Christ our Lord.

John 1:29-42

[29]The next day he saw Jesus coming toward him and declared, "Here is the Lamb of God who takes away the sin of the world! [30]This is he of whom I said, 'After me comes a man who ranks ahead of me because he was before me.' [31]I myself did not know him; but I came baptizing with water for this reason, that he might be revealed to Israel." [32]And John testified, "I saw the Spirit descending from heaven like a dove, and it remained on him. [33]I myself did not know him, but the one who sent me to baptize with water said to me, 'He on whom you see the Spirit descend and remain is the one who baptizes with the Holy Spirit.' [34]And I myself have seen and have testified that this is the Son of God."

[35]The next day John again was standing with two of his disciples, [36]and as he watched Jesus walk by, he exclaimed, "Look, here is the Lamb of God!" [37]The two disciples heard him say this, and they followed Jesus. [38]When Jesus turned and saw them following, he said to them, "What are you looking for?" They said to him, "Rabbi" (which translated means Teacher), "where are you staying?" [39]He said to them, "Come and see." They came and saw where he was staying, and they remained with him that day. It was about four o'clock in the afternoon. [40]One of the two who heard John speak and followed him was Andrew, Simon Peter's brother. [41]He first found his brother Simon and said to him, "We have found the Messiah" (which is translated Anointed). [42]He brought Simon to Jesus, who looked at him and said, "You are Simon son of John. You are to be called Cephas" (which is translated Peter).

Hymn and Keyboard Suggestions
O– "Holy God, We Praise Thy Name" (Isa.)
　　　E366 (PD), F385, L535, P460, UM79, W524
　　　　S-1　　#151-52. Harmonization with descant
　　　　　　　#153. Descant
　　　　K-1(I)　#28. Prelude or postlude (may be played on manuals only)
"O Gladsome Light" (Isa.)
　　　E36, L279, P549, UM686 (PD), W679
"Ye Servants of God" (Isa., John)
　　　B589 (PD)
　　　　H-1　　#37. Harmonization
　　　　S-1　　#223-26. Various treatments
　　　　K-8　　p. 17. Introduction
　　　E535 (PD)
　　　　S-2　　#145. Descant
　　　　　　　#146. Harmonization
　　　F360, P477, UM181 (PD)
　　　　H-1　　#45. Harmonization in G major
　　　　S-2　　#71. Introduction
　　　　　　　#72-74. Harmonizations
　　　　K-2　　p. 10. Short prelude/postlude
　　　　K-10　p. 13. Prelude/postlude
"O Zion, Haste" (Isa.)
　　　B583, E539, F658, L397, UM573 (PD)
　　　　S-2　　#174-75. Introduction and harmonization
"Christ for the World We Sing" (1 Cor.)
　　　E537, F686, UM568 (PD)
　　　　S-1　　#185. Harmonization
　　　　　　　#186. Descant
　　　　K-1(II)　#37. Prelude/postlude
　　　　K-2　　p. 20. Short prelude/meditation
　　　　K-14　p. 8. Piano prelude/postlude
"Lord God, Your Love Has Called Us Here" (1 Cor.)
　　　UM579
　　　　S-1　　#57-61. Various treatments
　　　P353
"Jesus! the Name High over All" (John)
　　　UM193 (PD)
　　　　S-1　　#149. Descant
　　　　S-2　　#67. Harmonization
　　　　K-1(II)　#55. Prelude/postlude (manuals only)
"Just as I Am, Without One Plea" (John)
　　　B307, E693, F417, L296, P370, UM357 (PD)
　　　　K-15　p. 66. Piano prelude/meditation
"Jesus, Priceless Treasure" (John)
　　　F277, L457, P365, UM532 (PD)
　　　　K-4　　p. 109. Variations, through p. 119
　　　　K-9　　p. 33. Prelude/meditation
　　　　K-14　p. 48. Prelude/meditation/postlude
　　　L458 (PD)

C– "Immortal, Invisible, God Only Wise" (Isa.)
　　　B6, E423, F319, L526, P263, UM103 (PD), W512
　　　　H-2　　p. 28. Harmonization with descant
　　　　S-1　　#300. Harmonization

Vocal Solos
"Ye Servants of God" (Isa., John)
V-1　　p. 41
"Patiently Have I Waited for the Lord" (Ps.)
V-4　　p. 24
"Just As I Am" (John)
V-3　　p. 23

Anthems
"Sing, O Heavens" (Isa.)
Emma Lou Diemer
Carl Fischer CM 7923
SATB *a cappella*

"I Waited for the Lord" (Ps.)
F. Mendelssohn
Carl Fischer CM 6250
SATB with piano

"Behold the Lamb of God" (John)
Healey Willan
Concordia 98-1509
SATB with organ

Hymn Anthem Suggestions
"This Little Light of Mine" (Isa.)
52IHA　#45
"I Sing a Song of the Saints of God" (1 Cor., John)
52IHA　#26

Other Suggestions
　Use some of the keyboard variations on "Jesus, Priceless Treasure" listed above as a prelude, followed by the choir singing the hymn, stanza 1 as an introit, stanza 2 as a prayer response, and stanza 3 as a benediction response. Close with final variations as postlude.
Canticle: UM82. "Canticle of God's Glory" (John)
Canticle: UM83. "Canticle of God's Glory" (John)
Response: UM300. "O the Lamb" (John)

Isaiah 9:1-4

[1]But there will be no gloom for those who were in anguish. In the former time he brought into contempt the land of Zebulun and the land of Naphtali, but in the latter time he will make glorious the way of the sea, the land beyond the Jordan, Galilee of the nations. [2]The people who walked in darkness have seen a great light; those who lived in a land of deep darkness—on them light has shined. [3]You have multiplied the nation, you have increased its joy; they rejoice before you as with joy at the harvest, as people exult when dividing plunder. [4]For the yoke of their burden, and the bar across their shoulders, the rod of their oppressor, you have broken as on the day of Midian.

Psalm 27:1, 4-9

[1]The LORD is my light and my salvation;
  whom shall I fear?
The LORD is the stronghold of my life;
  of whom shall I be afraid?
[4]One thing I asked of the LORD,
  that will I seek after:
to live in the house of the LORD
  all the days of my life,
to behold the beauty of the LORD,
  and to inquire in his temple.
[5]For he will hide me in his shelter
  in the day of trouble;
he will conceal me under the
    cover of his tent;
  he will set me high on a rock.
[6]Now my head is lifted up
  above my enemies all around me,
and I will offer in his tent
  sacrifices with shouts of joy;
I will sing and make melody to the LORD.
[7]Hear, O LORD, when I cry aloud,
  be gracious to me and answer me!
[8]"Come," my heart says, "seek his face!"
  Your face, LORD, do I seek.
[9]Do not hide your face from me.
Do not turn your servant away in anger,
  you who have been my help.
Do not cast me off, do not forsake me,
  O God of my salvation!

1 Corinthians 1:10-18

[10]Now I appeal to you, brothers and sisters, by the name of our Lord Jesus Christ, that all of you be in agreement and that there be no divisions among you, but that you be united in the same mind and the same purpose. [11]For it has been reported to me by Chloe's people that there are quarrels among you, my brothers and sisters. [12]What I mean is that each of you says, "I belong to Paul," or "I belong to Apollos," or "I belong to Cephas," or "I belong to Christ." [13]Has Christ been divided? Was Paul crucified for you? Or were you baptized in the name of Paul? [14]I thank God that I baptized none of you except Crispus and Gaius, [15]so that no one can say that you were baptized in my name. [16](I did baptize also the household of Stephanas; beyond that, I do not know whether I baptized anyone else.) [17]For Christ did not send me to baptize but to proclaim the gospel, and not with eloquent wisdom, so that the cross of Christ might not be emptied of its power.

[18]For the message about the cross is foolishness to those who are perishing, but to us who are being saved it is the power of God.

Matthew 4:12-23

[12]Now when Jesus heard that John had been arrested, he withdrew to Galilee. [13]He left Nazareth and made his home in Capernaum by the sea, in the territory of Zebulun and Naphtali, [14]so that what had been spoken through the prophet Isaiah might be fulfilled: [15]"Land of Zebulun, land of Naphtali, on the road by the sea, across the Jordan, Galilee of the Gentiles—[16]the people who sat in darkness have seen a great light, and for those who sat in the region and shadow of death light has dawned." [17]From that time Jesus began to proclaim, "Repent, for the kingdom of heaven has come near."

[18]As he walked by the Sea of Galilee, he saw two brothers, Simon, who is called Peter, and Andrew his brother, casting a net into the sea—for they were fishermen. [19]And he said to them, "Follow me, and I will make you fish for people." [20]Immediately they left their nets and followed him. [21]As he went from there, he saw two other brothers, James son of Zebedee and his brother John, in the boat with their father Zebedee, mending their nets, and he called them. [22]Immediately they left the boat and their father, and followed him.

[23]Jesus went throughout Galilee, teaching in their synagogues and proclaiming the good news of the kingdom and curing every disease and every sickness among the people.

Hymn and Keyboard Suggestions

O– "Christ, Whose Glory Fills the Skies" (Isa.)
      E7, L265, P462, UM173 (PD)
      H-1   #29. Harmonization
      S-1   #278. Harmonization
                #279. Harmonization
      E6, F293 (PD), P463
"The People Who In Darkness Walked" (Isa.)
      E126 (PD)
      H-1   #63. Harmonization
      K-1(I)   #17. Prelude/meditation
      E125
"I Want to Walk as a Child of the Light" (Isa., Matt.)
      E490, UM206, W510
      S-2   #91. Descant
"God Is My Strong Salvation" (Ps.)
      P179 (PD)
"Rock of Ages, Cleft for Me" (Ps.)
      B342, E685, F108, L327, UM361 (PD)
      S-2   #179. Harmonization
"Jesus, Lover of My Soul" (Ps.)
      E699, F222, P303, UM479 (PD)
      S-1   #6. Descant
      K-9   p. 10. Prelude/postlude
      B180
"All My Hope Is Firmly Grounded" (1 Cor.)
      E665, UM132
"The Church's One Foundation" (1 Cor.)
      B350, E525, F547, L369, P442, UM545 (PD) and
      UM546
      H-1   #62. Harmonization
      S-1   #25. Descant
                #26. Harmonization
      K-1(I)   #8. Prelude/postlude
"Tú Has Venido a la Orilla" ("Lord, You Have Come to
   the Lakeshore") (Matt.)
      P377, UM344
"Softly and Tenderly Jesus Is Calling" (Matt.)
      B312, F432, UM348 (PD)
      K-13   p. 60. Piano prelude/meditation
"Dear Lord and Father of Mankind" (Matt.)
      B267, E652, F422, L506, P345, UM358 (PD)
      H-1   #70. Harmonization
      S-2   #151. Introduction
                #152. Violin descant
      E653 (PD)
"Jesus Calls Us" (Matt.)
      B293, F399, L494, UM398 (PD)
      S-2   #65. Harmonization
      E550 (PD)
      E549

C– "Blest Be the Tie That Binds" (1 Cor.)
      B387, F560, L370, P438, UM557 (PD)
      H-1   #78. Harmonization

Vocal Solos

"The People That Walked in Darkness" (Isa.)
V-2
"Jesus, Lover of My Soul" (Ps.)
V-1   p. 37
"Serenity" (Matt.)
UM499

Anthems

"A Great Light" (Isa.)
James Fritschel
Hinshaw HMC 147
SATB *a cappella*

"God Is My Strong Salvation" (Ps.)
Robert Powell
Augsburg 1378
SAB *a cappella*

"Come, Follow Me" (Matt.)
Don Besig
Alfred Publishing 7150
SATB with piano and optional flute (also available in SSA
  or SAB)

Hymn Anthem Suggestions

"I Want to Walk as a Child of the Light" (Isa., Matt.)
52IHA   #27
"O Thou, in Whose Presence" (Ps.)
52IHA   #38
"Tú Has Venido a la Orilla" ("Lord, You Have Come to the
Lakeshore") (Matt.)
52IHA   #47

Other Suggestions

Canticle: UM205. "Canticle of Light and Darkness" (Isa.)
Benediction: B96, E107 (PD), F177, L55, P28, UM224,
  W391, stanza 3. "Good Christian Friends, Rejoice"
  (Matt.)

Micah 6:1-8

[1]Hear what the LORD says: Rise, plead your case before the mountains, and let the hills hear your voice. [2]Hear, you mountains, the controversy of the LORD, and you enduring foundations of the earth; for the LORD has a controversy with his people, and he will contend with Israel. [3]"O my people, what have I done to you? In what have I wearied you? Answer me! [4]For I brought you up from the land of Egypt, and redeemed you from the house of slavery; and I sent before you Moses, Aaron, and Miriam. [5]O my people, remember now what King Balak of Moab devised, what Balaam son of Beor answered him, and what happened from Shittim to Gilgal, that you may know the saving acts of the LORD."

[6]"With what shall I come before the LORD, and bow myself before God on high? Shall I come before him with burnt offerings, with calves a year old? [7]Will the LORD be pleased with thousands of rams, with ten thousands of rivers of oil? Shall I give my firstborn for my transgression, the fruit of my body for the sin of my soul?" [8]He has told you, O mortal, what is good; and what does the LORD require of you but to do justice, and to love kindness, and to walk humbly with your God?

Psalm 15

[1]O LORD, who may abide in your tent?
　　Who may dwell on your holy hill?
[2]Those who walk blamelessly,
　　and do what is right,
　　and speak the truth from their heart;
[3]who do not slander with their tongue,
　　and do no evil to their friends,
　　nor take up a reproach against their neighbors;
[4]in whose eyes the wicked are despised,
　　but who honor those who fear the LORD;
who stand by their oath even to their hurt;
[5]who do not lend money at interest,
　　and do not take a bribe against the innocent.
Those who do these things shall never be moved.

1 Corinthians 1:18-31

[18]For the message about the cross is foolishness to those who are perishing, but to us who are being saved it is the power of God. [19]For it is written, "I will destroy the wisdom of the wise, and the discernment of the discerning I will thwart." [20]Where is the one who is wise? Where is the scribe? Where is the debater of this age? Has not God made foolish the wisdom of the world? [21]For since, in the wisdom of God, the world did not know God through wisdom, God decided, through the foolishness of our proclamation, to save those who believe. [22]For Jews demand signs and Greeks desire wisdom, [23]but we proclaim Christ crucified, a stumbling block to Jews and foolishness to Gentiles, [24]but to those who are the called, both Jews and Greeks, Christ the power of God and the wisdom of God. [25]For God's foolishness is wiser than human wisdom, and God's weakness is stronger than human strength.

[26]Consider your own call, brothers and sisters: not many of you were wise by human standards, not many were powerful, not many were of noble birth. [27]But God chose what is foolish in the world to shame the wise; God chose what is weak in the world to shame the strong; [28]God chose what is low and despised in the world, things that are not, to reduce to nothing things that are, [29]so that no one might boast in the presence of God. [30]He is the source of your life in Christ Jesus, who became for us wisdom from God, and righteousness and sanctification and redemption, [31]in order that, as it is written, "Let the one who boasts, boast in the Lord."

Matthew 5:1-12

[1]When Jesus saw the crowds, he went up the mountain; and after he sat down, his disciples came to him. [2]Then he began to speak, and taught them, saying:

[3]"Blessed are the poor in spirit, for theirs is the kingdom of heaven.

[4]"Blessed are those who mourn, for they will be comforted.

[5]"Blessed are the meek, for they will inherit the earth.

[6]"Blessed are those who hunger and thirst for righteousness, for they will be filled.

[7]"Blessed are the merciful, for they will receive mercy.

[8]"Blessed are the pure in heart, for they will see God.

[9]"Blessed are the peacemakers, for they will be called children of God.

[10]"Blessed are those who are persecuted for righteousness' sake, for theirs is the kingdom of heaven.

[11]"Blessed are you when people revile you and persecute you and utter all kinds of evil against you falsely on my account. [12]Rejoice and be glad, for your reward is great in heaven, for in the same way they persecuted the prophets who were before you."

Hymn and Keyboard Suggestions
O– "All My Hope Is Firmly Grounded" (1 Cor.)
    E665, UM132
O– "Lord, You Give the Great Commission" (Mic., Ps.)
    P429, UM584, W470
      S-1   #4-5. Descants
                #5. Vocal descant
    E528
"O Master, Let Me Walk with Thee" (Mic.)
    B279, E660, F442, L492, P357, UM430 (PD)
      S-2   #118. Descant
    E659
"What Does the Lord Require" (Mic.)
    E605, P405, UM441, W624
      K-12   p. 31. Prelude
"All Who Love and Serve Your City" (Mic., Matt., Ecumenical Sunday)
    E571, P413, UM433
      S-1   #62. Descant
    E570, L436, W621
"Cuando El Pobre" ("When the Poor Ones") (Mic., Matt.)
    P407, UM434
"I Will Trust in the Lord" (Ps.)
    B420, UM464
"Lord, Who May Dwell Within Your House" (Ps.)
    P164
"Ask Ye What Great Thing I Know" (1 Cor., Ecumenical Sunday)
    B538, UM163 (PD)
      S-2   #78-80. Various treatments
"When I Survey the Wondrous Cross" (1 Cor.)
    B144, F258, P101, UM298 (PD)
      H-1   #36. Harmonization
      S-1   #155. Descant
      K-1(II) #31. Prelude/meditation
      K-15   p. 73. Piano prelude/meditation
    E474, L482, P100, UM299 (PD), W433
      H-1   #19. Harmonization
      S-1   #288. Transposition to E-flat major
"Thine Be the Glory" (1 Cor.)
    B163, F291, L145, P122, UM308
      S-1   #190. Arrangement for choir, handbells, trumpets, organ
      S-2   #95. Brass/percussion arrangement, descant and harmonization
"The Old Rugged Cross" (1 Cor.)
    B141, F256, UM504 (PD)
"By Gracious Powers" (Matt.)
    E695 and E696, P342, UM517, W577
"I Sing a Song of the Saints of God" (Matt., Ecumenical Sunday)
    E293, P364, UM712 (PD)
      S-2   #68. Flute descant

C– "Be Thou My Vision" (1 Cor.)
    B60, E488, F468, P339, UM451
      S-1   #319. Arrangement for organ and voices in canon
      K-12   p. 9. Prelude/meditation

Vocal Solos
"Sing a Song of Joy" (General)
V-4   p. 2
"God, Our Ever Faithful Shepherd" (General)
V-4   p. 15

Anthems
"All I Ask of You" (Mic.)
Mary MacDonald
Purifoy Publishing 26013
SATB with keyboard

"The Gift Most Treasured" (Mic.)
Hal Hopson
Choristers Guild A-196
Unison with keyboard and opt. instruments

"Offertory" (Mic.)
John Ness Beck
Beckenhorst BP 1280
SATB with keyboard

"Undivided" (Ecumenical Sunday)
Melanie Tunney, Word
SATB with keyboard

Hymn Anthem Suggestions
"What Does the Lord Require" (Mic.)
52IHA #49
"Cuando El Pobre" ("When the Poor Ones") (Mic., Matt.)
52IHA #12
"All Who Love and Serve Your City" (Mic., Matt.)
52IHA #1

Other Suggestions
    The hymn "What Does the Lord Require" may be sung by choir only with the congregation joining on "Do justly; love mercy; walk humbly with your God." This phrase may also be used as a psalm antiphon.
Greeting: Psalm 15. Who shall abide in God's tent? (Ps.)
Reading and/or Canticle: B119, E560, F589, L17, W620. "The Beatitudes" (Matt.)
Reading: F553. "Psalm 15" (Ps.)
Prayer: UM392. Prayer for a New Heart (Matt.)
Prayer: UM461. For Those Who Mourn (Matt.)
Prayer: UM564. For the Unity of Christ's Body (Ecumenical Sunday)
Litany: UM556. Litany for Christian Unity (Ecumenical Sunday)

Isaiah 58:1-9a (9b-12)

[1]Shout out, do not hold back! Lift up your voice like a trumpet! Announce to my people their rebellion, to the house of Jacob their sins. [2]Yet day after day they seek me and delight to know my ways, as if they were a nation that practiced righteousness and did not forsake the ordinance of their God; they ask of me righteous judgments, they delight to draw near to God. [3]"Why do we fast, but you do not see? Why humble ourselves, but you do not notice?" Look, you serve your own interest on your fast day, and oppress all your workers. [4]Look, you fast only to quarrel and to fight and to strike with a wicked fist. Such fasting as you do today will not make your voice heard on high. [5]Is such the fast that I choose, a day to humble oneself? Is it to bow down the head like a bulrush, and to lie in sackcloth and ashes? Will you call this a fast, a day acceptable to the LORD? [6]Is not this the fast that I choose: to loose the bonds of injustice, to undo the thongs of the yoke, to let the oppressed go free, and to break every yoke? [7]Is it not to share your bread with the hungry, and bring the homeless poor into your house; when you see the naked, to cover them, and not to hide yourself from your own kin? [8]Then your light shall break forth like the dawn, and your healing shall spring up quickly; your vindicator shall go before you, the glory of the LORD shall be your rear guard. [9]Then you shall call, and the LORD will answer; you shall cry for help, and he will say, Here I am. If you remove the yoke from among you, the pointing of the finger, the speaking of evil, [10]if you offer your food to the hungry and satisfy the needs of the afflicted, then your light shall rise in the darkness and your gloom be like the noonday. [11]The LORD will guide you continually, and satisfy your needs in parched places, and make your bones strong; and you shall be like a watered garden, like a spring of water, whose waters never fail. [12]Your ancient ruins shall be rebuilt; you shall raise up the foundations of many generations; you shall be called the repairer of the breach, the restorer of streets to live in.

Psalm 112:1-10

[1]Praise the LORD! Happy are those who fear the LORD, who greatly delight in his commandments. [2]Their descendants will be mighty in the land; the generation of the upright will be blessed. [3]Wealth and riches are in their houses, and their righteousness endures forever. [4]They rise in the darkness as a light for the upright; they are gracious, merciful, and righteous. [5]It is well with those who deal generously and lend, who conduct their affairs with justice. [6]For the righteous will never be moved; they will be remembered forever. [7]They are not afraid of evil tidings; their hearts are firm, secure in the LORD. [8]Their hearts are steady, they will not be afraid; in the end they will look in triumph on their foes. [9]They have distributed freely, they have given to the poor; their righteousness endures forever; their horn is exalted in honor. [10]The wicked see it and are angry; they gnash their teeth and melt away; the desire of the wicked comes to nothing.

1 Corinthians 2:1-12 (13-16)

[1]When I came to you, brothers and sisters, I did not come proclaiming the mystery of God to you in lofty words or wisdom. [2]For I decided to know nothing among you except Jesus Christ, and him crucified. [3]And I came to you in weakness and in fear and in much trembling. [4]My speech and my proclamation were not with plausible words of wisdom, but with a demonstration of the Spirit and of power, [5]so that your faith might rest not on human wisdom but on the power of God.

[6]Yet among the mature we do speak wisdom, though it is not a wisdom of this age or of the rulers of this age, who are doomed to perish. [7]But we speak God's wisdom, secret and hidden, which God decreed before the ages for our glory. [8]None of the rulers of this age understood this; for if they had, they would not have crucified the Lord of glory. [9]But, as it is written, "What no eye has seen, nor ear heard, nor the human heart conceived, what God has prepared for those who love him"—[10]these things God has revealed to us through the Spirit; for the Spirit searches everything, even the depths of God. [11]For what human being knows what is truly human except the human spirit that is within? So also no one comprehends what is truly God's except the Spirit of God. [12]Now we have received not the spirit of the world, but the Spirit that is from God, so that we may understand the gifts bestowed on us by God. [13]And we speak of these things in words not taught by human wisdom but taught by the Spirit, interpreting spiritual things to those who are spiritual.

[14]Those who are unspiritual do not receive the gifts of God's Spirit, for they are foolishness to them, and they are unable to understand them because they are spiritually discerned. [15]Those who are spiritual discern all things, and they are themselves subject to no one else's scrutiny. [16]"For who has known the mind of the Lord so as to instruct him?" But we have the mind of Christ.

Matthew 5:13-20

[13]"You are the salt of the earth; but if salt has lost its taste, how can its saltiness be restored? It is no longer good for anything, but is thrown out and trampled under foot.

[14]"You are the light of the world. A city built on a hill cannot be hid. [15]No one after lighting a lamp puts it under the bushel basket, but on the lampstand, and it gives light to all in the house. [16]In the same way, let your light shine before others, so that they may see your good works and give glory to your Father in heaven.

[17]"Do not think that I have come to abolish the law or the prophets; I have come not to abolish but to fulfill. [18]For truly I tell you, until heaven and earth pass away, not one letter, not one stroke of a letter, will pass from the law until all is accomplished. [19]Therefore, whoever breaks one of the least of these commandments, and teaches others to do the same, will be called least in the kingdom of heaven; but whoever does them and teaches them will be called great in the kingdom of heaven. [20]For I tell you, unless your righteousness exceeds that of the scribes and Pharisees, you will never enter the kingdom of heaven."

Hymn and Keyboard Suggestions

O– "Ask Ye What Great Thing I Know" (1 Cor.)
      B538, UM163 (PD)
          S-2   #78-80. Various treatments

O– "O For a Thousand Tongues to Sing" (Isa.)
      B216, E493, F349, L559, P466, UM57 and 59
      (PD)
          S-1   #33-38. Various treatments

O– "O That I Had a Thousand Voices" (Isa.)
      L560, P475, W546
          K-1(II) #61. Prelude/postlude

"Lord, Whose Love Through Humble Service" (Isa.)
      L423, UM581
          S-2   #22. Descant
          K-8   p. 2. Prelude
      W630
          H-1   #25. Harmonization
          S-1   #178. Harmonization
                    #179. Harmonization
      E610, P427

"Now Quit Your Care" (Isa.)
      E145 (PD)

"We've a Story to Tell to the Nations" (Isa.)
      B586, F659, UM569 (PD)
          K-8   p. 26. Introduction

"Hope of the World" (Isa., Ps., 1 Cor.)
      UM178
          S-1   #343. Descant
          S-2   #189. Introduction
      E472, L493, P360, W565

"Eat This Bread" (Isa., Ps., 1 Cor., Communion)
      UM628, W734

"Seek Ye First" (Ps.)
      B478, E711, P333, UM405, W580
          K-15   p. 111. Piano prelude/meditation

"Spirit of God, Descend upon My Heart" (1 Cor.)
      B245, F147, L486, P326, UM500 (PD)
          S-2   #125-28. Various treatments
          K-8   p. 24. Prelude/meditation

"Spirit of the Living God" (1 Cor.)
      B244, F155, P322, UM393
          S-1   #212. Vocal descant idea

"Forth in Thy Name, O Lord" (1 Cor.)
      UM438 (PD)
          K-1(I) #16. Use as interlude (manuals only)
          H-1   #83. Harmonization
          S-1   #100-103. Various treatments
          K-1(I) #16. Prelude/postlude
          K-2   p. 8. Short prelude
          K-10   p. 32. Prelude/postlude
      L505

"Blest Be the Dear Uniting Love" (1 Cor.)
      UM566 (PD)

"O Morning Star, How Fair and Bright" (Matt.)
      E497, L76, P69, UM247, W390
          K-1(IV) #97. Prelude
          K-3   p. 32. Short postlude
          K-5   p. 159. Various keyboard treatments,
                        through p. 173

C– "O Word of God Incarnate" (Matt.)
      E632, L231, P327, UM598 (PD)
          H-1   #64. Harmonization in D major
          S-1   #243. Harmonization
          K-1(II) #63. Prelude/meditation

C– "Sent Forth by God's Blessing" (Isa.)
      L221, UM664
          S-1   #327. Descant
          K-8   p. 8. Prelude/meditation

Vocal Solos

"O For a Thousand Tongues to Sing" (Isa.)
V-1   p. 32
"Spirit of Faith Come Down" (1 Cor.)
V-1   p. 43
"Jesus, Thou Art Watching Ever" (General)
V-4   p. 6

Anthems

"True Fasting" (Isa.)
arr. George Brandon
Abingdon APM 522
Two-part with keyboard

"Light and Salt" (Matt.)
Erik Routley
Gregorian Institute of America G-2300
SATB with organ

Hymn Anthem Suggestions

"This Little Light of Mine" (Matt.)
52IHA #45
"This Is the Feast of Victory" (Communion)
52IHA #44

Other Suggestions

Reading: F252. 1 Corinthians 2:1-5 (1 Cor.)
Reading: F156. 1 Corinthians 2:10-16 (1 Cor.)
Response: B244, F155, P322, UM393. "Spirit of the Living
  God"

Deuteronomy 30:15-20

[15]See, I have set before you today life and prosperity, death and adversity. [16]If you obey the commandments of the LORD your God that I am commanding you today, by loving the LORD your God, walking in his ways, and observing his commandments, decrees, and ordinances, then you shall live and become numerous, and the LORD your God will bless you in the land that you are entering to possess. [17]But if your heart turns away and you do not hear, but are led astray to bow down to other gods and serve them, [18]I declare to you today that you shall perish; you shall not live long in the land that you are crossing the Jordan to enter and possess. [19]I call heaven and earth to witness against you today that I have set before you life and death, blessings and curses. Choose life so that you and your descendants may live, [20]loving the LORD your God, obeying him, and holding fast to him; for that means life to you and length of days, so that you may live in the land that the LORD swore to give to your ancestors, to Abraham, to Isaac, and to Jacob.

Psalm 119:1-8

[1]Happy are those whose way is blameless,
   who walk in the law of the LORD.
[2]Happy are those who keep his decrees,
   who seek him with their whole heart,
[3]who also do no wrong, but walk in his ways.
[4]You have commanded your precepts
   to be kept diligently.
[5]O that my ways may be steadfast
   in keeping your statutes!
[6]Then I shall not be put to shame,
   having my eyes fixed on all
      your commandments.
[7]I will praise you with an upright heart,
   when I learn your righteous ordinances.
[8]I will observe your statutes;
   do not utterly forsake me.

1 Corinthians 3:1-9

[1]And so, brothers and sisters, I could not speak to you as spiritual people, but rather as people of the flesh, as infants in Christ. [2]I fed you with milk, not solid food, for you were not ready for solid food. Even now you are still not ready, [3]for you are still of the flesh. For as long as there is jealousy and quarreling among you, are you not of the flesh, and behaving according to human inclinations? [4]For when one says, "I belong to Paul," and another, "I belong to Apollos," are you not merely human?

[5]What then is Apollos? What is Paul? Servants through whom you came to believe, as the Lord assigned to each. [6]I planted, Apollos watered, but God gave the growth. [7]So neither the one who plants nor the one who waters is anything, but only God who gives the growth. [8]The one who plants and the one who waters have a common purpose, and each will receive wages according to the labor of each. [9]For we are God's servants, working together; you are God's field, God's building.

Matthew 5:21-37

[21]"You have heard that it was said to those of ancient times, 'You shall not murder'; and 'whoever murders shall be liable to judgment.' [22]But I say to you that if you are angry with a brother or sister, you will be liable to judgment; and if you insult a brother or sister, you will be liable to the council; and if you say, 'You fool,' you will be liable to the hell of fire. [23]So when you are offering your gift at the altar, if you remember that your brother or sister has something against you, [24]leave your gift there before the altar and go; first be reconciled to your brother or sister, and then come and offer your gift. [25]Come to terms quickly with your accuser while you are on the way to court with him, or your accuser may hand you over to the judge, and the judge to the guard, and you will be thrown into prison. [26]Truly I tell you, you will never get out until you have paid the last penny.

[27]"You have heard that it was said, 'You shall not commit adultery.' [28]But I say to you that everyone who looks at a woman with lust has already committed adultery with her in his heart. [29]If your right eye causes you to sin, tear it out and throw it away; it is better for you to lose one of your members than for your whole body to be thrown into hell. [30]And if your right hand causes you to sin, cut it off and throw it away; it is better for you to lose one of your members than for your whole body to go into hell.

[31]"It was also said, 'Whoever divorces his wife, let him give her a certificate of divorce.' [32]But I say to you that anyone who divorces his wife, except on the ground of unchastity, causes her to commit adultery; and whoever marries a divorced woman commits adultery.

[33]"Again, you have heard that it was said to those of ancient times, 'You shall not swear falsely, but carry out the vows you have made to the Lord.' [34]But I say to you, Do not swear at all, either by heaven, for it is the throne of God, [35]or by the earth, for it is his footstool, or by Jerusalem, for it is the city of the great King. [36]And do not swear by your head, for you cannot make one hair white or black. [37]Let your word be 'Yes, Yes' or 'No, No'; anything more than this comes from the evil one."

Hymn and Keyboard Suggestions

O– "Wonderful Words of Life" (Deut., Ps.)
  B261, F29, UM600 (PD)

O– "Come, Thou Fount of Every Blessing" (Deut.)
  B15, E686, F318, L499, P356, UM400 (PD)
    S-1   #244. Descant
  B18
  "We Utter Our Cry" (Deut.)
  B631
    H-1   #37. Harmonization
    S-1   #223-26. Various treatments
    K-8   p. 17. Introduction
  UM439
    S-2   #145. Descant
           #146. Harmonization
"O Word of God Incarnate" (Deut., Ps.)
  E632, L231, P327, UM598 (PD)
    H-1   #64. Harmonization in D major
    S-1   #243. Harmonization
    K-1(II) #63. Prelude/meditation
"Camina, Pueblo de Dios" ("Walk on, O People of
  God") (Deut., Ps., Matt.)
  P296, UM305
"Blest Are the Uncorrupt in Heart" (Ps.)
  P233
    S-1   #286. Descant
    K-2   p. 25. Short prelude/postlude
"O Lord, May Church and Home Combine" (Ps.,
  Matt.)
  B510, UM695
    S-2   #105. Flute/violin descant
           #106. Harmonization
    K-8   p. 22. Prelude/meditation
"Christ, from Whom All Blessings Flow" (1 Cor.)
  UM550 (PD)
    S-1   #53. Descant
"For the Fruits of This Creation" (1 Cor.)
  B643
    S-2   #14. Descant
  E424, L563, P553, UM97, W562
"Forgive Our Sins as We Forgive" (Matt.)
  E674, L307, P347, UM390, W754
    S-1   #85. Choral harmonization
"O For a Heart to Praise My God" (Matt.)
  F357, UM417
    S-1   #286. Descant
    K-2   p. 25. Short prelude/postlude
  W591
C– "O Master, Let Me Walk With Thee" (Deut., Ps.)
  B279, E660, F442, L492, P357, UM430 (PD)
    S-2   #118. Descant
  E659

Vocal Solos
"Stan' Still Jordan" (Deut.)
V-5   p. 34
"O Lord, Our God" (General)
V-10   p. 24

Anthems
"The New Covenant" (Deut.)
Dana F. Wells
Abingdon APM-619
SATB with piano

"Blessed Are Those Whose Way Is Blameless" (Ps.)
Roger Petrich
Augsburg PS 614
SAB with keyboard

"For We Are Laborers Together with God" (1 Cor.)
Leo Sowerby
H. W. Gray CMR 2888
SATB with organ and bass solo

Hymn Anthem Suggestion
"Come, Thou Fount of Every Blessing"
52IHA   #9

Other Suggestions
Response: B261, F29, UM600 (PD), refrain. "Wonderful
  Words of Life"
Response: UM601, refrain. "Thy Word Is a Lamp"
Benediction: UM439, stanza 6. "We Utter Our Cry"

Exodus 24:12-18

[12]The LORD said to Moses, "Come up to me on the mountain, and wait there; and I will give you the tablets of stone, with the law and the commandment, which I have written for their instruction." [13]So Moses set out with his assistant Joshua, and Moses went up into the mountain of God. [14]To the elders he had said, "Wait here for us, until we come to you again; for Aaron and Hur are with you; whoever has a dispute may go to them."

[15]Then Moses went up on the mountain, and the cloud covered the mountain. [16]The glory of the LORD settled on Mount Sinai, and the cloud covered it for six days; on the seventh day he called to Moses out of the cloud. [17]Now the appearance of the glory of the LORD was like a devouring fire on the top of the mountain in the sight of the people of Israel. [18]Moses entered the cloud, and went up on the mountain. Moses was on the mountain for forty days and forty nights.

Psalm 99

[1]The LORD is king; let the peoples tremble!
  He sits enthroned upon the
    cherubim; let the earth quake!
[2]The LORD is great in Zion;
  he is exalted over all the peoples.
[3]Let them praise your great and awesome name.
  Holy is he!
[4]Mighty King, lover of justice,
  you have established equity;
you have executed justice
  and righteousness in Jacob.
[5]Extol the LORD our God;
  worship at his footstool.
  Holy is he!
[6]Moses and Aaron were among his priests,
  Samuel also was among those
    who called on his name.
  They cried to the LORD, and he
    answered them.
[7]He spoke to them in the pillar of cloud;
  they kept his decrees,
  and the statutes that he gave them.
[8]O LORD our God, you answered them;
  you were a forgiving God to them,
  but an avenger of their wrongdoings.
[9]Extol the LORD our God,
  and worship at his holy mountain;
  for the LORD our God is holy.

2 Peter 1:16-21

[16]For we did not follow cleverly devised myths when we made known to you the power and coming of our Lord Jesus Christ, but we had been eyewitnesses of his majesty. [17]For he received honor and glory from God the Father when that voice was conveyed to him by the Majestic Glory, saying, "This is my Son, my Beloved, with whom I am well pleased." [18]We ourselves heard this voice come from heaven, while we were with him on the holy mountain.

[19]So we have the prophetic message more fully confirmed. You will do well to be attentive to this as to a lamp shining in a dark place, until the day dawns and the morning star rises in your hearts. [20]First of all you must understand this, that no prophecy of scripture is a matter of one's own interpretation, [21]because no prophecy ever came by human will, but men and women moved by the Holy Spirit spoke from God.

Matthew 17:1-9

[1]Six days later, Jesus took with him Peter and James and his brother John and led them up a high mountain, by themselves. [2]And he was transfigured before them, and his face shone like the sun, and his clothes became dazzling white. [3]Suddenly there appeared to them Moses and Elijah, talking with him. [4]Then Peter said to Jesus, "Lord, it is good for us to be here; if you wish, I will make three dwellings here, one for you, one for Moses, and one for Elijah." [5]While he was still speaking, suddenly a bright cloud overshadowed them, and from the cloud a voice said, "This is my Son, the Beloved; with him I am well pleased; listen to him!" [6]When the disciples heard this, they fell to the ground and were overcome by fear. [7]But Jesus came and touched them, saying, "Get up and do not be afraid." [8]And when they looked up, they saw no one except Jesus himself alone.

[9]As they were coming down the mountain, Jesus ordered them, "Tell no one about the vision until after the Son of Man has been raised from the dead."

Hymn and Keyboard Suggestions

O– "Guide Me, O Thou Great Jehovah" (Exod.)
      B56, E690, F608, L343, P281, UM127 (PD)

S-1	#76.	Descant
	#77.	Harmonization
K-6	p. 30.	Prelude/postlude

"Praise to the Lord, the Almighty" (Ps.)
      B14 (PD), E390, F337, L543, P482, UM139, W547

H-1	#88.	Harmonization in G major
H-2	p. 18.	Harmonization with descant
S-1	#218-22.	Various treatments
K-4	p. 140.	Various keyboard treatments, through p. 146
K-8	p. 10.	Interlude
K-14	p. 44.	Piano prelude/postlude

"The God of Abraham Praise" (Exod., Matt.)
      B34, E401, L544, P488, UM116 (PD), W537

H-1	#44.	Harmonization
S-1	#211.	Harmonization

"Every Time I Feel the Spirit" (Exod., Matt.)
      P315, UM404

"Christ, Whose Glory Fills the Skies" (2 Pet., Matt.)
      E7, L265, P462, UM173 (PD)

H-1	#29.	Harmonization
S-1	#278.	Harmonization
	#279.	Harmonization

      E6, F293 (PD), P463

"O Wondrous Sight! O Vision Fair" (2 Pet., Matt.)
      E137, UM258 (PD)

S-2	#191.	Harmonization

      L80, P75

S-1	#82-84.	Various treatments

      E136 (PD)

"Christ, upon the Mountain Peak" (2 Pet., Matt.)
      E129 or E130, P74, UM260, W701

"O Morning Star, How Fair and Bright" (2 Pet., Matt.)
      E497, L76, P69, UM247, W390

K-1(IV)	#97.	Prelude
K-3	p. 32.	Short postlude
K-5	p. 159.	Various keyboard treatments, through p. 173

"Jesus, Joy of Our Desiring" (Matt.)
      UM644 (PD)

K-1(IV)	#96.	Short prelude or meditation
K-5	p. 153.	Various keyboard treatments, through p. 158
K-14	p. 5.	Piano prelude/postlude

"I Stand Amazed in the Presence" (Matt.)
      B547, F223, UM371 (PD)

C– "Glorious Things of Thee Are Spoken" (Exod.)
      B398, E522 or 523, F376, L358, P446, UM731
      (PD)

H-1	#59.	Harmonization
S-1	#27.	Descant
	#28.	Harmonization in F major
K-10	p. 6.	Variations
K-14	p. 29.	Piano variations

Vocal Solos

"Hymn of Praise" (Ps.)
V-10   p. 48
"Every Time I Feel the Spirit" (Exod., Matt.)
V-5   p. 5

Anthems

"This Is My Beloved Son" (Matt.)
Knut Nystedt
Concordia 98-1805
SAB with organ

"And as They Came Down from the Mountain" (Matt.)
Alan Hovhaness
C. F. Peters 6545
SATB with tenor solo *a cappella*

"Goin' to the Mountain" (Matt.)
Boyd Bacon
Beckenhorst Press BP1184
SATB with keyboard

Hymn Anthem Suggestions

"Christ, Upon the Mountain Peak" (2 Pet., Matt.)
52IHA   #8
"Jesus, Joy of Our Desiring" (Matt.)
52IHA   #29

Other Suggestions

Introit: UM644, stanza 1. "Jesus, Joy of Our Desiring." Precede with one of the keyboard versions as a prelude.
Prayer: UM259. Transfiguration
Scripture Response: B56, E690, F608, L343, P281, UM127 (PD), stanza 3. "Guide Me, O Thou Great Jehovah"
Benediction Response: E497, L76, P69, UM247, W390, stanza 3. "O Morning Star, How Fair and Bright." Last section "Amen! Amen! . . .")

Joel 2:1-2, 12-17

[1]Blow the trumpet in Zion; sound the alarm on my holy mountain! Let all the inhabitants of the land tremble, for the day of the LORD is coming, it is near—[2]a day of darkness and gloom, a day of clouds and thick darkness! Like blackness spread upon the mountains a great and powerful army comes; their like has never been from of old, nor will be again after them in ages to come.

[12]Yet even now, says the LORD, return to me with all your heart, with fasting, with weeping, and with mourning; [13]rend your hearts and not your clothing. Return to the LORD, your God, for he is gracious and merciful, slow to anger, and abounding in steadfast love, and relents from punishing. [14]Who knows whether he will not turn and relent, and leave a blessing behind him, a grain offering and a drink offering for the LORD, your God? [15]Blow the trumpet in Zion; sanctify a fast; call a solemn assembly; [16]gather the people. Sanctify the congregation; assemble the aged; gather the children, even infants at the breast. Let the bridegroom leave his room, and the bride her canopy. [17]Between the vestibule and the altar let the priests, the ministers of the LORD, weep. Let them say, "Spare your people, O LORD, and do not make your heritage a mockery, a byword among the nations. Why should it be said among the peoples, 'Where is their God?' "

Psalm 51:1-17

[1]Have mercy on me, O God, according to your steadfast love; according to your abundant mercy blot out my transgressions. [2]Wash me thoroughly from my iniquity, and cleanse me from my sin. [3]For I know my transgressions, and my sin is ever before me. [4]Against you, you alone, have I sinned, and done what is evil in your sight, so that you are justified in your sentence and blameless when you pass judgment. [5]Indeed, I was born guilty, a sinner when my mother conceived me. [6]You desire truth in the inward being; therefore teach me wisdom in my secret heart. [7]Purge me with hyssop, and I shall be clean; wash me, and I shall be whiter than snow. [8]Let me hear joy and gladness; let the bones that you have crushed rejoice. [9]Hide your face from my sins, and blot out all my iniquities. [10]Create in me a clean heart, O God, and put a new and right spirit within me. [11]Do not cast me away from your presence, and do not take your holy spirit from me. [12]Restore to me the joy of your salvation, and sustain in me a willing spirit. [13]Then I will teach transgressors your ways, and sinners will return to you. [14]Deliver me from bloodshed, O God, O God of my salvation, and my tongue will sing aloud of your deliverance. [15]O Lord, open my lips, and my mouth will declare your praise. [16]For you have no delight in sacrifice; if I were to give a burnt offering, you would not be pleased. [17]The sacrifice acceptable to God is a broken spirit; a broken and contrite heart, O God, you will not despise.

2 Corinthians 5:20b–6:10

[20]We entreat you on behalf of Christ, be reconciled to God. [21]For our sake he made him to be sin who knew no sin, so that in him we might become the righteousness of God.

[1]As we work together with him, we urge you also not to accept the grace of God in vain. [2]For he says,

"At an acceptable time I have listened to you,
    and on a day of salvation I have helped you."

See, now is the acceptable time; see, now is the day of salvation! [3]We are putting no obstacle in anyone's way, so that no fault may be found with our ministry, [4]but as servants of God we have commended ourselves in every way: through great endurance, in afflictions, hardships, calamities, [5]beatings, imprisonments, riots, labors, sleepless nights, hunger; [6]by purity, knowledge, patience, kindness, holiness of spirit, genuine love, [7]truthful speech, and the power of God; with the weapons of righteousness for the right hand and for the left; [8]in honor and dishonor, in ill repute and good repute. We are treated as impostors, and yet are true; [9]as unknown, and yet are well known; as dying, and see—we are alive; as punished, and yet not killed; [10]as sorrowful, yet always rejoicing; as poor, yet making many rich; as having nothing, and yet possessing everything.

Matthew 6:1-6, 16-21

[1]"Beware of practicing your piety before others in order to be seen by them; for then you have no reward from your Father in heaven.

[2]"So whenever you give alms, do not sound a trumpet before you, as the hypocrites do in the synagogues and in the streets, so that they may be praised by others. Truly I tell you, they have received their reward. [3]But when you give alms, do not let your left hand know what your right hand is doing, [4]so that your alms may be done in secret; and your Father who sees in secret will reward you.

[5]"And whenever you pray, do not be like the hypocrites; for they love to stand and pray in the synagogues and at the street corners, so that they may be seen by others. Truly I tell you, they have received their reward. [6]But whenever you pray, go into your room and shut the door and pray to your Father who is in secret; and your Father who sees in secret will reward you.

[16]"And whenever you fast, do not look dismal, like the hypocrites, for they disfigure their faces so as to show others that they are fasting. Truly I tell you, they have received their reward. [17]But when you fast, put oil on your head and wash your face, [18]so that your fasting may be seen not by others but by your Father who is in secret; and your Father who sees in secret will reward you.

[19]"Do not store up for yourselves treasures on earth, where moth and rust consume and where thieves break in and steal; [20]but store up for yourselves treasures in heaven, where neither moth nor rust consumes and where thieves do not break in and steal. [21]For where your treasure is, there your heart will be also."

Hymn and Keyboard Suggestions
O– "Sing, My Tongue, the Glorious Battle" (Joel)
        UM296 (PD), W437
        H-1   #33. Harmonization
        S-1   #268. Handbell part
                 #269. Descant
        K-3   p. 14. Prelude/meditation
        E165, E166 (PD), L118
    "Weary of All Trumpeting" (Joel, Matt.)
        E572, UM442, W635
    "Lord, I Want to Be a Christian" (Joel, Matt.)
        B489, F421, P372 (PD), UM402
        K-7   p. 10. Prelude
    "Have Mercy on Us, Living Lord" (Ps.)
        P195, P196
    "O For a Heart to Praise My God" (Ps.)
        F357, UM417 (PD)
        S-1   #286. Descant
        K-2   p. 25. Short prelude/postlude
        W591
    "Alas! and Did My Savior Bleed" (2 Cor.)
        B145, F274, L98, P78, UM294 (PD)
        S-2   #116-17. Harmonizations
        K-6   p. 12. Prelude/meditation/postlude
        B139, UM359 (PD)
    "Creator of the Earth and Skies" (2 Cor.)
        E148, UM450
    "The Church's One Foundation" (2 Cor.)
        B350, E525, F547, L369, P442, UM545 (PD),
        UM546
        H-1   #62. Harmonization
        S-1   #25. Descant
                 #26. Harmonization
        K-1(I)   #8. Prelude/postlude
    "The Lord's Prayer" (Matt.)
        B462, F440, P589, UM271
    "More Love to Thee, O Christ" (Matt.)
        B473, F476, P359, UM453 (PD)
    "Prayer Is the Soul's Sincere Desire" (Matt.)
        UM492 (PD)
        S-2   #31. Flute/violin descant
                 #32. Descant
        F446
    "Sweet Hour of Prayer" (Matt.)
        B445, F439, UM496 (PD)
C– "What Wondrous Love Is This" (2 Cor.)
        B143 (PD), E439, F283, L385, P85, UM292, W600
        S-1   #347. Harmonization
        K-6   p. 28. Prelude/meditation
        K-12   p. 42. Prelude/meditation

Vocal Solos
"A Contrite Heart" (Ps.)
V-4   p. 10
"Come Thou and with Us Dwell" (Confession)
V-8   p. 1

Anthems
"Wash Me Throughly from My Wickedness" (Ps.)
Samuel Wesley
Novello 29.0111.00
SATB with soprano solo and organ

"Forgive Us" in *A Season to Celebrate* (Ps.)
Allen Pote
Hinshaw Music HMB 144
SATB with piano, optional guitar and flute

"Wondrous Love" (2 Cor.)
arr. Harold Owen
Columbia Pictures Publications SV8330
SATB *a cappella*

"Teach Me to Pray" (Matt.)
Jessie Mae Jewett (arr. Reddick)
M. Witmark 5-W2625
SATB with piano

Hymn Anthem Suggestions
"Out of the Depths I Cry to You" (Ps.)
52IHA   #39
"What Wondrous Love Is This" (2 Cor.)
52IHA   #50

Other Suggestions
Hymn Idea: E165, E166 (PD), L118, UM296 (PD), W437. "Sing, My Tongue, the Glorious Battle." Sing *a cappella* for a stark but prayerful and thoughtful rendition.
Introit and Benediction: E572, UM442, W635. "Weary of All Trumpeting." Use this hymn to begin and end the service. A male soloist, strongly declaiming stanza 1 from the rear of the worship space would be effective. Have the same soloist sing stanza 3 as a benediction response, also from behind the congregation.
Greeting: Joel 2:1. The day of the Lord is coming.
Greeting: 2 Corinthians 6:2. Now is the acceptable time.
Call to Confession: Psalm 51:16-17
Prayer of Confession: Psalm 51:1-15
Prayer: UM353. Ash Wednesday (Ps.)
Isaiah 58:1-12 gives another interpretation of fasting.
If this service includes the imposition of ashes, sing appropriate hymns as the congregation participates.

Genesis 2:15-17; 3:1-7

[15]The LORD God took the man and put him in the garden of Eden to till it and keep it. [16]And the LORD God commanded the man, "You may freely eat of every tree of the garden; [17]but of the tree of the knowledge of good and evil you shall not eat, for in the day that you eat of it you shall die."

[1]Now the serpent was more crafty than any other wild animal that the LORD God had made. He said to the woman, "Did God say, 'You shall not eat from any tree in the garden'?" [2]The woman said to the serpent, "We may eat of the fruit of the trees in the garden; [3]but God said, 'You shall not eat of the fruit of the tree that is in the middle of the garden, nor shall you touch it, or you shall die.' " [4]But the serpent said to the woman, "You will not die; [5]for God knows that when you eat of it your eyes will be opened, and you will be like God, knowing good and evil." [6]So when the woman saw that the tree was good for food, and that it was a delight to the eyes, and that the tree was to be desired to make one wise, she took of its fruit and ate; and she also gave some to her husband, who was with her, and he ate. [7]Then the eyes of both were opened, and they knew that they were naked; and they sewed fig leaves together and made loincloths for themselves.

Psalm 32

[1]Happy are those whose transgression is forgiven, whose sin is covered. [2]Happy are those to whom the LORD imputes no iniquity, and in whose spirit there is no deceit. [3]While I kept silence, my body wasted away through my groaning all day long. [4]For day and night your hand was heavy upon me; my strength was dried up as by the heat of summer. [5]Then I acknowledged my sin to you, and I did not hide my iniquity; I said, "I will confess my transgressions to the LORD," and you forgave the guilt of my sin. [6]Therefore let all who are faithful offer prayer to you; at a time of distress, the rush of mighty waters shall not reach them. [7]You are a hiding place for me; you preserve me from trouble; you surround me with glad cries of deliverance. [8]I will instruct you and teach you the way you should go; I will counsel you with my eye upon you. [9]Do not be like a horse or a mule, without understanding, whose temper must be curbed with bit and bridle, else it will not stay near you. [10]Many are the torments of the wicked, but steadfast love surrounds those who trust in the LORD. [11]Be glad in the LORD and rejoice, O righteous, and shout for joy, all you upright in heart.

Romans 5:12-19

[12]Therefore, just as sin came into the world through one man, and death came through sin, and so death spread to all because all have sinned—[13]sin was indeed in the world before the law, but sin is not reckoned when there is no law. [14]Yet death exercised dominion from Adam to Moses, even over those whose sins were not like the transgression of Adam, who is a type of the one who was to come.

[15]But the free gift is not like the trespass. For if the many died through the one man's trespass, much more surely have the grace of God and the free gift in the grace of the one man, Jesus Christ, abounded for the many. [16]And the free gift is not like the effect of the one man's sin. For the judgment following one trespass brought condemnation, but the free gift following many trespasses brings justification. [17]If, because of the one man's trespass, death exercised dominion through that one, much more surely will those who receive the abundance of grace and the free gift of righteousness exercise dominion in life through the one man, Jesus Christ.

[18]Therefore just as one man's trespass led to condemnation for all, so one man's act of righteousness leads to justification and life for all. [19]For just as by the one man's disobedience the many were made sinners, so by the one man's obedience the many will be made righteous.

Matthew 4:1-11

[1]Then Jesus was led up by the Spirit into the wilderness to be tempted by the devil. [2]He fasted forty days and forty nights, and afterwards he was famished. [3]The tempter came and said to him, "If you are the Son of God, command these stones to become loaves of bread." [4]But he answered, "It is written,

'One does not live by bread alone,
  but by every word that comes
    from the mouth of God.'"

[5]Then the devil took him to the holy city and placed him on the pinnacle of the temple, [6]saying to him, "If you are the Son of God, throw yourself down; for it is written,

'He will command his angels
    concerning you,'
  and 'On their hands they will
    bear you up,
so that you will not dash your
    foot against a stone.'"

[7]Jesus said to him, "Again it is written, 'Do not put the Lord your God to the test.'"

[8]Again, the devil took him to a very high mountain and showed him all the kingdoms of the world and their splendor; [9]and he said to him, "All these I will give you, if you will fall down and worship me." [10]Jesus said to him, "Away with you, Satan! for it is written,

'Worship the Lord your God,
    and serve only him.'"

[11]Then the devil left him, and suddenly angels came and waited on him.

Hymn and Keyboard Suggestions
O– "O Worship the King" (Gen., Rom.)
      B16, F336, P476, UM73 (PD)
      H-1   #37. Harmonization
      S-1   #223-26. Various treatments
      K-8   p. 17. Introduction
      E388, L548 (PD)
      H-1   #45. Harmonization in G major
      S-2   #71. Introduction
                #72-74. Harmonizations
      K-2   p. 10. Short prelude/postlude
      K-10   p. 13. Prelude/postlude
"God, Who Stretched the Spangled Heavens" (Gen.)
      E580, L463, P268, UM150, W648
      S-1   #160-62. Various treatments
      S-2   #87-88. Brass and timpani introduction and arrangement
      B47
      S-1   #173-76. Various treatments
      K-8   p. 23. Harmonization
      K-13   p. 16. Piano prelude/postlude
      K-15   p. 122. Piano prelude/postlude
"Creator of the Stars of Night" (Gen.)
      E60, L323, P4, UM692 (PD), W368
      S-2   #41. Handbell arrangement
"How Blest Are Those" (Ps.)
      P184
"Grace Greater than Our Sin" (Ps., Rom.)
      B329, F105, UM365 (PD)
      S-1   #240. Descant idea
      S-2   #124. Harmonization
"Amazing Grace" (Ps., Rom.)
      B330, E671, F107, L448, P280, UM378 (PD), W583
      S-2   #5-7. Various treatments
      K-15   p. 146. Piano prelude/meditation
"Forty Days and Forty Nights" (Matt.)
      E150, P77, W419
      H-1   #18. Harmonization
"O Love, How Deep" (Matt.)
      E449, L88, P83, UM267 (PD)
      S-1   #82-84. Various treatments
      E448 (PD)
      S-2   #48. Descant
                #49. Harmonization

"Lord, Who Throughout These Forty Days" (Matt.)
      E142, P81, W417 (PD)
      K-2   p. 28. Short prelude/meditation
      UM269
      S-2   #105. Flute/violin descant
                #106. Harmonization
      K-8   p. 22. Prelude/meditation
"Come, Sinners, to the Gospel Feast" (Communion)
      UM616 (PD)
      S-1   #164. Transposition in E-flat major
                #165-66. Harmonization with descant
      K-1(I)   #28. Prelude or postlude
      K-2   p. 11. Short prelude
"There Is a Fountain Filled with Blood" (Communion)
      B142, UM622 (PD)
C– "Lord, Dismiss Us with Thy Blessing" (Rom.)
      E344, F520, L259, P538, UM671 (PD)
      H-1   #79. Harmonization

Vocal Solos
"Forsake Me Not" (Gen., Ps.)
V-9   p. 60
"Amazing Grace" (Rom.)
V-3   p. 8
"What Was Thy Transgression?"
V-8   p. 18

Anthems
"Jesus Christ, the Apple Tree" (Gen.)
Elizabeth Poston (arr. Schalk)
Concordia 98-2664
SATB and handbells

"Amazing Grace" (Rom.)
John Newton (arr. Fred Bock)
Fred Bock G-195
SATB with piano

Hymn Anthem Suggestions
"Come, Thou Fount of Every Blessing" (Gen., Rom.)
52IHA   #9
"Blessed Be the God of Israel" (Gen., Rom.)
52IHA   #3
"Freely, Freely" (Gen., Rom.)
52IHA   #16

Other Suggestions
Prayer: UM366. For Guidance (Gen., Rom.)
Canticle: UM167. "Canticle of Christ's Obedience" (Rom.)
Canticle: UM516. "Canticle of Redemption" (Ps.)

Genesis 12:1-4a

[1]Now the LORD said to Abram, "Go from your country and your kindred and your father's house to the land that I will show you. [2]I will make of you a great nation, and I will bless you, and make your name great, so that you will be a blessing. [3]I will bless those who bless you, and the one who curses you I will curse; and in you all the families of the earth shall be blessed."

[4]So Abram went, as the LORD had told him; and Lot went with him.

Psalm 121

[1]I lift up my eyes to the hills—
    from where will my help come?
[2]My help comes from the LORD,
    who made heaven and earth.
[3]He will not let your foot be moved;
    he who keeps you will not slumber.
[4]He who keeps Israel
    will neither slumber nor sleep.
[5]The LORD is your keeper;
    the LORD is your shade at your right hand.
[6]The sun shall not strike you by day,
    nor the moon by night.
[7]The LORD will keep you from all evil;
    he will keep your life.
[8]The LORD will keep
    your going out and your coming in
    from this time on and forevermore.

Romans 4:1-5, 13-17

[1]What then are we to say was gained by Abraham, our ancestor according to the flesh? [2]For if Abraham was justified by works, he has something to boast about, but not before God. [3]For what does the scripture say? "Abraham believed God, and it was reckoned to him as righteousness." [4]Now to one who works, wages are not reckoned as a gift but as something due. [5]But to one who without works trusts him who justifies the ungodly, such faith is reckoned as righteousness.

[13]For the promise that he would inherit the world did not come to Abraham or to his descendants through the law but through the righteousness of faith. [14]If it is the adherents of the law who are to be the heirs, faith is null and the promise is void. [15]For the law brings wrath; but where there is no law, neither is there violation.

[16]For this reason it depends on faith, in order that the promise may rest on grace and be guaranteed to all his descendants, not only to the adherents of the law but also to those who share the faith of Abraham (for he is the father of all of us, [17]as it is written, "I have made you the father of many nations")—in the presence of the God in whom he believed, who gives life to the dead and calls into existence the things that do not exist.

John 3:1-17

[1]Now there was a Pharisee named Nicodemus, a leader of the Jews. [2]He came to Jesus by night and said to him, "Rabbi, we know that you are a teacher who has come from God; for no one can do these signs that you do apart from the presence of God." [3]Jesus answered him, "Very truly, I tell you, no one can see the kingdom of God without being born from above." [4]Nicodemus said to him, "How can anyone be born after having grown old? Can one enter a second time into the mother's womb and be born?" [5]Jesus answered, "Very truly, I tell you, no one can enter the kingdom of God without being born of water and Spirit. [6]What is born of the flesh is flesh, and what is born of the Spirit is spirit. [7]Do not be astonished that I said to you, 'You must be born from above.' [8]The wind blows where it chooses, and you hear the sound of it, but you do not know where it comes from or where it goes. So it is with everyone who is born of the Spirit." [9]Nicodemus said to him, "How can these things be?" [10]Jesus answered him, "Are you a teacher of Israel, and yet you do not understand these things?

[11]"Very truly, I tell you, we speak of what we know and testify to what we have seen; yet you do not receive our testimony. [12]If I have told you about earthly things and you do not believe, how can you believe if I tell you about heavenly things? [13]No one has ascended into heaven except the one who descended from heaven, the Son of Man. [14]And just as Moses lifted up the serpent in the wilderness, so must the Son of Man be lifted up, [15]that whoever believes in him may have eternal life.

[16]"For God so loved the world that he gave his only Son, so that everyone who believes in him may not perish but may have eternal life.

[17]"Indeed, God did not send the Son into the world to condemn the world, but in order that the world might be saved through him."

Hymn and Keyboard Suggestions
O– "The God of Abraham Praise" (Gen.)
        B34, E401, L544, P488, UM116 (PD), W537
        H-1   #44. Harmonization
        S-1   #211. Harmonization
"If Thou But Suffer God to Guide Thee" (Gen., Ps.)
        B57, E635, L453, P282, UM142 (PD)
        K-5   p. 141. Harmonization in A minor
        K-1(IV) #94. Prelude/meditation
        K-5   p. 141. Various keyboard treatments, through p. 152
"Sing Praise to God Who Reigns Above" (Gen., Ps.)
        B20, E408, F343, P483, UM126 (PD), W528
        S-1   #237. Descant
"I to the Hills Will Lift My Eyes" (Ps.)
        P234 (PD)
        H-1   #63. Harmonization
        K-1(I) #17. Prelude/meditation
        E668 (PD)
"O God, Our Help in Ages Past" (Ps.)
        B74, E680, F370, L320, P210, UM117 (PD), W579
        H-1   #46. Harmonization
        S-1   #293-96. Various treatments
        K-1(III) #74. Short prelude/postlude
        K-14   p. 34. Piano variations
"Give to the Winds Thy Fears" (Ps.)
        UM129 (PD)
        S-1   #129. Descant
        P286 (PD)
"Jesus, Lover of My Soul" (Ps.)
        E699, F222, P303, UM479 (PD)
        S-1   #6. Descant
        K-9   p. 10. Prelude/postlude
        B180 (PD)
"Faith of Our Fathers" (or "Faith of the Martyrs") (Rom.)
        B352, F526, L500, UM710 (PD), W571
        H-1   #60. Harmonization in G major
"All Glory Be to God on High" (John)
        E421 (PD), L166, P133, W527
        H-2   p. 4. Harmonization with descant
        K-1(I) #1. Prelude/postlude
"Lift High the Cross" (John, Baptism)
        B594, E473, L377, P371, UM159, W704
        S-1   #71-75. Various treatments
        K-15   p. 88. Piano prelude/postlude
"Of the Father's Love Begotten" (John)
        B251, E82, F172 (PD), L42, P309, UM184, W398
        S-1   #92. Handbell arrangement
        K-9   p. 4. Prelude/meditation

"Now Let Us from This Table Rise" (John, Communion)
        UM634, W625
        S-2   #48. Descant
                 #49. Harmonization
C– "To God Be the Glory" (John)
        B4, F363, P485, UM98 (PD)
        S-2   #176. Piano arrangement
        K-15   p. 42. Prelude/postlude

Vocal Solos
"Jesus, Lover of My Soul" (Ps.)
V-1   p. 37
"Of the Father's Love Begotten" (John)
V-3   p. 17
"And Can It Be That I Should Gain" (John)
V-1   p. 29

Anthems
"He Watching Over Israel" (Ps.)
F. Mendelssohn
Carl Fisher CM-7245
SATB with keyboard

"Speak to One Another" (John)
Allen Pote
Beckenhorst BP1284
SATB with piano and optional handbells

"Jesu, Blessed Jesu" (John)
Gordon Young
Harold Flammer A-6357
SATB with keyboard

Hymn Anthem Suggestions
"He Leadeth Me: O Blessed Thought" (Gen.)
52IHA #21
"This Is a Day of New Beginnings" (John)
52IHA #43
"What Wondrous Love Is This" (John)
52IHA #50

Other Suggestions
   The scripture from John makes today an excellent day to schedule baptisms.
Introit: B34, E401, L544, P488, UM116 (PD), W537, stanza 4. "The God of Abraham Praise"
Introit: B74, E680, F370, L320, P210, UM117 (PD), W579, stanza 1. "O God, Our Help in Ages Past"
Words of Assurance: Psalm 121
Benediction: B74, E680, F370, L320, P210, UM117 (PD), W579, last stanza. "O God, Our Help in Ages Past"

Exodus 17:1-7

¹From the wilderness of Sin the whole congregation of the Israelites journeyed by stages, as the LORD commanded. They camped at Rephidim, but there was no water for the people to drink. ²The people quarreled with Moses, and said, "Give us water to drink." Moses said to them, "Why do you quarrel with me? Why do you test the LORD?" ³But the people thirsted there for water; and the people complained against Moses and said, "Why did you bring us out of Egypt, to kill us and our children and livestock with thirst?" ⁴So Moses cried out to the LORD, "What shall I do with this people? They are almost ready to stone me." ⁵The LORD said to Moses, "Go on ahead of the people, and take some of the elders of Israel with you; take in your hand the staff with which you struck the Nile, and go. ⁶I will be standing there in front of you on the rock at Horeb. Strike the rock, and water will come out of it, so that the people may drink." Moses did so, in the sight of the elders of Israel. ⁷He called the place Massah and Meribah, because the Israelites quarreled and tested the LORD, saying, "Is the LORD among us or not?"

Psalm 95

¹O come, let us sing to the LORD; let us make a joyful noise to the rock of our salvation! ²Let us come into his presence with thanksgiving; let us make a joyful noise to him with songs of praise! ³For the LORD is a great God, and a great King above all gods. ⁴In his hand are the depths of the earth; the heights of the mountains are his also. ⁵The sea is his, for he made it, and the dry land, which his hands have formed. ⁶O come, let us worship and bow down, let us kneel before the LORD, our Maker! ⁷For he is our God, and we are the people of his pasture, and the sheep of his hand. O that today you would listen to his voice! ⁸Do not harden your hearts, as at Meribah, as on the day at Massah in the wilderness, ⁹when your ancestors tested me, and put me to the proof, though they had seen my work. ¹⁰For forty years I loathed that generation and said, "They are a people whose hearts go astray, and they do not regard my ways." ¹¹Therefore in my anger I swore, "They shall not enter my rest."

Romans 5:1-11

¹Therefore, since we are justified by faith, we have peace with God through our Lord Jesus Christ, ²through whom we have obtained access to this grace in which we stand; and we boast in our hope of sharing the glory of God. ³And not only that, but we also boast in our sufferings, knowing that suffering produces endurance, ⁴and endurance produces character, and character produces hope, ⁵and hope does not disappoint us, because God's love has been poured into our hearts through the Holy Spirit that has been given to us.

⁶For while we were still weak, at the right time Christ died for the ungodly. ⁷Indeed, rarely will anyone die for a righteous person—though perhaps for a good person someone might actually dare to die. ⁸But God proves his love for us in that while we still were sinners Christ died for us. ⁹Much more surely then, now that we have been justified by his blood, will we be saved through him from the wrath of God. ¹⁰For if while we were enemies, we were reconciled to God through the death of his Son, much more surely, having been reconciled, will we be saved by his life. ¹¹But more than that, we even boast in God through our Lord Jesus Christ, through whom we have now received reconciliation.

John 4:5-42

⁵So he came to a Samaritan city called Sychar, near the plot of ground that Jacob had given to his son Joseph. ⁶Jacob's well was there, and Jesus, tired out by his journey, was sitting by the well. It was about noon.

⁷A Samaritan woman came to draw water, and Jesus said to her, "Give me a drink." ⁸(His disciples had gone to the city to buy food.) ⁹The Samaritan woman said to him, "How is it that you, a Jew, ask a drink of me, a woman of Samaria?" (Jews do not share things in common with Samaritans.) ¹⁰Jesus answered her, "If you knew the gift of God, and who it is that is saying to you, 'Give me a drink,' you would have asked him, and he would have given you living water." ¹¹The woman said to him, "Sir, you have no bucket, and the well is deep. Where do you get that living water? ¹²Are you greater than our ancestor Jacob, who gave us the well, and with his sons and his flocks drank from it?" ¹³Jesus said to her, "Everyone who drinks of this water will be thirsty again, ¹⁴but those who drink of the water that I will give them will never be thirsty. The water that I will give will become in them a spring of water gushing up to eternal life." ¹⁵The woman said to him, "Sir, give me this water, so that I may never be thirsty or have to keep coming here to draw water."

¹⁶Jesus said to her, "Go, call your husband, and come back." ¹⁷The woman answered him, "I have no husband." Jesus said to her, "You are right in saying, 'I have no husband'; ¹⁸for you have had five husbands, and the one you have now is not your husband. What you have said is true!" ¹⁹The woman said to him, "Sir, I see that you are a prophet. ²⁰Our ancestors worshiped on this mountain, but you say that the place where people must worship is in Jerusalem." ²¹Jesus said to her, "Woman, believe me, the hour is coming when you will worship the Father neither on this mountain nor in Jerusalem. ²²You worship what you do not know; we worship what we know, for salvation is from the Jews. ²³But the hour is coming, and is now here, when the true worshipers will worship the Father in spirit and truth, for the Father seeks such as these to worship him. ²⁴God is spirit, and those who worship him must worship in spirit

and truth." [25]The woman said to him, "I know that Messiah is coming" (who is called Christ). "When he comes, he will proclaim all things to us." [26]Jesus said to her, "I am he, the one who is speaking to you."

[27]Just then his disciples came. They were astonished that he was speaking with a woman, but no one said, "What do you want?" or, "Why are you speaking with her?" [28]Then the woman left her water jar and went back to the city. She said to the people, [29]"Come and see a man who told me everything I have ever done! He cannot be the Messiah, can he?" [30]They left the city and were on their way to him.

[31]Meanwhile the disciples were urging him, "Rabbi, eat something." [32]But he said to them, "I have food to eat that you do not know about." [33]So the disciples said to one another, "Surely no one has brought him something to eat?" [34]Jesus said to them, "My food is to do the will of him who sent me and to complete his work. [35]Do you not say,

'Four months more, then comes the harvest'? But I tell you, look around you, and see how the fields are ripe for harvesting. [36]The reaper is already receiving wages and is gathering fruit for eternal life, so that sower and reaper may rejoice together. [37]For here the saying holds true, 'One sows and another reaps.' [38]I sent you to reap that for which you did not labor. Others have labored, and you have entered into their labor."

[39]Many Samaritans from that city believed in him because of the woman's testimony, "He told me everything I have ever done." [40]So when the Samaritans came to him, they asked him to stay with them; and he stayed there two days. [41]And many more believed because of his word. [42]They said to the woman, "It is no longer because of what you said that we believe, for we have heard for ourselves, and we know that this is truly the Savior of the world."

Hymn and Keyboard Suggestions

O– "Joyful, Joyful, We Adore Thee" (Ps., John)
        B7, E376, F377, L551, P464, UM89 (PD), W525
          S-1   #173-76. Various treatments
          K-8   p. 23. Harmonization
          K-13   p. 16. Piano prelude/postlude
          K-15   p. 122. Piano prelude/postlude
"A Charge to Keep I Have" (Exod., John, Girl Scout Sunday)
        UM413 (PD)
          S-1   #46. Choral harmonization
          K-1(I)   #10. Short prelude/postlude/hymn interlude
"O Food to Pilgrims Given" (Exod., John)
        E309, UM631
          K-1(III) #67. Prelude/postlude
          K-5   p. 51. Various keyboard treatments, through p. 53
          K-10   p. 18. Variations
        E308
"O Come and Sing Unto the Lord" (Ps.)
        P214 (PD)
"'Tis Finished! The Messiah Dies" (Rom.)
        B148, UM282 (PD)
"Jesus, Thine All-Victorious Love" (Rom.)
        UM422 (PD)
          S-1   #33-38. Various treatments
"O Love That Wilt Not Let Me Go" (Rom.)
        B292, F404, L324, P384, UM480 (PD)
"Rescue the Perishing" (Rom.)
        B559, F661, UM591 (PD)
          K-8   p. 21. Introduction
"Christ Is the World's Light" (John)
        UM188, W543
          S-1   #64. Descant
"The First One Ever" (John)
        E673, UM276
"Jesus, Lover of My Soul" (John)
        E699, F222, P303, UM479 (PD)
          S-1   #6. Descant
          K-9   p. 10. Prelude/postlude
        B180 (PD)
"Deck Thyself, My Soul, with Gladness" (John)
        E339, L224, P506, UM612 (PD)
          K-1(III) #80. Prelude/meditation (manuals only)
          K-5   p. 55. Various keyboard treatments, through p. 64
"You Satisfy the Hungry Heart" (John)
        P521, UM629, W736
          S-1   #144. Four-part setting of refrain
"Jesus, Joy of Our Desiring" (John)
        UM644 (PD)
          K-1(IV) #96. Short prelude or meditation
          K-5   p. 153. Various keyboard treatments, through p. 158
          K-14   p. 5. Piano prelude/postlude
C– "Guide Me, O Thou Great Jehovah" (Exod., John)
        B56, E690, F608, L343, P281, UM127 (PD)
          S-1   #76. Descant
                     #77. Harmonization
          K-6   p. 30. Prelude/postlude

Vocal Solos

"'Tis Finished! The Messiah Dies" (Rom.)
V-1   p. 63
"O Love, That Wilt Not Let Me Go" (Rom.)
V-7   p. 49
"Abide with Me" (John)
V-10   p. 64

Anthems

"Credo" (Exod.)
Jane Marshall
AMSI 264
SAB and unison choir with keyboard

"The Love of God Flows Deep and Strong" (Rom.)
Sue Ellen Page
Hinshaw Music HMC-208
SAB with keyboard

"Living Water" (John)
Lloyd Larson
Beckenhorst BP 1271
SATB with keyboard

"Galilee Man" in *A Season to Celebrate* (John)
Allen Pote
Hinshaw Music HMB 144
Unison women with piano and optional soprano solo

Hymn Anthem Suggestions

"You Satisfy the Hungry Heart" (John)
52IHA   #52
"Jesus, Joy of Our Desiring" (John)
52IHA   #29

Other Suggestions

Introit: B56, E690, F608, L343, P281, UM127 (PD), stanza 1. "Guide Me, O Thou Great Jehovah"
Call to Worship: Psalm 95. Call to worship and obedience
Canticle: UM91. "Canticle of Praise to God" (Ps.)
Response: F481, UM641. "Fill My Cup, Lord" (John)
Benediction: B56, E690, F608, L343, P281, UM127 (PD), stanza 3. "Guide Me, O Thou Great Jehovah"

1 Samuel 16:1-13

[1]The LORD said to Samuel, "How long will you grieve over Saul? I have rejected him from being king over Israel. Fill your horn with oil and set out; I will send you to Jesse the Bethlehemite, for I have provided for myself a king among his sons." [2]Samuel said, "How can I go? If Saul hears of it, he will kill me." And the LORD said, "Take a heifer with you, and say, 'I have come to sacrifice to the LORD.' [3]Invite Jesse to the sacrifice, and I will show you what you shall do; and you shall anoint for me the one whom I name to you." [4]Samuel did what the LORD commanded, and came to Bethlehem. The elders of the city came to meet him trembling, and said, "Do you come peaceably?" [5]He said, "Peaceably; I have come to sacrifice to the LORD; sanctify yourselves and come with me to the sacrifice." And he sanctified Jesse and his sons and invited them to the sacrifice.

[6]When they came, he looked on Eliab and thought, "Surely the LORD's anointed is now before the LORD." [7]But the LORD said to Samuel, "Do not look on his appearance or on the height of his stature, because I have rejected him; for the LORD does not see as mortals see; they look on the outward appearance, but the LORD looks on the heart." [8]Then Jesse called Abinadab, and made him pass before Samuel. He said, "Neither has the LORD chosen this one." [9]Then Jesse made Shammah pass by. And he said, "Neither has the LORD chosen this one." [10]Jesse made seven of his sons pass before Samuel, and Samuel said to Jesse, "The LORD has not chosen any of these." [11]Samuel said to Jesse, "Are all your sons here?" And he said, "There remains yet the youngest, but he is keeping the sheep." And Samuel said to Jesse, "Send and bring him; for we will not sit down until he comes here." [12]He sent and brought him in. Now he was ruddy, and had beautiful eyes, and was handsome. The LORD said, "Rise and anoint him; for this is the one." [13]Then Samuel took the horn of oil, and anointed him in the presence of his brothers; and the spirit of the LORD came mightily upon David from that day forward. Samuel then set out and went to Ramah.

Psalm 23

[1]The LORD is my shepherd, I shall not want. [2]He makes me lie down in green pastures; he leads me beside still waters; [3]he restores my soul. He leads me in right paths for his name's sake. [4]Even though I walk through the darkest valley, I fear no evil; for you are with me; your rod and your staff—they comfort me. [5]You prepare a table before me in the presence of my enemies; you anoint my head with oil; my cup overflows. [6]Surely goodness and mercy shall follow me all the days of my life, and I shall dwell in the house of the LORD my whole life long.

Ephesians 5:8-14

[8]For once you were darkness, but now in the Lord you are light. Live as children of light—[9]for the fruit of the light is found in all that is good and right and true. [10]Try to find out what is pleasing to the Lord. [11]Take no part in the unfruitful works of darkness, but instead expose them. [12]For it is shameful even to mention what such people do secretly; [13]but everything exposed by the light becomes visible, [14]for everything that becomes visible is light. Therefore it says,

> "Sleeper, awake!
> Rise from the dead,
> and Christ will shine on you."

John 9:1-41

[1]As he walked along, he saw a man blind from birth. [2]His disciples asked him, "Rabbi, who sinned, this man or his parents, that he was born blind?" [3]Jesus answered, "Neither this man nor his parents sinned; he was born blind so that God's works might be revealed in him. [4]We must work the works of him who sent me while it is day; night is coming when no one can work. [5]As long as I am in the world, I am the light of the world." [6]When he had said this, he spat on the ground and made mud with the saliva and spread the mud on the man's eyes, [7]saying to him, "Go, wash in the pool of Siloam" (which means Sent). Then he went and washed and came back able to see. [8]The neighbors and those who had seen him before as a beggar began to ask, "Is this not the man who used to sit and beg?" [9]Some were saying, "It is he." Others were saying, "No, but it is someone like him." He kept saying, "I am the man." [10]But they kept asking him, "Then how were your eyes opened?" [11]He answered, "The man called Jesus made mud, spread it on my eyes, and said to me, 'Go to Siloam and wash.' Then I went and washed and received my sight." [12]They said to him, "Where is he?" He said, "I do not know."

[13]They brought to the Pharisees the man who had formerly been blind. [14]Now it was a sabbath day when Jesus made the mud and opened his eyes. [15]Then the Pharisees also began to ask him how he had received his sight. He said to them, "He put mud on my eyes. Then I washed, and now I see." [16]Some of the Pharisees said, "This man is not from God, for he does not observe the sabbath." But others said, "How can a man who is a sinner perform such signs?" And they were divided. [17]So they said again to the blind man, "What do you say about him? It was your eyes he opened." He said, "He is a prophet."

[18]The Jews did not believe that he had been blind and had received his sight until they called the parents of the man who had received his sight [19]and asked them, "Is this your son, who you say was born blind? How then does he now see?" [20]His parents answered, "We know that this is our son, and that he was born blind; [21]but we do not know how it is that now he sees, nor do we know who opened his eyes. Ask him; he is of age. He will speak for himself." [22]His parents said this because they were afraid of the Jews; for the Jews had already agreed that anyone who confessed Jesus to be the Messiah would be put out of the synagogue. [23]Therefore his parents said, "He is of age; ask him."

[24]So for the second time they called the man who had been blind, and they said to him, "Give glory to God! We know that this man is a sinner." [25]He answered, "I do not know whether he is a sinner. One thing I do know, that though I was blind, now I see." [26]They said to him, "What did he do to you? How did he open your eyes?" [27]He answered them, "I have told you already, and you would not listen. Why do you want to hear it again? Do you also want to become his disciples?" [28]Then they reviled him, saying, "You are his disciple, but we are disciples of Moses. [29]We know that God has spoken to Moses, but as for this man, we do not know where he comes from." [30]The man answered, "Here is an astonishing thing! You do not know where he comes from, and yet he opened my eyes. [31]We know that God does not listen to sinners, but he does listen to one who worships him and obeys his will. [32]Never since the world began has it been heard that anyone opened the eyes of a person born blind. [33]If this man were not from God, he could do nothing." [34]They answered him, "You were born entirely in sins, and are you trying to teach us?" And they drove him out.

[35]Jesus heard that they had driven him out, and when he found him, he said, "Do you believe in the Son of Man?" [36]He answered, "And who is he, sir? Tell me, so that I may believe in him." [37]Jesus said to him, "You have seen him, and the one speaking with you is he." [38]He said, "Lord, I believe." And he worshiped him. [39]Jesus said, "I came into this world for judgment so that those who do not see may see, and those who do see may become blind." [40]Some of the Pharisees near him heard this and said to him, "Surely we are not blind, are we?" [41]Jesus said to them, "If you were blind, you would not have sin. But now that you say, 'We see,' your sin remains."

Hymn and Keyboard Suggestions
O– "God of Love and God of Power" (1 Sam.)
 UM578 (PD)
  H-2 p. 23. Harmonization with descant
  S-1 #338. Descant
    #341. Descant
O– "He Leadeth Me: O Blessed Thought" (1 Sam., Ps.)
 B52, F606, L501, UM128 (PD)
 "Close to Thee" (1 Sam., Ps.)
 B464, F405, UM407 (PD)
 "Precious Lord, Take My Hand" (1 Sam., Ps.)
 B456, F611, P404, UM474
 "The Lord's My Shepherd, I'll Not Want" (Ps.)
 F40, P170, UM136
 F42, L451
 "The King of Love My Shepherd Is" (Ps.)
 E645, L456, P171, UM138 (PD), W609
  S-1 #298. Harmonization
    #299. Harmonization
  K-2 p. 27. Short prelude/postlude
  K-9 p. 47. Prelude/meditation
 E646
 "Savior, Like a Shepherd Lead Us" (Ps.)
 B61, F601, P387, UM381 (PD)
  S-2 #29. Harmonization
  K-13 p. 51. Piano prelude/meditation
 E708
  H-1 #79. Harmonization
 "I Want to Walk as a Child of the Light" (Eph.)
 E490, UM206, W510
  S-2 #91. Descant
 "Awake, O Sleeper" (Eph.)
 E547, UM551
  S-2 #115. Descant
 W586
  S-1 #33-38. Various treatments
 "O Zion, Haste" (Eph.)
 B583, E539, F658, L397, UM573 (PD)
  S-2 #174-75. Introduction and harmo-
      nization
 "O Christ, the Healer" (John)
 P380, UM265, W747
  K-1(I) #23. Short prelude (may be played
       manuals only)
 L360
 "Open My Eyes, That I May See" (John)
 B502, F486, P324, UM454

C– "Lord, Whose Love Through Humble Service" (John)
 L423, UM581
  S-2 #22. Descant
  K-8 p. 2. Prelude
 W630
  H-1 #25. Harmonization
  S-1 #178. Harmonization
    #179. Harmonization
 E610, P427

Vocal Solos
"God Is my Shepherd" (Ps.)
V-9 p. 52
"The Shepherd" (Ps., John)
V-7 p. 59
"God, Our Ever Faithful Shepherd" (Ps.)
V-4 p. 15
De Blin' Man Stood on de Road An' Cried (John)
V-5 p. 99

Anthems
"Brother James's Air" (Ps.)
arr. Gordon Jacob
Oxford OCS 763
SATB *a cappella*

"The Pool of Bethsaida" (John)
Leo Sowerby
H. W. Gray CMR 2851
SATB with organ

Hymn Anthem Suggestions
"He Leadeth Me: O Blessed Thought" (1 Sam., Ps.)
52IHA #21
"How Like a Gentle Spirit" (Ps.)
52IHA #24
"O Thou, in Whose Presence" (Ps., John)
52IHA #38
"I Want to Walk as a Child of the Light" (Eph.)
52IHA #27

Other Suggestions
 You may wish to schedule a healing service today using the reading from John.
Prayer: UM460. In Time of Illness (Ps., John)
Response: B52, F606, L501, UM128 (PD). "He Leadeth Me: O Blessed Thought." Sing the refrain before and/or after each scripture reading.

Ezekiel 37:1-14

[1]The hand of the LORD came upon me, and he brought me out by the spirit of the LORD and set me down in the middle of a valley; it was full of bones. [2]He led me all around them; there were very many lying in the valley, and they were very dry. [3]He said to me, "Mortal, can these bones live?" I answered, "O Lord GOD, you know." [4]Then he said to me, "Prophesy to these bones, and say to them: O dry bones, hear the word of the LORD. [5]Thus says the Lord GOD to these bones: I will cause breath to enter you, and you shall live. [6]I will lay sinews on you, and will cause flesh to come upon you, and cover you with skin, and put breath in you, and you shall live; and you shall know that I am the LORD."

[7]So I prophesied as I had been commanded; and as I prophesied, suddenly there was a noise, a rattling, and the bones came together, bone to its bone. [8]I looked, and there were sinews on them, and flesh had come upon them, and skin had covered them; but there was no breath in them. [9]Then he said to me, "Prophesy to the breath, prophesy, mortal, and say to the breath: Thus says the Lord GOD: Come from the four winds, O breath, and breathe upon these slain, that they may live." [10]I prophesied as he commanded me, and the breath came into them, and they lived, and stood on their feet, a vast multitude.

[11]Then he said to me, "Mortal, these bones are the whole house of Israel. They say, 'Our bones are dried up, and our hope is lost; we are cut off completely.' [12]Therefore prophesy, and say to them, Thus says the Lord GOD: I am going to open your graves, and bring you up from your graves, O my people; and I will bring you back to the land of Israel. [13]And you shall know that I am the LORD, when I open your graves, and bring you up from your graves, O my people. [14]I will put my spirit within you, and you shall live, and I will place you on your own soil; then you shall know that I, the LORD, have spoken and will act," says the LORD.

Psalm 130

[1]Out of the depths I cry to you, O LORD. [2]Lord, hear my voice! Let your ears be attentive to the voice of my supplications! [3]If you, O LORD, should mark iniquities, Lord, who could stand? [4]But there is forgiveness with you, so that you may be revered. [5]I wait for the LORD, my soul waits, and in his word I hope; [6]my soul waits for the Lord more than those who watch for the morning, more than those who watch for the morning. [7]O Israel, hope in the LORD! For with the LORD there is steadfast love, and with him is great power to redeem. [8]It is he who will redeem Israel from all its iniquities.

Romans 8:6-11

[6]To set the mind on the flesh is death, but to set the mind on the Spirit is life and peace. [7]For this reason the mind that is set on the flesh is hostile to God; it does not submit to God's law—indeed it cannot, [8]and those who are in the flesh cannot please God.

[9]But you are not in the flesh; you are in the Spirit, since the Spirit of God dwells in you. Anyone who does not have the Spirit of Christ does not belong to him. [10]But if Christ is in you, though the body is dead because of sin, the Spirit is life because of righteousness. [11]If the Spirit of him who raised Jesus from the dead dwells in you, he who raised Christ from the dead will give life to your mortal bodies also through his Spirit that dwells in you.

John 11:1-45

[1]Now a certain man was ill, Lazarus of Bethany, the village of Mary and her sister Martha. [2]Mary was the one who anointed the Lord with perfume and wiped his feet with her hair; her brother Lazarus was ill. [3]So the sisters sent a message to Jesus, "Lord, he whom you love is ill." [4]But when Jesus heard it, he said, "This illness does not lead to death; rather it is for God's glory, so that the Son of God may be glorified through it." [5]Accordingly, though Jesus loved Martha and her sister and Lazarus, [6]after having heard that Lazarus was ill, he stayed two days longer in the place where he was.

[7]Then after this he said to the disciples, "Let us go to Judea again." [8]The disciples said to him, "Rabbi, the Jews were just now trying to stone you, and are you going there again?" [9]Jesus answered, "Are there not twelve hours of daylight? Those who walk during the day do not stumble, because they see the light of this world. [10]But those who walk at night stumble, because the light is not in them." [11]After saying this, he told them, "Our friend Lazarus has fallen asleep, but I am going there to awaken him." [12]The disciples said to him, "Lord, if he has fallen asleep, he will be all right." [13]Jesus, however, had been speaking about his death, but they thought that he was referring merely to sleep. [14]Then Jesus told them plainly, "Lazarus is dead. [15]For your sake I am glad I was not there, so that you may believe. But let us go to him." [16]Thomas, who was called the Twin, said to his fellow disciples, "Let us also go, that we may die with him."

[17]When Jesus arrived, he found that Lazarus had already been in the tomb four days. [18]Now Bethany was near Jerusalem, some two miles away, [19]and many of the Jews had come to Martha and Mary to console them about their brother. [20]When Martha heard that Jesus was coming, she went and met him, while Mary stayed at home. [21]Martha said to Jesus, "Lord, if you had been here, my brother would not have died. [22]But even now I know that God will give you whatever you ask of him." [23]Jesus said to her, "Your brother will rise again." [24]Martha said to him, "I know that he will rise again in the resurrection on the last day." [25]Jesus said to her, "I am the resurrection and the life. Those who believe in me, even though they die, will live,

[26]and everyone who lives and believes in me will never die. Do you believe this?" [27]She said to him, "Yes, Lord, I believe that you are the Messiah, the Son of God, the one coming into the world."

[28]When she had said this, she went back and called her sister Mary, and told her privately, "The Teacher is here and is calling for you." [29]And when she heard it, she got up quickly and went to him. [30]Now Jesus had not yet come to the village, but was still at the place where Martha had met him. [31]The Jews who were with her in the house, consoling her, saw Mary get up quickly and go out. They followed her because they thought that she was going to the tomb to weep there. [32]When Mary came where Jesus was and saw him, she knelt at his feet and said to him, "Lord, if you had been here, my brother would not have died." [33]When Jesus saw her weeping, and the Jews who came with her also weeping, he was greatly disturbed in spirit and deeply moved. [34]He said, "Where have you laid him?" They said to him, "Lord, come and see." [35]Jesus began to weep. [36]So the Jews said, "See how he loved him!" [37]But some of them said, "Could not he who opened the eyes of the blind man have kept this man from dying?"

[38]Then Jesus, again greatly disturbed, came to the tomb. It was a cave, and a stone was lying against it. [39]Jesus said, "Take away the stone." Martha, the sister of the dead man, said to him, "Lord, already there is a stench because he has been dead four days." [40]Jesus said to her, "Did I not tell you that if you believed, you would see the glory of God?" [41]So they took away the stone. And Jesus looked upward and said, "Father, I thank you for having heard me. [42]I knew that you always hear me, but I have said this for the sake of the crowd standing here, so that they may believe that you sent me." [43]When he had said this, he cried with a loud voice, "Lazarus, come out!" [44]The dead man came out, his hands and feet bound with strips of cloth, and his face wrapped in a cloth. Jesus said to them, "Unbind him, and let him go."

[45]Many of the Jews therefore, who had come with Mary and had seen what Jesus did, believed in him.

Hymn and Keyboard Suggestions

O– "Spirit of Faith, Come Down" (John, Rom.)
　　　UM332 (PD)
　　　　　S-2　　　#24. Harmonization
O– "Holy Spirit, Truth Divine" (Rom.)
　　　L257, P321, UM465 (PD)
　　　　　S-1　　　#53. Descant
"Camina, Pueblo de Dios" ("Walk On, O People of
　　God") (Ezek., John)
　　　P296, UM305
"Out of the Depths I Cry to You" (Ps.)
　　　L295, P240, UM515
　　　　　K-14　　　p. 18. Piano prelude
"Alas! and Did My Savior Bleed" (Rom.)
　　　B145, F274, L98, P78, UM294 (PD)
　　　　　S-2　　　#116-17. Harmonizations
　　　　　K-6　　　p. 12. Prelude/meditation/postlude
"Trust and Obey" (Rom., John)
　　　B447, F454, UM467 (PD)
　　　　　S-1　　　#336. Harmonization
"Lord of the Dance" (John)
　　　P302, UM261, W636
"O Christ, the Healer" (John)
　　　P380, UM265, W747
　　　　　K-1(I)　　#23. Short prelude (may be played
　　　　　　　　　　　manuals only)
　　　L360
"O Happy Day, That Fixed My Choice" (John)
　　　B349, F647, UM391 (PD)
C– "Now the Green Blade Riseth" (Ezek., John)
　　　E204, L148, UM311, W453
　　　　　S-1　　　#136. Orff instrument arrangement
C– "This Is a Day of New Beginnings" (Ezek., John)
　　　B370, UM383, W661

Vocal Solos

"Spirit of Faith Come Down" (John, Rom.)
V-1　　　p. 43
"There Is a Balm in Gilead" (John)
V-5　　　p. 111
"Give Me Jesus"
V-5　　　p. 39

Anthems

"Ye Shall Dwell in the Land" (Ezek.)
John Stainer
G. Schirmer 4468
SATB with organ and incidental solos

"I Am the Resurrection and the Life" (John)
Ronald Nelson
Augsburg ACL 1511
SATB *a cappella*

Hymn Anthem Suggestions

"Now the Green Blade Riseth" (Ezek., John)
52IHA　　#35
"This Is a Day of New Beginnings" (Ezek., John)
52IHA　　#43
"Out of the Depths I Cry to You" (Ps.)
52IHA　　#39
"Lord of the Dance" (John)
52IHA　　#31

Other Suggestions

　　Plan this service so that it moves from the quietness of
the tomb and the psalm to the joy of Lazarus' resurrection.
Introit: B370, UM383, W661, stanza 1. "This Is a Day of
　　New Beginnings." Use final ending for last word.
Canticle: UM516. "Canticle of Redemption" (Ps.)
Prayer: UM461. For Those Who Mourn (John)
Benediction: B370, UM383, W661, stanza 2. "This Is a Day
　　of New Beginnings." Use final ending for last word.

Matthew 21:1-11 (Palms Liturgy)

[1]When they had come near Jerusalem and had reached Bethphage, at the Mount of Olives, Jesus sent two disciples, [2]saying to them, "Go into the village ahead of you, and immediately you will find a donkey tied, and a colt with her; untie them and bring them to me. [3]If anyone says anything to you, just say this, 'The Lord needs them.' And he will send them immediately." [4]This took place to fulfill what had been spoken through the prophet, saying,

[5]"Tell the daughter of Zion,
Look, your king is coming to you,
   humble, and mounted on a donkey,
   and on a colt, the foal of a donkey."

[6]The disciples went and did as Jesus had directed them; [7]they brought the donkey and the colt, and put their cloaks on them, and he sat on them. [8]A very large crowd spread their cloaks on the road, and others cut branches from the trees and spread them on the road. [9]The crowds that went ahead of him and that followed were shouting,

"Hosanna to the Son of David!
Blessed is the one who comes
   in the name of the Lord!
Hosanna in the highest heaven!"

[10]When he entered Jerusalem, the whole city was in turmoil, asking, "Who is this?" [11]The crowds were saying, "This is the prophet Jesus from Nazareth in Galilee."

Psalm 118:1-2, 19-29 (Palms Liturgy)

[1]O give thanks to the LORD, for he is good; his steadfast love endures forever! [2]Let Israel say, "His steadfast love endures forever."

[19]Open to me the gates of righteousness, that I may enter through them and give thanks to the LORD. [20]This is the gate of the LORD; the righteous shall enter through it. [21]I thank you that you have answered me and have become my salvation. [22]The stone that the builders rejected has become the chief cornerstone. [23]This is the LORD's doing; it is marvelous in our eyes. [24]This is the day that the LORD has made; let us rejoice and be glad in it. [25]Save us, we beseech you, O LORD! O LORD, we beseech you, give us success! [26]Blessed is the one who comes in the name of the LORD. We bless you from the house of the LORD. [27]The LORD is God, and he has given us light. Bind the festal procession with branches, up to the horns of the altar. [28]You are my God, and I will give thanks to you; you are my God, I will extol you. [29]O give thanks to the LORD, for he is good, for his steadfast love endures forever.

Isaiah 50:4-9a (Passion Liturgy)

[4]The Lord GOD has given me the tongue of a teacher, that I may know how to sustain the weary with a word. Morning by morning he wakens—wakens my ear to listen as those who are taught. [5]The Lord GOD has opened my ear, and I was not rebellious, I did not turn backward. [6]I gave my back to those who struck me, and my cheeks to those who pulled out the beard; I did not hide my face from insult and spitting. [7]The Lord GOD helps me; therefore I have not been disgraced; therefore I have set my face like flint, and I know that I shall not be put to shame; [8]he who vindicates me is near. Who will contend with me? Let us stand up together. Who are my adversaries? Let them confront me. [9]It is the Lord GOD who helps me; who will declare me guilty?

Psalm 31:9-16 (Passion Liturgy)

[9]Be gracious to me, O LORD, for I am in distress; my eye wastes away from grief, my soul and body also. [10]For my life is spent with sorrow, and my years with sighing; my strength fails because of my misery, and my bones waste away. [11]I am the scorn of all my adversaries, a horror to my neighbors, an object of dread to my acquaintances; those who see me in the street flee from me. [12]I have passed out of mind like one who is dead; I have become like a broken vessel. [13]For I hear the whispering of many—terror all around!—as they scheme together against me, as they plot to take my life. [14]But I trust in you, O LORD; I say, "You are my God." [15]My times are in your hand; deliver me from the hand of my enemies and persecutors. [16]Let your face shine upon your servant; save me in your steadfast love.

Philippians 2:5-11 (Passion Liturgy)

[5]Let the same mind be in you that was in Christ Jesus, [6]who, though he was in the form of God, did not regard equality with God as something to be exploited, [7]but emptied himself, taking the form of a slave, being born in human likeness. And being found in human form, [8]he humbled himself and became obedient to the point of death—even death on a cross. [9]Therefore God also highly exalted him and gave him the name that is above every name, [10]so that at the name of Jesus every knee should bend, in heaven and on earth and under the earth, [11]and every tongue should confess that Jesus Christ is Lord, to the glory of God the Father.

Matthew 26:14–27:66 (Passion Liturgy)

¹⁴Then one of the twelve, who was called Judas Iscariot, went to the chief priests ¹⁵and said, "What will you give me if I betray him to you?" They paid him thirty pieces of silver. ¹⁶And from that moment he began to look for an opportunity to betray him.

¹⁷On the first day of Unleavened Bread the disciples came to Jesus, saying, "Where do you want us to make the preparations for you to eat the Passover?" ¹⁸He said, "Go into the city to a certain man, and say to him, 'The Teacher says, My time is near; I will keep the Passover at your house with my disciples.' " ¹⁹So the disciples did as Jesus had directed them, and they prepared the Passover meal.

²⁰When it was evening, he took his place with the twelve; ²¹and while they were eating, he said, "Truly I tell you, one of you will betray me." ²²And they became greatly distressed and began to say to him one after another, "Surely not I, Lord?" ²³He answered, "The one who has dipped his hand into the bowl with me will betray me. ²⁴The Son of Man goes as it is written of him, but woe to that one by whom the Son of Man is betrayed! It would have been better for that one not to have been born." ²⁵Judas, who betrayed him, said, "Surely not I, Rabbi?" He replied, "You have said so."

²⁶While they were eating, Jesus took a loaf of bread, and after blessing it he broke it, gave it to the disciples, and said, "Take, eat; this is my body." ²⁷Then he took a cup, and after giving thanks he gave it to them, saying, "Drink from it, all of you; ²⁸for this is my blood of the covenant, which is poured out for many for the forgiveness of sins. ²⁹I tell you, I will never again drink of this fruit of the vine until that day when I drink it new with you in my Father's kingdom."

³⁰When they had sung the hymn, they went out to the Mount of Olives.

³¹Then Jesus said to them, "You will all become deserters because of me this night; for it is written, 'I will strike the shepherd, and the sheep of the flock will be scattered.' ³²But after I am raised up, I will go ahead of you to Galilee." ³³Peter said to him, "Though all become deserters because of you, I will never desert you." ³⁴Jesus said to him, "Truly I tell you, this very night, before the cock crows, you will deny me three times." ³⁵Peter said to him, "Even though I must die with you, I will not deny you." And so said all the disciples.

³⁶Then Jesus went with them to a place called Gethsemane; and he said to his disciples, "Sit here while I go over there and pray." ³⁷He took with him Peter and the two sons of Zebedee, and began to be grieved and agitated. ³⁸Then he said to them, "I am deeply grieved, even to death; remain here, and stay awake with me." ³⁹And going a little farther, he threw himself on the ground and prayed, "My Father, if it is possible, let this cup pass from me; yet not what I want but what you want." ⁴⁰Then he came to the disciples and found them sleeping; and he said to Peter, "So, could you not stay awake with me one hour? ⁴¹Stay awake and pray that you may not come into the time of trial; the spirit indeed is willing, but the flesh is weak." ⁴²Again he went away for the second time and prayed, "My Father, if this cannot pass unless I drink it, your will be done." ⁴³Again he came and found them sleeping, for their eyes were heavy. ⁴⁴So leaving them again, he went away and prayed for the third time, saying the same words. ⁴⁵Then he came to the disciples and said to them, "Are you still sleeping and taking your rest? See, the hour is at hand, and the Son of Man is betrayed into the hands of sinners. ⁴⁶Get up, let us be going. See, my betrayer is at hand."

⁴⁷While he was still speaking, Judas, one of the twelve, arrived; with him was a large crowd with swords and clubs, from the chief priests and the elders of the people. ⁴⁸Now the betrayer had given them a sign, saying, "The one I will kiss is the man; arrest him." ⁴⁹At once he came up to Jesus and said, "Greetings, Rabbi!" and kissed him. ⁵⁰Jesus said to him, "Friend, do what you are here to do." Then they came and laid hands on Jesus and arrested him. ⁵¹Suddenly, one of those with Jesus put his hand on his sword, drew it, and struck the slave of the high priest, cutting off his ear. ⁵²Then Jesus said to him, "Put your sword back into its place; for all who take the sword will perish by the sword. ⁵³Do you think that I cannot appeal to my Father, and he will at once send me more than twelve legions of angels? ⁵⁴But how then would the scriptures be fulfilled, which say it must happen in this way?" ⁵⁵At that hour Jesus said to the crowds, "Have you come out with swords and clubs to arrest me as though I were a bandit? Day after day I sat in the temple teaching, and you did not arrest me. ⁵⁶But all this has taken place, so that the scriptures of the prophets may be fulfilled." Then all the disciples deserted him and fled.

⁵⁷Those who had arrested Jesus took him to Caiaphas the high priest, in whose house the scribes and the elders had gathered. ⁵⁸But Peter was following him at a distance, as far as the courtyard of the high priest; and going inside, he sat with the guards in order to see how this would end. ⁵⁹Now the chief priests and the whole council were looking for false testimony against Jesus so that they might put him to death, ⁶⁰but they found none, though many false witnesses came forward. At last two came forward ⁶¹and said, "This fellow said, 'I am able to destroy the temple of God and to build it in three days.' " ⁶²The high priest stood up and said, "Have you no answer? What is it that they testify against you?" ⁶³But Jesus was silent. Then the high priest said to him, "I put you under oath before the living God, tell us if you are the Messiah, the Son of God." ⁶⁴Jesus said to him, "You have said so. But I tell you, From now on you

will see the Son of Man seated at the right hand of Power and coming on the clouds of heaven." [65]Then the high priest tore his clothes and said, "He has blasphemed! Why do we still need witnesses? You have now heard his blasphemy. [66]What is your verdict?" They answered, "He deserves death." [67]Then they spat in his face and struck him; and some slapped him, [68]saying, "Prophesy to us, you Messiah! Who is it that struck you?"

[69]Now Peter was sitting outside in the courtyard. A servant-girl came to him and said, "You also were with Jesus the Galilean." [70]But he denied it before all of them, saying, "I do not know what you are talking about." [71]When he went out to the porch, another servant-girl saw him, and she said to the bystanders, "This man was with Jesus of Nazareth." [72]Again he denied it with an oath, "I do not know the man." [73]After a little while the bystanders came up and said to Peter, "Certainly you are also one of them, for your accent betrays you." [74]Then he began to curse, and he swore an oath, "I do not know the man!" At that moment the cock crowed. [75]Then Peter remembered what Jesus had said: "Before the cock crows, you will deny me three times." And he went out and wept bitterly.

[1]When morning came, all the chief priests and the elders of the people conferred together against Jesus in order to bring about his death. [2]They bound him, led him away, and handed him over to Pilate the governor.

[3]When Judas, his betrayer, saw that Jesus was condemned, he repented and brought back the thirty pieces of silver to the chief priests and the elders. [4]He said, "I have sinned by betraying innocent blood." But they said, "What is that to us? See to it yourself." [5]Throwing down the pieces of silver in the temple, he departed; and he went and hanged himself. [6]But the chief priests, taking the pieces of silver, said, "It is not lawful to put them into the treasury, since they are blood money." [7]After conferring together, they used them to buy the potter's field as a place to bury foreigners. [8]For this reason that field has been called the Field of Blood to this day. [9]Then was fulfilled what had been spoken through the prophet Jeremiah, "And they took the thirty pieces of silver, the price of the one on whom a price had been set, on whom some of the people of Israel had set a price, [10]and they gave them for the potter's field, as the Lord commanded me."

[11]Now Jesus stood before the governor; and the governor asked him, "Are you the King of the Jews?" Jesus said, "You say so." [12]But when he was accused by the chief priests and elders, he did not answer. [13]Then Pilate said to him, "Do you not hear how many accusations they make against you?" [14]But he gave him no answer, not even to a single charge, so that the governor was greatly amazed.

[15]Now at the festival the governor was accustomed to release a prisoner for the crowd, anyone whom they wanted. [16]At that time they had a notorious prisoner, called Jesus Barabbas. [17]So after they had gathered, Pilate said to them, "Whom do you want me to release for you, Jesus Barabbas or Jesus who is called the Messiah?" [18]For he realized that it was out of jealousy that they had handed him over. [19]While he was sitting on the judgment seat, his wife sent word to him, "Have nothing to do with that innocent man, for today I have suffered a great deal because of a dream about him." [20]Now the chief priests and the elders persuaded the crowds to ask for Barabbas and to have Jesus killed. [21]The governor again said to them, "Which of the two do you want me to release for you?" And they said, "Barabbas." [22]Pilate said to them, "Then what should I do with Jesus who is called the Messiah?" All of them said, "Let him be crucified!" [23]Then he asked, "Why, what evil has he done?" But they shouted all the more, "Let him be crucified!"

[24]So when Pilate saw that he could do nothing, but rather that a riot was beginning, he took some water and washed his hands before the crowd, saying, "I am innocent of this man's blood; see to it yourselves." [25]Then the people as a whole answered, "His blood be on us and on our children!" [26]So he released Barabbas for them; and after flogging Jesus, he handed him over to be crucified.

[27]Then the soldiers of the governor took Jesus into the governor's headquarters, and they gathered the whole cohort around him. [28]They stripped him and put a scarlet robe on him, [29]and after twisting some thorns into a crown, they put it on his head. They put a reed in his right hand and knelt before him and mocked him, saying, "Hail, King of the Jews!" [30]They spat on him, and took the reed and struck him on the head. [31]After mocking him, they stripped him of the robe and put his own clothes on him. Then they led him away to crucify him.

[32]As they went out, they came upon a man from Cyrene named Simon; they compelled this man to carry his cross. [33]And when they came to a place called Golgotha (which means Place of a Skull), [34]they offered him wine to drink, mixed with gall; but when he tasted it, he would not drink it. [35]And when they had crucified him, they divided his clothes among themselves by casting lots; [36]then they sat down there and kept watch over him. [37]Over his head they put the charge against him, which read, "This is Jesus, the King of the Jews."

[38]Then two bandits were crucified with him, one on his right and one on his left. [39]Those who passed by derided him, shaking their heads [40]and saying, "You who would destroy the temple and build it in three days, save yourself! If you are the Son of God, come down from the cross." [41]In the same way the chief priests also, along with the scribes and elders, were mocking him, saying, [42]"He saved others; he cannot save himself. He is the King of Israel; let him come down from the cross now, and we will believe in him. [43]He trusts in God; let God deliver him now, if he wants to;

for he said, 'I am God's Son.' " [44]The bandits who were crucified with him also taunted him in the same way.

[45]From noon on, darkness came over the whole land until three in the afternoon. [46]And about three o'clock Jesus cried with a loud voice, "Eli, Eli, lema sabachthani?" that is, "My God, my God, why have you forsaken me?" [47]When some of the bystanders heard it, they said, "This man is calling for Elijah." [48]At once one of them ran and got a sponge, filled it with sour wine, put it on a stick, and gave it to him to drink. [49]But the others said, "Wait, let us see whether Elijah will come to save him." [50]Then Jesus cried again with a loud voice and breathed his last. [51]At that moment the curtain of the temple was torn in two, from top to bottom. The earth shook, and the rocks were split. [52]The tombs also were opened, and many bodies of the saints who had fallen asleep were raised. [53]After his resurrection they came out of the tombs and entered the holy city and appeared to many. [54]Now when the centurion and those with him, who were keeping watch over Jesus, saw the earthquake and what took place, they were terrified and said, "Truly this man was God's Son!"

[55]Many women were also there, looking on from a distance; they had followed Jesus from Galilee and had provided for him. [56]Among them were Mary Magdalene, and Mary the mother of James and Joseph, and the mother of the sons of Zebedee.

[57]When it was evening, there came a rich man from Arimathea, named Joseph, who was also a disciple of Jesus. [58]He went to Pilate and asked for the body of Jesus; then Pilate ordered it to be given to him. [59]So Joseph took the body and wrapped it in a clean linen cloth [60]and laid it in his own new tomb, which he had hewn in the rock. He then rolled a great stone to the door of the tomb and went away. [61]Mary Magdalene and the other Mary were there, sitting opposite the tomb.

[62]The next day, that is, after the day of Preparation, the chief priests and the Pharisees gathered before Pilate [63]and said, "Sir, we remember what that impostor said while he was still alive, 'After three days I will rise again.' [64]Therefore command the tomb to be made secure until the third day; otherwise his disciples may go and steal him away, and tell the people, [6]He has been raised from the dead,' and the last deception would be worse than the first." [65]Pilate said to them, "You have a guard of soldiers; go, make it as secure as you can." [66]So they went with the guard and made the tomb secure by sealing the stone.

Hymn and Keyboard Suggestions

O– "All Glory, Laud, and Honor" (Palms Gospel)
        B126, E154, F249, L108, P88, UM280 (PD), W428

H-2	p. 30.	Harmonization with descant
S-1	#309-10.	Harmonization with descant
K-1(III)	#85.	Prelude/postlude
K-5	p. 70.	Various keyboard treatments, through p. 72

        E155, W805

"This Is the Day" (Ps. 118)
        B359, UM657
        B358 (PD)

S-1	#22.	Descant
	#23.	Harmonization

        P230 (PD)

K-1(II)	#55.	Prelude/postlude

        E50 (PD), UM658 (PD)

"Tell Me the Stories of Jesus" (Palms Gospel)
        B129, F212, UM277 (PD)

"Hosanna, Loud Hosanna" (Palms Gospel)
        B130, F248, P89, UM278 (PD)

S-1	#115.	Harmonization

"He Never Said a Mumbalin' Word" (Isa.)
        P95 (PD), UM291

"At the Name of Jesus" (Phil.)
        B198

K-6	p. 7.	Prelude

        E435, F351, L179, P148, UM168, W499

S-2	#99.	Descant

"Creator of the Stars of Night" (Phil.)
        E60, L323, P4, UM692 (PD), W368

S-2	#41.	Handbell arrangement

"Sing of Mary, Pure and Lowly" (Passion Gospel)
        E277, UM272

S-1	#274-75.	Harmonization with descant

        W404

"To Mock Your Reign, O Dearest Lord" (Passion Gospel)
        UM285

S-2	#100-103.	Various treatments

        E170

"O Sacred Head, Now Wounded" (Passion Gospel)
        B137, E168 or E169, F284, L116 or L117, P98, UM286, W434

K-1(II)	#34.	Prelude/postlude/meditation (manuals only)
K-4	p. 68.	Various keyboard treatments, through p. 81
K-14	p. 16.	Piano prelude
K-15	p. 86.	Piano prelude/postlude

C– "Rejoice, Ye Pure in Heart" (Phil.)
        B39, E556, F394, P145, UM160 (PD)

H-1	#92.	Harmonization in G major
S-1	#228.	Descant

        E557, P146, UM161

Vocal Solos

"Glad Hosannas" (Palms Gospel)
V-7   p. 26
"Ride on King Jesus" (Palms Gospel)
V-5   p. 147
"Jerusalem"
V-8   p. 32

Anthems

"Hosanna" in *A Season to Celebrate* (Palms Liturgy)
Allen Pote
Hinshaw Music HMB 144
SATB with keyboard

"Hosanna!" (Palms Liturgy)
Don Besig
Shawnee Press A-6456
SATB with keyboard

"Lift High the Cross" (Passion Liturgy)
arr. James Christensen
National Music CH-32
SATB with organ and optional brass

Hymn Anthem Suggestions

"Mantos y Palmas" ("Filled with Excitement")
52IHA   #32
HA   p. 22

Other Suggestions

This Sunday is celebrated in a variety of ways and the lectionary provides for different emphases. Since storytelling is such an important part of our heritage, you are encouraged to read all the lessons in their entirety, telling the story of Jesus' last week on earth. Ask someone familiar with storytelling or readers theater to assist a group of readers in proclaiming the Word. You may celebrate this day as Palm Sunday by substituting the opening Gospel and Psalm for the later ones.

If you have a "palm processional" allow both adults and children to participate.
Canticle: UM167. "Canticle of Christ's Obedience" (Phil.)
Response: B178, F234, UM177, refrain. "He Is Lord" (Phil.)
Prayer: UM281. Passion/Palm Sunday
Prayer: UM283. Holy Thursday (Passion Gospel)

Exodus 12:1-4 (5-10), 11-14

[1]The LORD said to Moses and Aaron in the land of Egypt: [2]This month shall mark for you the beginning of months; it shall be the first month of the year for you. [3]Tell the whole congregation of Israel that on the tenth of this month they are to take a lamb for each family, a lamb for each household. [4]If a household is too small for a whole lamb, it shall join its closest neighbor in obtaining one; the lamb shall be divided in proportion to the number of people who eat of it. [5]Your lamb shall be without blemish, a year-old male; you may take it from the sheep or from the goats. [6]You shall keep it until the fourteenth day of this month; then the whole assembled congregation of Israel shall slaughter it at twilight. [7]They shall take some of the blood and put it on the two doorposts and the lintel of the houses in which they eat it. [8]They shall eat the lamb that same night; they shall eat it roasted over the fire with unleavened bread and bitter herbs. [9]Do not eat any of it raw or boiled in water, but roasted over the fire, with its head, legs, and inner organs. [10]You shall let none of it remain until the morning; anything that remains until the morning you shall burn. [11]This is how you shall eat it: your loins girded, your sandals on your feet, and your staff in your hand; and you shall eat it hurriedly. It is the passover of the LORD. [12]For I will pass through the land of Egypt that night, and I will strike down every firstborn in the land of Egypt, both human beings and animals; on all the gods of Egypt I will execute judgments: I am the LORD. [13]The blood shall be a sign for you on the houses where you live: when I see the blood, I will pass over you, and no plague shall destroy you when I strike the land of Egypt.

[14]This day shall be a day of remembrance for you. You shall celebrate it as a festival to the LORD; throughout your generations you shall observe it as a perpetual ordinance.

Psalm 116:1-4, 12-19

[1]I love the LORD, because he has heard my voice and my supplications. [2]Because he inclined his ear to me, therefore I will call on him as long as I live. [3]The snares of death encompassed me; the pangs of Sheol laid hold on me; I suffered distress and anguish. [4]Then I called on the name of the LORD: "O LORD, I pray, save my life!"

[12]What shall I return to the LORD for all his bounty to me? [13]I will lift up the cup of salvation and call on the name of the LORD, [14]I will pay my vows to the LORD in the presence of all his people. [15]Precious in the sight of the LORD is the death of his faithful ones. [16]O LORD, I am your servant; I am your servant, the child of your serving girl. You have loosed my bonds. [17]I will offer to you a thanksgiving sacrifice and call on the name of the LORD. [18]I will pay my vows to the LORD in the presence of all his people, [19]in the courts of the house of the LORD, in your midst, O Jerusalem. Praise the LORD!

1 Corinthians 11:23-26

[23]For I received from the Lord what I also handed on to you, that the Lord Jesus on the night when he was betrayed took a loaf of bread, [24]and when he had given thanks, he broke it and said, "This is my body that is for you. Do this in remembrance of me." [25]In the same way he took the cup also, after supper, saying, "This cup is the new covenant in my blood. Do this, as often as you drink it, in remembrance of me." [26]For as often as you eat this bread and drink the cup, you proclaim the Lord's death until he comes.

John 13:1-17, 31b-35

[1]Now before the festival of the Passover, Jesus knew that his hour had come to depart from this world and go to the Father. Having loved his own who were in the world, he loved them to the end. [2]The devil had already put it into the heart of Judas son of Simon Iscariot to betray him. And during supper [3]Jesus, knowing that the Father had given all things into his hands, and that he had come from God and was going to God, [4]got up from the table, took off his outer robe, and tied a towel around himself. [5]Then he poured water into a basin and began to wash the disciples' feet and to wipe them with the towel that was tied around him. [6]He came to Simon Peter, who said to him, "Lord, are you going to wash my feet?" [7]Jesus answered, "You do not know now what I am doing, but later you will understand." [8]Peter said to him, "You will never wash my feet." Jesus answered, "Unless I wash you, you have no share with me." [9]Simon Peter said to him, "Lord, not my feet only but also my hands and my head!" [10]Jesus said to him, "One who has bathed does not need to wash, except for the feet, but is entirely clean. And you are clean, though not all of you." [11]For he knew who was to betray him; for this reason he said, "Not all of you are clean."

[12]After he had washed their feet, had put on his robe, and had returned to the table, he said to them, "Do you know what I have done to you? [13]You call me Teacher and Lord—and you are right, for that is what I am. [14]So if I, your Lord and Teacher, have washed your feet, you also ought to wash one another's feet. [15]For I have set you an example, that you also should do as I have done to you. [16]Very truly, I tell you, servants are not greater than their master, nor are messengers greater than the one who sent them. [17]If you know these things, you are blessed if you do them."

[31b]"Now the Son of Man has been glorified, and God has been glorified in him. [32]If God has been glorified in him, God will also glorify him in himself and will glorify him at once. [33]Little children, I am with you only a little longer. You will look for me; and as I said to the Jews so now I say to you, 'Where I am going, you cannot come.' [34]I give you a new commandment, that you love one another. Just as I have loved you, you also should love one another. [35]By this everyone will know that you are my disciples, if you have love for one another."

Hymn and Keyboard Suggestions

O– "O God, Our Help in Ages Past" (Exod.)

       B74, E680, F370, L320, P210, UM117 (PD), W579

         H-1   #46. Harmonization

         S-1   #293-96. Various treatments

         K-1(III) #74. Short prelude/postlude

         K-14   p. 34. Piano variations

   "The Church of Christ, in Every Age" (1 Cor.)

       B402

         S-1   #141. Harmonization

                   #142-43. Descant and transposition
                             in A major

       L433, P421

         S-2   #191. Harmonization

       UM589

         K-12   p. 14. Prelude/meditation

       W626

         S-2   #53. Descant

   "Lord God, Your Love Has Called Us Here" (John)

       UM579

         S-1   #57-61. Various treatments

       P353

   "Jesu, Jesu" (John)

       B501, E602, P367, UM432, W431

         S-1   #63. Vocal part

   "What Wondrous Love Is This" (John)

       B143 (PD), E439, F283, L385, P85, UM292, W600

         S-1   #347. Harmonization

         K-6   p. 28. Prelude/meditation

         K-12   p. 42. Prelude/meditation

   "Draw Us in the Spirit's Tether" (John, Communion)

       P504, UM632, W731

         S-1   #337. Performance note

   "Let Us Break Bread Together" (1 Cor., Communion)

       B366, E325 (PD), F564, L212, P513, UM618,
       W727

         K-7   p. 17. Prelude/postlude/meditation

         K-11   p. 42. Prelude/meditation

   "For the Bread Which You Have Broken" (1 Cor.,
   Communion)

       E340, UM615

         S-1   #43. Performance note

         S-2   #25. Orff instrument arrangement

       P508, UM614

         S-2   #63. Descant

                   #64. Harmonization

       E341, L200, P509

C– "Ah, Holy Jesus" (John)

       E158, L123, P93, UM289 (PD)

         S-2   #81-85. Harmonizations

                   #86. Instrumental descant

         K-1(II) #32. Short prelude/postlude

Vocal Solos

"Author of Life Divine" (1 Cor., John)

V-1   p. 39

"And Can It Be That I Should Gain" (John)

V-1   p. 29

"What Wondrous Love Is This" (John)

B143 (PD), E439, F283, L385, P85, UM292, W600, sung
   freely, *a cappella*

Anthems

"This Do in Remembrance of Me" (1 Cor.)
Austin Lovelace
Agape AG 7189
SATB with organ

"Jesu, Jesu Fill Us with Your Love" (John)
arr. Cindy Johnston
GIA Publications G-3000
Two-part mixed with keyboard and flute

Hymn Anthem Suggestion

"What Wondrous Love Is This" (John)
52IHA   #50

Other Suggestions

   You may choose to design a very quiet, and/or more
intimate service. The following hymns would be appropriate and may be sung *a cappella* or accompanied by guitar
only:

     "What Wondrous Love Is This"

     "Jesu, Jesu"

     "Let Us Break Bread Together"

     "Come, Let Us Eat" (L214, UM625)

Introit: E333, L205, UM619, W668. "Now the Silence"
   (Communion)

Prayer: UM283. Holy Thursday (John, 1 Cor.)

Isaiah 52:13–53:12

[13]See, my servant shall prosper; he shall be exalted and lifted up, and shall be very high. [14]Just as there were many who were astonished at him—so marred was his appearance, beyond human semblance, and his form beyond that of mortals—[15]so he shall startle many nations; kings shall shut their mouths because of him; for that which had not been told them they shall see, and that which they had not heard they shall contemplate.

[1]Who has believed what we have heard? And to whom has the arm of the LORD been revealed? [2]For he grew up before him like a young plant, and like a root out of dry ground; he had no form or majesty that we should look at him, nothing in his appearance that we should desire him. [3]He was despised and rejected by others; a man of suffering and acquainted with infirmity; and as one from whom others hide their faces he was despised, and we held him of no account. [4]Surely he has borne our infirmities and carried our diseases; yet we accounted him stricken, struck down by God, and afflicted. [5]But he was wounded for our transgressions, crushed for our iniquities; upon him was the punishment that made us whole, and by his bruises we are healed. [6]All we like sheep have gone astray; we have all turned to our own way, and the LORD has laid on him the iniquity of us all. [7]He was oppressed, and he was afflicted, yet he did not open his mouth; like a lamb that is led to the slaughter, and like a sheep that before its shearers is silent, so he did not open his mouth. [8]By a perversion of justice he was taken away. Who could have imagined his future? For he was cut off from the land of the living, stricken for the transgression of my people. [9]They made his grave with the wicked and his tomb with the rich, although he had done no violence, and there was no deceit in his mouth. [10]Yet it was the will of the LORD to crush him with pain. When you make his life an offering for sin, he shall see his offspring, and shall prolong his days; through him the will of the LORD shall prosper. [11]Out of his anguish he shall see light; he shall find satisfaction through his knowledge. The righteous one, my servant, shall make many righteous, and he shall bear their iniquities. [12]Therefore I will allot him a portion with the great, and he shall divide the spoil with the strong; because he poured out himself to death, and was numbered with the transgressors; yet he bore the sin of many, and made intercession for the transgressors.

Psalm 22

[1]My God, my God, why have you forsaken me? Why are you so far from helping me, from the words of my groaning? [2]O my God, I cry by day, but you do not answer; and by night, but find no rest. [3]Yet you are holy, enthroned on the praises of Israel. [4]In you our ancestors trusted; they trusted, and you delivered them. [5]To you they cried, and were saved; in you they trusted, and were not put to shame. [6]But I am a worm, and not human; scorned by others, and despised by the people. [7]All who see me mock at me; they make mouths at me, they shake their heads; [8]"Commit your cause to the LORD; let him deliver—let him rescue the one in whom he delights!" [9]Yet it was you who took me from the womb; you kept me safe on my mother's breast. [10]On you I was cast from my birth, and since my mother bore me you have been my God. [11]Do not be far from me, for trouble is near and there is no one to help. [12]Many bulls encircle me, strong bulls of Bashan surround me; [13]they open wide their mouths at me, like a ravening and roaring lion. [14]I am poured out like water, and all my bones are out of joint; my heart is like wax; it is melted within my breast; [15]my mouth is dried up like a potsherd, and my tongue sticks to my jaws; you lay me in the dust of death. [16]For dogs are all around me; a company of evildoers encircles me. My hands and feet have shriveled; [17]I can count all my bones. They stare and gloat over me; [18]they divide my clothes among themselves, and for my clothing they cast lots. [19]But you, O LORD, do not be far away! O my help, come quickly to my aid! [20]Deliver my soul from the sword, my life from the power of the dog! [21]Save me from the mouth of the lion! From the horns of the wild oxen you have rescued me. [22]I will tell of your name to my brothers and sisters; in the midst of the congregation I will praise you: [23]You who fear the LORD, praise him! All you offspring of Jacob, glorify him; stand in awe of him, all you offspring of Israel! [24]For he did not despise or abhor the affliction of the afflicted; he did not hide his face from me, but heard when I cried to him. [25]From you comes my praise in the great congregation; my vows I will pay before those who fear him. [26]The poor shall eat and be satisfied; those who seek him shall praise the LORD. May your hearts live forever! [27]All the ends of the earth shall remember and turn to the LORD; and all the families of the nations shall worship before him. [28]For dominion belongs to the LORD, and he rules over the nations. [29]To him, indeed, shall all who sleep in the earth bow down; before him shall bow all who go down to the dust, and I shall live for him. [30]Posterity will serve him; future generations will be told about the Lord, [31]and proclaim his deliverance to a people yet unborn, saying that he has done it.

Hebrews 10:16-25

[16]"This is the covenant that I will
make with them
after those days, says the Lord:
I will put my laws in their hearts,
and I will write them on their
minds,"

[17]he also adds,

> "I will remember their sins and
> their lawless deeds no more."

[18]Where there is forgiveness of these, there is no longer any offering for sin.

[19]Therefore, my friends, since we have confidence to enter the sanctuary by the blood of Jesus, [20]by the new and living way that he opened for us through the curtain (that is, through his flesh), [21]and since we have a great priest over the house of God, [22]let us approach with a true heart in full assurance of faith, with our hearts sprinkled clean from an evil conscience and our bodies washed with pure water. [23]Let us hold fast to the confession of our hope without wavering, for he who has promised is faithful. [24]And let us consider how to provoke one another to love and good deeds, [25]not neglecting to meet together, as is the habit of some, but encouraging one another, and all the more as you see the Day approaching.

John 18:1–19:42

[1]After Jesus had spoken these words, he went out with his disciples across the Kidron valley to a place where there was a garden, which he and his disciples entered. [2]Now Judas, who betrayed him, also knew the place, because Jesus often met there with his disciples. [3]So Judas brought a detachment of soldiers together with police from the chief priests and the Pharisees, and they came there with lanterns and torches and weapons. [4]Then Jesus, knowing all that was to happen to him, came forward and asked them, "Whom are you looking for?" [5]They answered, "Jesus of Nazareth." Jesus replied, "I am he." Judas, who betrayed him, was standing with them. [6]When Jesus said to them, "I am he," they stepped back and fell to the ground. [7]Again he asked them, "Whom are you looking for?" And they said, "Jesus of Nazareth." [8]Jesus answered, "I told you that I am he. So if you are looking for me, let these men go." [9]This was to fulfill the word that he had spoken, "I did not lose a single one of those whom you gave me." [10]Then Simon Peter, who had a sword, drew it, struck the high priest's slave, and cut off his right ear. The slave's name was Malchus. [11]Jesus said to Peter, "Put your sword back into its sheath. Am I not to drink the cup that the Father has given me?"

[12]So the soldiers, their officer, and the Jewish police arrested Jesus and bound him. [13]First they took him to Annas, who was the father-in-law of Caiaphas, the high priest that year. [14]Caiaphas was the one who had advised the Jews that it was better to have one person die for the people.

[15]Simon Peter and another disciple followed Jesus. Since that disciple was known to the high priest, he went with Jesus into the courtyard of the high priest, [16]but Peter was standing outside at the gate. So the other disciple, who was known to the high priest, went out, spoke to the woman who guarded the gate, and brought Peter in. [17]The woman said to Peter, "You are not also one of this man's disciples, are you?" He said, "I am not." [18]Now the slaves and the police had made a charcoal fire because it was cold, and they were standing around it and warming themselves. Peter also was standing with them and warming himself.

[19]Then the high priest questioned Jesus about his disciples and about his teaching. [20]Jesus answered, "I have spoken openly to the world; I have always taught in synagogues and in the temple, where all the Jews come together. I have said nothing in secret. [21]Why do you ask me? Ask those who heard what I said to them; they know what I said." [22]When he had said this, one of the police standing nearby struck Jesus on the face, saying, "Is that how you answer the high priest?" [23]Jesus answered, "If I have spoken wrongly, testify to the wrong. But if I have spoken rightly, why do you strike me?" [24]Then Annas sent him bound to Caiaphas the high priest.

[25]Now Simon Peter was standing and warming himself. They asked him, "You are not also one of his disciples, are you?" He denied it and said, "I am not." [26]One of the slaves of the high priest, a relative of the man whose ear Peter had cut off, asked, "Did I not see you in the garden with him?" [27]Again Peter denied it, and at that moment the cock crowed.

[28]Then they took Jesus from Caiaphas to Pilate's headquarters. It was early in the morning. They themselves did not enter the headquarters, so as to avoid ritual defilement and to be able to eat the Passover. [29]So Pilate went out to them and said, "What accusation do you bring against this man?" [30]They answered, "If this man were not a criminal, we would not have handed him over to you." [31]Pilate said to them, "Take him yourselves and judge him according to your law." The Jews replied, "We are not permitted to put anyone to death." [32](This was to fulfill what Jesus had said when he indicated the kind of death he was to die.)

[33]Then Pilate entered the headquarters again, summoned Jesus, and asked him, "Are you the King of the Jews?" [34]Jesus answered, "Do you ask this on your own, or did others tell you about me?" [35]Pilate replied, "I am not a Jew, am I? Your own nation and the chief priests have handed you over to me. What have you done?" [36]Jesus answered, "My kingdom is not from this world. If my kingdom were from this world, my followers would be fighting to keep me from being handed over to the Jews. But as it is, my kingdom is not from here." [37]Pilate asked him, "So you are a king?" Jesus answered, "You say that I am a king. For this I was born, and for this I came into the world, to testify to the truth. Everyone who belongs to the truth listens to my voice." [38]Pilate asked him, "What is truth?"

After he had said this, he went out to the Jews again and

told them, "I find no case against him. [39]But you have a custom that I release someone for you at the Passover. Do you want me to release for you the King of the Jews?" [40]They shouted in reply, "Not this man, but Barabbas!" Now Barabbas was a bandit.

[1]Then Pilate took Jesus and had him flogged. [2]And the soldiers wove a crown of thorns and put it on his head, and they dressed him in a purple robe. [3]They kept coming up to him, saying, "Hail, King of the Jews!" and striking him on the face. [4]Pilate went out again and said to them, "Look, I am bringing him out to you to let you know that I find no case against him." [5]So Jesus came out, wearing the crown of thorns and the purple robe. Pilate said to them, "Here is the man!" [6]When the chief priests and the police saw him, they shouted, "Crucify him! Crucify him!" Pilate said to them, "Take him yourselves and crucify him; I find no case against him." [7]The Jews answered him, "We have a law, and according to that law he ought to die because he has claimed to be the Son of God."

[8]Now when Pilate heard this, he was more afraid than ever. [9]He entered his headquarters again and asked Jesus, "Where are you from?" But Jesus gave him no answer. [10]Pilate therefore said to him, "Do you refuse to speak to me? Do you not know that I have power to release you, and power to crucify you?" [11]Jesus answered him, "You would have no power over me unless it had been given you from above; therefore the one who handed me over to you is guilty of a greater sin." [12]From then on Pilate tried to release him, but the Jews cried out, "If you release this man, you are no friend of the emperor. Everyone who claims to be a king sets himself against the emperor."

[13]When Pilate heard these words, he brought Jesus outside and sat on the judge's bench at a place called The Stone Pavement, or in Hebrew Gabbatha. [14]Now it was the day of Preparation for the Passover; and it was about noon. He said to the Jews, "Here is your King!" [15]They cried out, "Away with him! Away with him! Crucify him!" Pilate asked them, "Shall I crucify your King?" The chief priests answered, "We have no king but the emperor." [16]Then he handed him over to them to be crucified.

So they took Jesus; [17]and carrying the cross by himself, he went out to what is called The Place of the Skull, which in Hebrew is called Golgotha. [18]There they crucified him, and with him two others, one on either side, with Jesus between them. [19]Pilate also had an inscription written and put on the cross. It read, "Jesus of Nazareth, the King of the Jews." [20]Many of the Jews read this inscription, because the place where Jesus was crucified was near the city; and it was written in Hebrew, in Latin, and in Greek. [21]Then the chief priests of the Jews said to Pilate, "Do not write, 'The King of the Jews,' but, 'This man said, I am King of the Jews.'" [22]Pilate answered, "What I have written I have writ-

ten." [23]When the soldiers had crucified Jesus, they took his clothes and divided them into four parts, one for each soldier. They also took his tunic; now the tunic was seamless, woven in one piece from the top. [24]So they said to one another, "Let us not tear it, but cast lots for it to see who will get it." This was to fulfill what the scripture says, "They divided my clothes among themselves, and for my clothing they cast lots." [25]And that is what the soldiers did.

Meanwhile, standing near the cross of Jesus were his mother, and his mother's sister, Mary the wife of Clopas, and Mary Magdalene. [26]When Jesus saw his mother and the disciple whom he loved standing beside her, he said to his mother, "Woman, here is your son." [27]Then he said to the disciple, "Here is your mother." And from that hour the disciple took her into his own home.

[28]After this, when Jesus knew that all was now finished, he said (in order to fulfill the scripture), "I am thirsty." [29]A jar full of sour wine was standing there. So they put a sponge full of the wine on a branch of hyssop and held it to his mouth. [30]When Jesus had received the wine, he said, "It is finished." Then he bowed his head and gave up his spirit.

[31]Since it was the day of Preparation, the Jews did not want the bodies left on the cross during the sabbath, especially because that sabbath was a day of great solemnity. So they asked Pilate to have the legs of the crucified men broken and the bodies removed. [32]Then the soldiers came and broke the legs of the first and of the other who had been crucified with him. [33]But when they came to Jesus and saw that he was already dead, they did not break his legs. [34]Instead, one of the soldiers pierced his side with a spear, and at once blood and water came out. [35](He who saw this has testified so that you also may believe. His testimony is true, and he knows that he tells the truth.) [36]These things occurred so that the scripture might be fulfilled, "None of his bones shall be broken." [37]And again another passage of scripture says, "They will look on the one whom they have pierced."

[38]After these things, Joseph of Arimathea, who was a disciple of Jesus, though a secret one because of his fear of the Jews, asked Pilate to let him take away the body of Jesus. Pilate gave him permission; so he came and removed his body. [39]Nicodemus, who had at first come to Jesus by night, also came, bringing a mixture of myrrh and aloes, weighing about a hundred pounds. [40]They took the body of Jesus and wrapped it with the spices in linen cloths, according to the burial custom of the Jews. [41]Now there was a garden in the place where he was crucified, and in the garden there was a new tomb in which no one had ever been laid. [42]And so, because it was the Jewish day of Preparation, and the tomb was nearby, they laid Jesus there.

Hymn and Keyboard Suggestions

O– "Hallelujah! What a Savior" (Isa.)
   B175, F246, UM165 (PD)
 "To Mock Your Reign, O Dearest Lord" (Isa., John)
   UM285
    S-2 #100-103. Various treatments
   E170
 "He Never Said a Mumbalin' Word" (Isa., John)
   P95 (PD), UM291
 "Out of the Depths I Cry to You" (Ps.)
   L295, P240, UM515
    K-14 p. 18. Piano prelude
 "Near to the Heart of God" (Heb.)
   B295, F35, P527, UM472 (PD)
    S-1 #230. Performance note
    K-13 p. 34. Piano prelude/meditation
 "'Tis Finished! The Messiah Dies" (John)
   B148, UM282 (PD)
 "O Sacred Head, Now Wounded" (John)
   B137, E168 or E169, F284, L116 or L117, P98,
   UM286, W434
    K-1(II) #34. Prelude/postlude/meditation
       (manuals only)
    K-4 p. 68. Various keyboard treatments,
       through p. 81
    K-14 p. 16. Piano prelude
    K-15 p. 86. Piano prelude/postlude
 "Ah, Holy Jesus" (John)
   E158, L123, P93, UM289 (PD)
    S-2 #81-85. Harmonizations
       #86. Instrumental descant
    K-1(II) #32. Short prelude/postlude
 "My God, I Love Thee" (John)
   UM470 (PD)
    S-2 #197. Descant
       #198. Harmonization
    K-1(IV) #100. Prelude/meditation/postlude
    K-2 p. 36. Prelude/meditation/postlude
 "The Bread of Life for All Is Broken" (John)
   E342, UM633
C– "Were You There" (John)
   B156, E172, F287, L92, P102, UM288, W436
    S-2 #195. Descant
       #196. Harmonization
    K-7 p. 2. Prelude/meditation
C– "I Am Thine, O Lord" (Heb.)
   B290, F455, UM419 (PD)

Vocal Solos

"He Was Despised" from *Messiah* (Isa.)
V-2
"Thy Rebuke Hath Broken His Heart" and
"Behold, and See If There Be Any Sorrow" (Isa.)
V-2
"'Tis Finished! The Messiah Dies" (John)
V-1 p. 63
"Were You There" (John)
V-3 p. 19
V-5 p. 46

Anthems

"Were You There" (John)
arr. Wayne Howorth
Belwin 1662
SAB with solo and keyboard

"O Holy Jesus" (John)
L. Beethoven (arr. Hopson)
Carl Fischer CM8030
SATB with organ

"I Wonder Why" (John)
Avery and Marsh (arr. Pfautsch)
Agape AG 7104
SATB with keyboard

Hymn Anthem Suggestions

"Out of the Depths I Cry to You" (Ps.)
52IHA #39
"O the Lamb" (John)
52IHA #37
"Were You There" (John)
HA p. 28

Other Suggestions

Greeting: Isaiah 53:6. All we like sheep have gone astray.
Prayer: UM284. Good Friday (John)
Poem: UM293. Behold the Savior of Mankind (John)
Hymn Idea: E171, F281, L109, P97, UM290. "Go to Dark
 Gethsemane." Use this hymn to supplement the reading
 of the John passage. Sing stanza 1 before beginning
 18:1. Sing stanza 2 after 19:3. Sing stanza 3 after 19:30.
 Sing "Were You There," stanza 5 ("when they laid him in
 the tomb") at the conclusion of the reading.

Acts 10:34-43

[34]Then Peter began to speak to them: "I truly understand that God shows no partiality, [35]but in every nation anyone who fears him and does what is right is acceptable to him. [36]You know the message he sent to the people of Israel, preaching peace by Jesus Christ—he is Lord of all. [37]That message spread throughout Judea, beginning in Galilee after the baptism that John announced: [38]how God anointed Jesus of Nazareth with the Holy Spirit and with power; how he went about doing good and healing all who were oppressed by the devil, for God was with him. [39]We are witnesses to all that he did both in Judea and in Jerusalem. They put him to death by hanging him on a tree; [40]but God raised him on the third day and allowed him to appear, [41]not to all the people but to us who were chosen by God as witnesses, and who ate and drank with him after he rose from the dead. [42]He commanded us to preach to the people and to testify that he is the one ordained by God as judge of the living and the dead. [43]All the prophets testify about him that everyone who believes in him receives forgiveness of sins through his name."

Psalm 118:1-2, 14-24

[1]O give thanks to the LORD, for he is good; his steadfast love endures forever! [2]Let Israel say, "His steadfast love endures forever."

[14]The LORD is my strength and my might; he has become my salvation. [15]There are glad songs of victory in the tents of the righteous: "The right hand of the LORD does valiantly; [16]the right hand of the LORD is exalted; the right hand of the LORD does valiantly." [17]I shall not die, but I shall live, and recount the deeds of the LORD. [18]The LORD has punished me severely, but he did not give me over to death. [19]Open to me the gates of righteousness, that I may enter through them and give thanks to the LORD. [20]This is the gate of the LORD; the righteous shall enter through it. [21]I thank you that you have answered me and have become my salvation. [22]The stone that the builders rejected has become the chief cornerstone. [23]This is the LORD's doing; it is marvelous in our eyes. [24]This is the day that the LORD has made; let us rejoice and be glad in it.

Colossians 3:1-4

[1]So if you have been raised with Christ, seek the things that are above, where Christ is, seated at the right hand of God. [2]Set your minds on things that are above, not on things that are on earth, [3]for you have died, and your life is hidden with Christ in God. [4]When Christ who is your life is revealed, then you also will be revealed with him in glory.

John 20:1-18

[1]Early on the first day of the week, while it was still dark, Mary Magdalene came to the tomb and saw that the stone had been removed from the tomb. [2]So she ran and went to Simon Peter and the other disciple, the one whom Jesus loved, and said to them, "They have taken the Lord out of the tomb, and we do not know where they have laid him." [3]Then Peter and the other disciple set out and went toward the tomb. [4]The two were running together, but the other disciple outran Peter and reached the tomb first. [5]He bent down to look in and saw the linen wrappings lying there, but he did not go in. [6]Then Simon Peter came, following him, and went into the tomb. He saw the linen wrappings lying there, [7]and the cloth that had been on Jesus' head, not lying with the linen wrappings but rolled up in a place by itself. [8]Then the other disciple, who reached the tomb first, also went in, and he saw and believed; [9]for as yet they did not understand the scripture, that he must rise from the dead. [10]Then the disciples returned to their homes.

[11]But Mary stood weeping outside the tomb. As she wept, she bent over to look into the tomb; [12]and she saw two angels in white, sitting where the body of Jesus had been lying, one at the head and the other at the feet. [13]They said to her, "Woman, why are you weeping?" She said to them, "They have taken away my Lord, and I do not know where they have laid him." [14]When she had said this, she turned around and saw Jesus standing there, but she did not know that it was Jesus. [15]Jesus said to her, "Woman, why are you weeping? Whom are you looking for?" Supposing him to be the gardener, she said to him, "Sir, if you have carried him away, tell me where you have laid him, and I will take him away." [16]Jesus said to her, "Mary!" She turned and said to him in Hebrew, "Rabbouni!" (which means Teacher). [17]Jesus said to her, "Do not hold on to me, because I have not yet ascended to the Father. But go to my brothers and say to them, 'I am ascending to my Father and your Father, to my God and your God.' " [18]Mary Magdalene went and announced to the disciples, "I have seen the Lord"; and she told them that he had said these things to her.

Hymn and Keyboard Suggestions
O– "Christ the Lord Is Risen Today" (John, Matt.)
    B159, F289, UM302 (PD)
    H-1   #22. Harmonization
    H-2   p. 8. Harmonization with descant in B-flat major
    S-1   #104-108. Various treatments
    K-1(I)   #18. Prelude/postlude/hymn introduction
    K-15   p. 50. Piano prelude/postlude
    L130
    S-1   #261. Instructions for children's drama (UM227 only)
    S-2   #144. Orff instrument arrangement
    K-1(III)   #70. Prelude/postlude
    K-12   p. 6. Prelude/meditation
    K-12   p. 18. Postlude
    P113, W463 (PD)
    S-1   #213-14. Transposition with descant in F major
    W462 (PD)
O– "Jesus Christ Is Risen Today" (John, Matt.)
    E207, F297, L151, P123, W442 (PD)
    (See above hymn for suggestions)
O– "Come, Ye Faithful, Raise the Strain" (Matt.)
    E199, P115, UM315 (PD)
    S-2   #161. Descant
    K-9   p. 27. Prelude/meditation/postlude
    E200, L132, P114 (PD), W456
    S-1   #29. Transposition to F major
    "This Is the Day" (Ps.)
    B359, UM657
    B358 (PD)
    S-1   #22. Descant
        #23. Harmonization
    P230 (PD)
    K-1(II)   #55. Prelude/postlude
    E50 (PD), UM658 (PD)
    "Cristo Vive" ("Christ Is Risen") (John)
    B167, P109, UM313
    "Christ Is Risen" (John, Col., Communion)
    P104 (Not PD)
    S-1   #173-76. Various treatments
    K-8   p. 23. Harmonization
    K-13   p. 16. Piano prelude/postlude
    K-15   p. 122. Piano prelude/postlude
    UM307
    S-1   #345. Handbell/keyboard arrangement
    "He Lives" (John)
    B533, F299, UM310

"O Sons and Daughters, Let Us Sing" (John)
    E203, L139, P116 (PD), UM317, W447
    S-2   #138-39. Harmonization with descant
    K-10   p. 3. Prelude/postlude
"Christ Is Alive" (Matt.)
    B173, E182, L363, P108, UM318
    S-1   #334. Descant
        #335. Harmonization
C– "Crown Him with Many Crowns" (John)
    B161, E494, F345, L170, P151, UM327 (PD)
    H-1   #55. Harmonization in D major
    H-2   p. 6. Harmonization with descant
    S-1   #86-88. Various treatments
    K-2   p. 7. Short harmonization/prelude/meditation/postlude
    K-13   p. 16. Piano prelude/postlude

Vocal Solos
"Christ Is Arisen" (John)
V-6   p. 12
"Jesus Christ Is Risen Today" (John, Matt.)
V-1   p. 50

Anthems
"Easter Day" in *A Season to Celebrate* (John, Matt.)
Allen Pote
Hinshaw Music HMB 144
SATB with keyboard and optional guitar

Hymn Anthem Suggestions
"Lord of the Dance" (Acts)
52IHA   #31
"O Sons and Daughters, Let Us Sing" (John)
HA   p. 37
"Easter People, Raise Your Voices" (Easter)
52IHA   #13
"Now the Green Blade Riseth" (John, Matt.)
52IHA   #35

Other Suggestions
Worship Opening design:
1. Worship space is unadorned and dark. This is especially effective if you removed all paraments and banners at the conclusion of your Good Friday service.
2. A reader reads John 20:1-18 or Luke 24:1-9.
3. A woman soloist sings either "In the Garden" (B187, F588, UM314), stanzas 1-2, or the entire choir may sing "Woman in the Night" (UM274), stanza 8.
4. During a lengthy introduction to the opening hymn, all of the paraments, banners, flowers, and so on, are brought in and the lights are brightened.
5. The choir and worship leaders process into the worship space.

Acts 2:14a, 22-32

[14a]But Peter, standing with the eleven, raised his voice and addressed them.

[22]"You that are Israelites, listen to what I have to say: Jesus of Nazareth, a man attested to you by God with deeds of power, wonders, and signs that God did through him among you, as you yourselves know—[23]this man, handed over to you according to the definite plan and foreknowledge of God, you crucified and killed by the hands of those outside the law. [24]But God raised him up, having freed him from death, because it was impossible for him to be held in its power. [25]For David says concerning him,

'I saw the Lord always before me,
    for he is at my right hand so
        that I will not be shaken;
[26]therefore my heart was glad,
        and my tongue rejoiced;
    moreover my flesh will live in hope.
[27]For you will not abandon my
        soul to Hades,
    or let your Holy One
        experience corruption.
[28]You have made known to me the
        ways of life;
    you will make me full of
        gladness with your presence.'

[29]"Fellow Israelites, I may say to you confidently of our ancestor David that he both died and was buried, and his tomb is with us to this day. [30]Since he was a prophet, he knew that God had sworn with an oath to him that he would put one of his descendants on his throne. [31]Foreseeing this, David spoke of the resurrection of the Messiah, saying,

'He was not abandoned to Hades,
    nor did his flesh experience corruption.'
[32]This Jesus God raised up, and of that all of us are witnesses."

Psalm 16

[1]Protect me, O God, for in you I take refuge. [2]I say to the LORD, "You are my Lord; I have no good apart from you." [3]As for the holy ones in the land, they are the noble, in whom is all my delight. [4]Those who choose another god multiply their sorrows; their drink offerings of blood I will not pour out or take their names upon my lips. [5]The LORD is my chosen portion and my cup; you hold my lot. [6]The boundary lines have fallen for me in pleasant places; I have a goodly heritage. [7]I bless the LORD who gives me counsel; in the night also my heart instructs me. [8]I keep the LORD always before me; because he is at my right hand, I shall not be moved. [9]Therefore my heart is glad, and my soul rejoices; my body also rests secure. [10]For you do not give me up to Sheol, or let your faithful one see the Pit. [11]You show me the path of life. In your presence there is fullness of joy; in your right hand are pleasures forevermore.

1 Peter 1:3-9

[3]Blessed be the God and Father of our Lord Jesus Christ! By his great mercy he has given us a new birth into a living hope through the resurrection of Jesus Christ from the dead, [4]and into an inheritance that is imperishable, undefiled, and unfading, kept in heaven for you, [5]who are being protected by the power of God through faith for a salvation ready to be revealed in the last time. [6]In this you rejoice, even if now for a little while you have had to suffer various trials, [7]so that the genuineness of your faith—being more precious than gold that, though perishable, is tested by fire—may be found to result in praise and glory and honor when Jesus Christ is revealed. [8]Although you have not seen him, you love him; and even though you do not see him now, you believe in him and rejoice with an indescribable and glorious joy, [9]for you are receiving the outcome of your faith, the salvation of your souls.

John 20:19-31

[19]When it was evening on that day, the first day of the week, and the doors of the house where the disciples had met were locked for fear of the Jews, Jesus came and stood among them and said, "Peace be with you." [20]After he said this, he showed them his hands and his side. Then the disciples rejoiced when they saw the Lord. [21]Jesus said to them again, "Peace be with you. As the Father has sent me, so I send you." [22]When he had said this, he breathed on them and said to them, "Receive the Holy Spirit. [23]If you forgive the sins of any, they are forgiven them; if you retain the sins of any, they are retained."

[24]But Thomas (who was called the Twin), one of the twelve, was not with them when Jesus came. [25]So the other disciples told him, "We have seen the Lord." But he said to them, "Unless I see the mark of the nails in his hands, and put my finger in the mark of the nails and my hand in his side, I will not believe."

[26]A week later his disciples were again in the house, and Thomas was with them. Although the doors were shut, Jesus came and stood among them and said, "Peace be with you." [27]Then he said to Thomas, "Put your finger here and see my hands. Reach out your hand and put it in my side. Do not doubt but believe." [28]Thomas answered him, "My Lord and my God!" [29]Jesus said to him, "Have you believed because you have seen me? Blessed are those who have not seen and yet have come to believe."

[30]Now Jesus did many other signs in the presence of his disciples, which are not written in this book. [31]But these are written so that you may come to believe that Jesus is the Messiah, the Son of God, and that through believing you may have life in his name.

Hymn and Keyboard Suggestions

O– "The Day of Resurrection" (1 Pet., John)
  B164, P118, UM303 (PD)
    H-1   #87. Harmonization
    S-1   #195-96. Harmonization with descant
           #197. Same harmonization in C major
  E210
    S-1   #115. Harmonization
  L141

O– "Hail the Day That Sees Him Rise" (Acts)
  E214, UM312, W471 (PD)
    S-1   #213-14. Transposition with descant in F major
  B165

"Hail Thee, Festival Day" (Acts)
  E175, L142, UM324, W444
    S-2   #164. Descant

"Like the Murmur of the Dove's Song" (Acts)
  E513, P314, UM544
    S-2   #30. Descant

"Easter People, Raise Your Voices" (1 Pet.)
  B360, UM304
    H-1   #7. Harmonization
    S-1   #280. Descant
           #281. Harmonization
    K-1(III) #72. Short prelude/postlude/interlude
    K-2   p. 24. Short prelude
    K-8   p. 28. Introduction/interlude

"O Sons and Daughters, Let Us Sing" (John)
  E203, L139, P116 (PD), UM317, W447
    S-2   #138-39. Harmonization with descant
    K-10   p. 3. Prelude/postlude

"Christ Jesus Lay in Death's Strong Band" (John)
  E186, L134, P110, UM319 (PD)

"Depth of Mercy" (John)
  UM355 (PD)
    S-1   #53. Descant
  B306

"Dona Nobis Pacem" (John)
  E712, UM376 (PD)

"Breathe on Me, Breath of God" (John)
  W725
    S-1   #298. Harmonization
           #299. Harmonization
    K-2   p. 27. Short prelude/postlude
    K-9   p. 47. Prelude/meditation
  E508, L488 (PD)
  B241, F161, P316, UM420 (PD)

"Holy Spirit, Truth Divine" (John)
  L257, P321, UM465 (PD)
    S-1   #53. Descant

"Come Down, O Love Divine" (John)
  E516, L508, P313, UM475 (PD), W472
    S-1   #98-99. Descants

C– "Thine Be the Glory" (Acts, John)
  B163, F291, L145, P122, UM308
    S-1   #190. Arrangement for choir, handbells, trumpets, organ
    S-2   #95. Brass/percussion arrangement, descant and harmonization

Vocal Solos

"Spirit of Faith Come Down" (Acts)
V-1   p. 43
"But Thou Didst Not Leave His Soul in Hell" (Acts)
V-2
"Praise, Praise the Lord" (1 Pet.)
V-6   p. 60
"Jesus, Author of Our Being" (1 Pet.)
V-9   p. 35

Anthems

"Love, Joy, and Peace" (John)
Jane Marshall
Choristers Guild CGA-503
Two-part mixed

"Alleluia! Christ Is Risen!" (John)
Gordon Young
Hope Publishing A 584
SATB with keyboard

Hymn Anthem Suggestions

"Hail Thee, Festival Day" (Acts)
HA   p. 48
"Easter People, Raise Your Voices" (1 Pet.)
52IHA   #13
"O Sons and Daughters, Let Us Sing" (John)
HA   p. 37
"Come Down, O Love Divine" (John)
HA   p. 56

Other Suggestions

Introit: E186, L134, P110, UM319 (PD), stanza 1. "Christ Jesus Lay in Death's Strong Band" (John)
Response: B208, E657, F21, P376, UM384, W588, stanza 1. "Love Divine, All Loves Excelling" (John)

Acts 2:14a, 36-41

[14a]But Peter, standing with the eleven, raised his voice and addressed them,

[36]"Therefore let the entire house of Israel know with certainty that God has made him both Lord and Messiah, this Jesus whom you crucified."

[37]Now when they heard this, they were cut to the heart and said to Peter and to the other apostles, "Brothers, what should we do?" [38]Peter said to them, "Repent, and be baptized every one of you in the name of Jesus Christ so that your sins may be forgiven; and you will receive the gift of the Holy Spirit. [39]For the promise is for you, for your children, and for all who are far away, everyone whom the Lord our God calls to him." [40]And he testified with many other arguments and exhorted them, saying, "Save yourselves from this corrupt generation." [41]So those who welcomed his message were baptized, and that day about three thousand persons were added.

Psalm 116:1-4, 12-19

[1]I love the LORD, because he has heard my voice and my supplications. [2]Because he inclined his ear to me, therefore I will call on him as long as I live. [3]The snares of death encompassed me; the pangs of Sheol laid hold on me; I suffered distress and anguish. [4]Then I called on the name of the LORD: "O LORD, I pray, save my life!"

[12]What shall I return to the LORD for all his bounty to me? [13]I will lift up the cup of salvation and call on the name of the LORD, [14]I will pay my vows to the LORD in the presence of all his people. [15]Precious in the sight of the LORD is the death of his faithful ones. [16]O LORD, I am your servant; I am your servant, the child of your serving girl. You have loosed my bonds. [17]I will offer to you a thanksgiving sacrifice and call on the name of the LORD. [18]I will pay my vows to the LORD in the presence of all his people, [19]in the courts of the house of the LORD, in your midst, O Jerusalem. Praise the LORD!

1 Peter 1:17-23

[17]If you invoke as Father the one who judges all people impartially according to their deeds, live in reverent fear during the time of your exile. [18]You know that you were ransomed from the futile ways inherited from your ancestors, not with perishable things like silver or gold, [19]but with the precious blood of Christ, like that of a lamb without defect or blemish. [20]He was destined before the foundation of the world, but was revealed at the end of the ages for your sake. [21]Through him you have come to trust in God, who raised him from the dead and gave him glory, so that your faith and hope are set on God.

[22]Now that you have purified your souls by your obedience to the truth so that you have genuine mutual love, love one another deeply from the heart. [23]You have been born anew, not of perishable but of imperishable seed, through the living and enduring word of God.

Luke 24:13-35

[13]Now on that same day two of them were going to a village called Emmaus, about seven miles from Jerusalem, [14]and talking with each other about all these things that had happened. [15]While they were talking and discussing, Jesus himself came near and went with them, [16]but their eyes were kept from recognizing him. [17]And he said to them, "What are you discussing with each other while you walk along?" They stood still, looking sad. [18]Then one of them, whose name was Cleopas, answered him, "Are you the only stranger in Jerusalem who does not know the things that have taken place there in these days?" [19]He asked them, "What things?" They replied, "The things about Jesus of Nazareth, who was a prophet mighty in deed and word before God and all the people, [20]and how our chief priests and leaders handed him over to be condemned to death and crucified him. [21]But we had hoped that he was the one to redeem Israel. Yes, and besides all this, it is now the third day since these things took place. [22]Moreover, some women of our group astounded us. They were at the tomb early this morning, [23]and when they did not find his body there, they came back and told us that they had indeed seen a vision of angels who said that he was alive. [24]Some of those who were with us went to the tomb and found it just as the women had said; but they did not see him." [25]Then he said to them, "Oh, how foolish you are, and how slow of heart to believe all that the prophets have declared! [26]Was it not necessary that the Messiah should suffer these things and then enter into his glory?" [27]Then beginning with Moses and all the prophets, he interpreted to them the things about himself in all the scriptures.

[28]As they came near the village to which they were going, he walked ahead as if he were going on. [29]But they urged him strongly, saying, "Stay with us, because it is almost evening and the day is now nearly over." So he went in to stay with them. [30]When he was at the table with them, he took bread, blessed and broke it, and gave it to them. [31]Then their eyes were opened, and they recognized him; and he vanished from their sight. [32]They said to each other, "Were not our hearts burning within us while he was talking to us on the road, while he was opening the scriptures to us?" [33]That same hour they got up and returned to Jerusalem; and they found the eleven and their companions gathered together. [34]They were saying, "The Lord has risen indeed, and he has appeared to Simon!" [35]Then they told what had happened on the road, and how he had been made known to them in the breaking of the bread.

Hymn and Keyboard Suggestions

O– "O Spirit of the Living God" (Acts)
    UM539 (PD)
      S-1   #131. Introduction
              #132. Descant
      K-3   p. 25. Short prelude/postlude (manuals only)
      K-6   p. 10. Prelude/postlude

O– "We Know That Christ Is Raised" (Acts)
    E296, L189, P495, UM610, W721
      S-1   #118-27. Various treatments

"O Thou, My Soul, Return in Peace" (Ps.)
    P228 (PD)
      S-2   #116-17. Harmonizations
      K-6   p. 12. Prelude/meditation/postlude

"Jesus, Priceless Treasure" (Ps., 1 Pet.)
    F277, L457, P365, UM532 (PD)
      K-4   p. 109. Variations, through p. 119
      K-9   p. 33. Prelude/meditation
      K-14   p. 48. Prelude/meditation/postlude
    L458 (PD)

"Just As I Am, Without One Plea" (1 Pet.)
    B307, E693, F417, L296, P370, UM357 (PD)
      K-15   p. 66. Piano prelude/meditation
    B303

"Blessed Assurance" (1 Pet.)
    B334, F67, P341, UM369 (PD)
      S-1   #24. Harmonization
      K-15   p. 38. Piano prelude/postlude

"Amazing Grace" (1 Pet.)
    B330, E671, F107, L448, P280, UM378 (PD), W583
      S-2   #5-7. Various treatments
      K-15   p. 146. Piano prelude/meditation

"My Faith Looks Up to Thee" (1 Pet.)
    B416, E691, F84, L479, P383, UM452 (PD)
      H-1   #72. Harmonization in D major
      S-2   #142. Flute/violin descant
      K-1(III)   #69. Prelude/meditation
      K-14   p. 12. Piano prelude/meditation

"Be Known to Us in Breaking Bread" (Luke)
    P505 (PD)
      K-2   p. 28. Short prelude/meditation

"Shepherd of Souls" (Luke)
    E343, W728
      H-1   #15. Harmonization
      S-1   #291. Descant
              #292. Harmonization
      K-2   p. 26. Short prelude/meditation
      K-6   p. 22. Prelude/meditation
      K-15   p. 63. Piano prelude/meditation

"We Meet You, O Christ" (Luke)
    UM257
      S-2   #166. Descant
    P311

"Cuando El Pobre" ("When the Poor Ones") (Luke)
    P407, UM434

C– "It Is Well with My Soul" (1 Pet.)
    B410, F495, L346, UM377 (PD)
      K-13   p. 21. Piano prelude/meditation
      K-15   p. 126. Piano prelude/meditation

C– "Nothing but the Blood" (1 Pet.)
    B135, F266, UM362 (PD)

Vocal Solos

"I Want to Be Ready" (Acts)
    V-5   p. 195

"Amazing Grace" (1 Pet.)
    V-3   p. 8

"Just As I Am" (1 Pet.)
    V-3   p. 23

"We Walk with God" (Luke)
    V-7   p. 42

Anthems

"The Heavens Are Telling" from *The Creation* (Ps.)
F. J. Haydn
E. C. Schirmer 1188
SATB with STB trio and keyboard

"Assurance" (1 Pet.)
John Ness Beck
Beckenhorst Press BP-1097-3
SATB with keyboard

Hymn Anthem Suggestions

"Children of the Heavenly Father" (Ps.)
52IHA   #7
"Cuando El Pobre" ("When the Poor Ones") (Luke)
52IHA   #12

Other Suggestions

    This would be an excellent day to schedule baptisms or a congregational reaffirmation of the baptismal covenant in response to the Acts reading.
Response: UM609, W112. "You Have Put On Christ." See
    S-1, #39, canon and instrumental parts.

Acts 2:42-47

[42]They devoted themselves to the apostles' teaching and fellowship, to the breaking of bread and the prayers.

[43]Awe came upon everyone, because many wonders and signs were being done by the apostles. [44]All who believed were together and had all things in common; [45]they would sell their possessions and goods and distribute the proceeds to all, as any had need. [46]Day by day, as they spent much time together in the temple, they broke bread at home and ate their food with glad and generous hearts, [47]praising God and having the goodwill of all the people. And day by day the Lord added to their number those who were being saved.

Psalm 23

[1]The LORD is my shepherd, I shall not want.
   [2]He makes me lie down in green pastures;
he leads me beside still waters;
   [3]he restores my soul.
He leads me in right paths for his name's sake.
[4]Even though I walk through the darkest valley,
   I fear no evil;
for you are with me;
   your rod and your staff—they comfort me.
[5]You prepare a table before me
   in the presence of my enemies;
you anoint my head with oil;
   my cup overflows.
[6]Surely goodness and mercy shall follow me
   all the days of my life,
and I shall dwell in the house of the LORD
   my whole life long.

1 Peter 2:19-25

[19]For it is a credit to you if, being aware of God, you endure pain while suffering unjustly. [20]If you endure when you are beaten for doing wrong, what credit is that? But if you endure when you do right and suffer for it, you have God's approval. [21]For to this you have been called, because Christ also suffered for you, leaving you an example, so that you should follow in his steps.

[22]"He committed no sin,
   and no deceit was found in his mouth."
[23]When he was abused, he did not return abuse; when he suffered, he did not threaten; but he entrusted himself to the one who judges justly. [24]He himself bore our sins in his body on the cross, so that, free from sins, we might live for righteousness; by his wounds you have been healed. [25]For you were going astray like sheep, but now you have returned to the shepherd and guardian of your souls.

John 10:1-10

[1]"Very truly, I tell you, anyone who does not enter the sheepfold by the gate but climbs in by another way is a thief and a bandit. [2]The one who enters by the gate is the shepherd of the sheep. [3]The gatekeeper opens the gate for him, and the sheep hear his voice. He calls his own sheep by name and leads them out. [4]When he has brought out all his own, he goes ahead of them, and the sheep follow him because they know his voice. [5]They will not follow a stranger, but they will run from him because they do not know the voice of strangers." [6]Jesus used this figure of speech with them, but they did not understand what he was saying to them.

[7]So again Jesus said to them, "Very truly, I tell you, I am the gate for the sheep. [8]All who came before me are thieves and bandits; but the sheep did not listen to them. [9]I am the gate. Whoever enters by me will be saved, and will come in and go out and find pasture. [10]The thief comes only to steal and kill and destroy. I came that they may have life, and have it abundantly."

Hymn and Keyboard Suggestions

O– "Savior, Like a Shepherd Lead Us" (Ps., John)
       B61, F601, P387, UM381 (PD)
         S-2   #29. Harmonization
         K-13   p. 51. Piano prelude/meditation
       E708
         H-1   #79. Harmonization
"Sweet, Sweet Spirit" (Acts)
       B243, F159, P398, UM334
"Filled with the Spirit's Power" (Acts)
       L160, UM537
"Praise the Spirit in Creation" (Acts)
       E507, W477
         S-1   #191. Descant
"He Leadeth Me: O Blessed Thought" (Ps.)
       B52, F606, L501, UM128 (PD)
"My Shepherd Will Supply My Need" (Ps., John))
       B68, E664, F66, P172, W606
         K-11   p. 28. Prelude/meditation
         K-11   p. 9. Prelude/meditation
"The Lord's My Shepherd, I'll Not Want" (Ps.)
       F40, P170, UM136
       F42, L451
"The King of Love My Shepherd Is" (Ps., John)
       E645, L456, P171, UM138 (PD), W609
         S-1   #298. Harmonization
                  #299. Harmonization
         K-2   p. 27. Short prelude/postlude
         K-9   p. 47. Prelude/meditation
       E646
"Close to Thee" (Ps.)
       B464, F405, UM407 (PD)
"Precious Lord, Take My Hand"
       B456, F611, P404, UM474
"Give Me the Faith Which Can Remove" (Ps., John)
       UM650 (PD)
         S-1   #57-61. Various treatments
C– "Christ Is Alive" (1 Pet.)
       B173, E182, L363, P108, UM318
         S-1   #334. Descant
                  #335. Harmonization

Vocal Solos

"The Shepherd" (Ps.)
V-6   p. 42
"God Is My Shepherd" (Ps.)
V-9   p. 52
"The Shepherd" (Ps.)
V-7   p. 59
"God, Our Ever Faithful Shepherd" (Ps.)
V-4   p. 15

Anthems

"Sweet, Sweet Spirit" (Acts)
Doris Akers (arr. Kaiser)
Manna/Word Music CS-2499
SATB *a cappella*

"Love Grows Here" (Acts)
Don and Nancy Besig
Glory Sound E-5215
Two-part with keyboard

"The Lord's My Shepherd" (Ps., John)
Carl Mueller
Carl Fischer 30874
SATB with keyboard

Hymn Anthem Suggestions

"He Leadeth Me: O Blessed Thought" (Ps.)
52IHA   #21
"How Like a Gentle Spirit" (Ps., John)
52IHA   #24
"O Thou, in Whose Presence" (Ps., John)
52IHA   #38

Other Suggestions

Introit: B243, F159, P398, UM334. "Sweet, Sweet Spirit"
Poem or Hymn: UM342 (PD) "Where Shall My Wondering Soul Begin." Use tune: ST. PETERSBURG (Ps., John)
Prayer Response: B61, F601, P387, UM381 (PD), stanza 2. "Savior, Like a Shepherd Lead Us." Begin at "Blessed Jesus. . . ."

Acts 7:55-60

⁵⁵But filled with the Holy Spirit, he gazed into heaven and saw the glory of God and Jesus standing at the right hand of God. ⁵⁶"Look," he said, "I see the heavens opened and the Son of Man standing at the right hand of God!" ⁵⁷But they covered their ears, and with a loud shout all rushed together against him. ⁵⁸Then they dragged him out of the city and began to stone him; and the witnesses laid their coats at the feet of a young man named Saul. ⁵⁹While they were stoning Stephen, he prayed, "Lord Jesus, receive my spirit." ⁶⁰Then he knelt down and cried out in a loud voice, "Lord, do not hold this sin against them." When he had said this, he died.

Psalm 31:1-5, 15-16

¹In you, O LORD, I seek refuge; do not let me ever be put to shame; in your righteousness deliver me. ²Incline your ear to me; rescue me speedily. Be a rock of refuge for me, a strong fortress to save me. ³You are indeed my rock and my fortress; for your name's sake lead me and guide me, ⁴take me out of the net that is hidden for me, for you are my refuge. ⁵Into your hand I commit my spirit; you have redeemed me, O LORD, faithful God.

¹⁵My times are in your hand; deliver me from the hand of my enemies and persecutors. ¹⁶Let your face shine upon your servant; save me in your steadfast love.

1 Peter 2:2-10

²Like newborn infants, long for the pure, spiritual milk, so that by it you may grow into salvation—³if indeed you have tasted that the Lord is good.

⁴Come to him, a living stone, though rejected by mortals yet chosen and precious in God's sight, and ⁵like living stones, let yourselves be built into a spiritual house, to be a holy priesthood, to offer spiritual sacrifices acceptable to God through Jesus Christ. ⁶For it stands in scripture:

"See, I am laying in Zion a stone,
a cornerstone chosen and precious;
and whoever believes in him
will not be put to shame."

⁷To you then who believe, he is precious; but for those who do not believe,

"The stone that the builders rejected
has become the very head of the corner,"

⁸and

"A stone that makes them stumble,
and a rock that makes them fall."

They stumble because they disobey the word, as they were destined to do.

⁹But you are a chosen race, a royal priesthood, a holy nation, God's own people, in order that you may proclaim the mighty acts of him who called you out of darkness into his marvelous light.

¹⁰Once you were not a people,
but now you are God's people;
once you had not received mercy,
but now you have received mercy.

John 14:1-14

¹"Do not let your hearts be troubled. Believe in God, believe also in me. ²In my Father's house there are many dwelling places. If it were not so, would I have told you that I go to prepare a place for you? ³And if I go and prepare a place for you, I will come again and will take you to myself, so that where I am, there you may be also. ⁴And you know the way to the place where I am going." ⁵Thomas said to him, "Lord, we do not know where you are going. How can we know the way?" ⁶Jesus said to him, "I am the way, and the truth, and the life. No one comes to the Father except through me. ⁷If you know me, you will know my Father also. From now on you do know him and have seen him."

⁸Philip said to him, "Lord, show us the Father, and we will be satisfied." ⁹Jesus said to him, "Have I been with you all this time, Philip, and you still do not know me? Whoever has seen me has seen the Father. How can you say, 'Show us the Father'? ¹⁰Do you not believe that I am in the Father and the Father is in me? The words that I say to you I do not speak on my own; but the Father who dwells in me does his works. ¹¹Believe me that I am in the Father and the Father is in me; but if you do not, then believe me because of the works themselves. ¹²Very truly, I tell you, the one who believes in me will also do the works that I do and, in fact, will do greater works than these, because I am going to the Father. ¹³I will do whatever you ask in my name, so that the Father may be glorified in the Son. ¹⁴If in my name you ask me for anything, I will do it."

Hymn and Keyboard Suggestions

O– "I'll Praise My Maker While I've Breath" (Acts)
     B35, E429 (PD), P253, UM60
        S-2   #141. Harmonization

O– "Only Trust Him" (Ps., John)
     B317, F629, UM337 (PD)
        K-8   p. 31. Harmonization

"God of Grace and God of Glory" (Acts)
     B395, E594, F528, L415, P420, UM577
        S-1   #76. Descant
                #77. Harmonization
        K-6   p. 30. Prelude/postlude
     E595

"Be Still My Soul" (Acts, Ps.)
     F77, UM534

"If Thou But Suffer God to Guide Thee" (Acts, Ps., 1 Pet.)
     B57, E635, L453, P282, UM142 (PD)
        K-5   p. 141. Harmonization in A minor
        K-1(IV)   #94. Prelude/meditation
        K-5   p. 141. Various keyboard treatments, through p. 152

"Here, O My Lord, I See Thee" (Acts, Ps., Communion)
     F567, UM623 (PD)
        S-1   #265. Descant
     E316 (PD), E317, E318, L211, P520

"The Church's One Foundation" (1 Pet., John)
     B350, E525, F547, L369, P442, UM545 (PD), UM546
        H-1   #62. Harmonization
        S-1   #25. Descant
                #26. Harmonization
        K-1(I)   #8. Prelude/postlude

"How Great Thou Art" (John)
     B10, F2, L532, P467, UM77
        S-1   #163. Harmonization
        K-15   p. 134. Piano prelude/meditation

"Come, My Way, My Truth, My Life" (John)
     E487, L513, UM164 (PD), W569
        K-12   p. 35. Prelude/meditation

"My Jesus, I Love Thee" (John)
     B210, F456, UM172 (PD)
        S-1   #148. Harmonization

"Christ Is the World's Light" (John)
     UM188, W543
        S-1   #64. Descant

"Here, O Lord, Your Servants Gather" (John)
     B179, P465, UM552
        S-1   #333. Orff arrangement
        S-2   #178. Flute descant

C– "Victory in Jesus" (John)
     B426, F82, UM370
        S-2   #75. Piano arrangement

C– "Christ Is Made the Sure Foundation" (1 Pet.)
     B356 (PD)
        H-2   p. 23. Harmonization with descant
        S-1   #338, 341. Descants
     E518, P416, UM559 (PD), W617
        S-1   #346. Descant
     F557, P417 (PD)
        H-1   #7. Harmonization
        S-1   #280. Descant
                #281. Harmonization
        K-1(III)   #72. Short prelude/postlude/interlude
        K-2   p. 24. Short prelude
        K-8   p. 28. Introduction/interlude
     L367

Vocal Solos

"Come My Way, My Truth, My Life" (John)
V-4   p. 31
"Heav'n Heav'n" (John)
V-5   p. 79
"The Master's Touch" (1 Pet.)
V-6   p. 5

Anthems

"Christ Is Our Cornerstone" (1 Pet.)
Edgar Aufdemberge (tr. Chandler)
Concordia 98-1591
SATB with organ

"A Vineyard Grows" (John)
arr. K. Lee Scott (text by Jaroslav Vajda)
Morning Star MSM-50-9010
SATB with organ

Hymn Anthem Suggestions

"How Firm a Foundation" (1 Pet.)
52IHA   #23
"Here, O Lord, Your Servants Gather" (John)
52IHA   #22
"I Want to Walk as a Child of the Light" (John)
52IHA   #27

Other Suggestion

Prayer: UM535. A Refuge amid Distraction (Acts, Ps.)

Acts 17:22-31

[22]Then Paul stood in front of the Areopagus and said, "Athenians, I see how extremely religious you are in every way. [23]For as I went through the city and looked carefully at the objects of your worship, I found among them an altar with the inscription, 'To an unknown god.' What therefore you worship as unknown, this I proclaim to you. [24]The God who made the world and everything in it, he who is Lord of heaven and earth, does not live in shrines made by human hands, [25]nor is he served by human hands, as though he needed anything, since he himself gives to all mortals life and breath and all things. [26]From one ancestor he made all nations to inhabit the whole earth, and he allotted the times of their existence and the boundaries of the places where they would live, [27]so that they would search for God and perhaps grope for him and find him— though indeed he is not far from each one of us. [28]For 'In him we live and move and have our being'; as even some of your own poets have said, 'For we too are his offspring.' [29]Since we are God's offspring, we ought not to think that the deity is like gold, or silver, or stone, an image formed by the art and imagination of mortals. [30]While God has overlooked the times of human ignorance, now he commands all people everywhere to repent, [31]because he has fixed a day on which he will have the world judged in righteousness by a man whom he has appointed, and of this he has given assurance to all by raising him from the dead."

Psalm 66:8-20

[8]Bless our God, O peoples, let the sound of his praise be heard, [9]who has kept us among the living, and has not let our feet slip. [10]For you, O God, have tested us; you have tried us as silver is tried. [11]You brought us into the net; you laid burdens on our backs; [12]you let people ride over our heads; we went through fire and through water; yet you have brought us out to a spacious place. [13]I will come into your house with burnt offerings; I will pay you my vows, [14]those that my lips uttered and my mouth promised when I was in trouble. [15]I will offer to you burnt offerings of fatlings, with the smoke of the sacrifice of rams; I will make an offering of bulls and goats. Selah [16]Come and hear, all you who fear God, and I will tell what he has done for me. [17]I cried aloud to him, and he was extolled with my tongue. [18]If I had cherished iniquity in my heart, the Lord would not have listened. [19]But truly God has listened; he has given heed to the words of my prayer. [20]Blessed be God, because he has not rejected my prayer or removed his steadfast love from me.

1 Peter 3:13-22

[13]Now who will harm you if you are eager to do what is good? [14]But even if you do suffer for doing what is right, you are blessed. Do not fear what they fear, and do not be intimidated, [15]but in your hearts sanctify Christ as Lord. Always be ready to make your defense to anyone who demands from you an accounting for the hope that is in you; [16]yet do it with gentleness and reverence. Keep your conscience clear, so that, when you are maligned, those who abuse you for your good conduct in Christ may be put to shame. [17]For it is better to suffer for doing good, if suffering should be God's will, than to suffer for doing evil. [18]For Christ also suffered for sins once for all, the righteous for the unrighteous, in order to bring you to God. He was put to death in the flesh, but made alive in the spirit, [19]in which also he went and made a proclamation to the spirits in prison, [20]who in former times did not obey, when God waited patiently in the days of Noah, during the building of the ark, in which a few, that is, eight persons, were saved through water. [21]And baptism, which this prefigured, now saves you—not as a removal of dirt from the body, but as an appeal to God for a good conscience, through the resurrection of Jesus Christ, [22]who has gone into heaven and is at the right hand of God, with angels, authorities, and powers made subject to him.

John 14:15-21

[15]"If you love me, you will keep my commandments. [16]And I will ask the Father, and he will give you another Advocate, to be with you forever. [17]This is the Spirit of truth, whom the world cannot receive, because it neither sees him nor knows him. You know him, because he abides with you, and he will be in you.

[18]"I will not leave you orphaned; I am coming to you. [19]In a little while the world will no longer see me, but you will see me; because I live, you also will live. [20]On that day you will know that I am in my Father, and you in me, and I in you. [21]They who have my commandments and keep them are those who love me; and those who love me will be loved by my Father, and I will love them and reveal myself to them."

Hymn and Keyboard Suggestions

O– "God Is Here" (Acts)
    P461, UM660, W667
        S-1   #4. Instrumental descant
                #5. Vocal descant

O– "For the Beauty of the Earth" (Acts)
    B44, F1, L561, P473, UM92 (PD)
        H-1   #16. Harmonization
        S-1   #93-96. Various treatments
        K-1(I)   #15. Short prelude/postlude
        K-3   p. 31. Postlude
    E416, W557

"O Zion, Haste" (Acts)
    B583, E539, F658, L397, UM573 (PD)
        S-2   #174-75. Introduction and harmo-
                        nization

"Draw Us in the Spirit's Tether" (Acts)
    P504, UM632, W731
        S-1   #337. Performance note

"I Sing the Almighty Power of God" (Acts, John)
    B42, E398, UM152 (PD)
        S-1   #131. Introduction
                #132. Descant
        K-3   p. 25. Short prelude/postlude (man-
                        uals only)
        K-6   p. 10. Prelude/postlude
    P288 (PD)
        S-1   #115. Harmonization
    W502 (PD)

"O For a Heart to Praise My God" (1 Pet.)
    F357, UM417 (PD)
        S-1   #286. Descant
        K-2   p. 25. Short prelude/postlude
    W591

"Thou Hidden Source of Calm Repose" (John)
    UM153 (PD)
        S-2   #163. Descant

"There's Within My Heart a Melody" (John)
    B425, UM380 (PD)
        S-2   #170. Descant

"Spirit of the Living God" (John)
    B244, F155, P322, UM393
        S-1   #212. Vocal descant idea

"Holy Spirit, Truth Divine" (John)
    L257, P321, UM465 (PD)
        S-1   #53. Descant

C– "All Creatures of Our God and King" (Acts)
    B27, E400, F347, L527, P455, UM62, W520
        H-1   #96. Harmonization
        S-1   #198-204. Various treatments
        K-1(II)   #46. Prelude/postlude
        K-8   p. 29. Harmonization
        K-9   p. 25. Prelude/postlude
        K-13   p. 3. Piano prelude/meditation
        K-15   p. 80. Piano prelude/postlude

C– "Easter People, Raise Your Voices" (Acts, 1 Pet.)
    B360, UM304
        H-1   #7. Harmonization
        S-1   #280. Descant
                 #281. Harmonization
        K-1(III)   #72. Short prelude/postlude/inter-
                        lude
        K-2   p. 24. Short prelude
        K-8   p. 28. Introduction/interlude

Vocal Solos

"Year's at the Spring" (Acts)
V-7   p. 35
"Rejoice, the Lord Is King" (Acts, 1 Pet.)
V-1   p. 66
"I Will Bless the Lord at All Times" (1 Pet.)
V-9   p. 37

Anthems

"All Breathing Life, Sing and Praise Ye the Lord" (Ps.)
J. S. Bach (arr. Williamson)
G. Schirmer 7470
SATB *a cappella*

"If Ye Love Me" (John)
Thomis Tallis
E. C. Schirmer 2992
SATB *a cappella*

Hymn Anthem Suggestion

"How Firm a Foundation" (Ps.)
52IHA   #23

Other Suggestions

Introit: P504, UM632, W731, stanza 1. "Draw Us in the
    Spirit's Tether" (Acts)
Prayer: UM255. Epiphany (Acts)
Benediction: B583, E539, F658, L397, UM573 (PD), stanza
    3. "O Zion, Haste" (Acts)

Acts 1:1-11

[1]In the first book, Theophilus, I wrote about all that Jesus did and taught from the beginning [2]until the day when he was taken up to heaven, after giving instructions through the Holy Spirit to the apostles whom he had chosen. [3]After his suffering he presented himself alive to them by many convincing proofs, appearing to them during forty days and speaking about the kingdom of God. [4]While staying with them, he ordered them not to leave Jerusalem, but to wait there for the promise of the Father. "This," he said, "is what you have heard from me; [5]for John baptized with water, but you will be baptized with the Holy Spirit not many days from now."

[6]So when they had come together, they asked him, "Lord, is this the time when you will restore the kingdom to Israel?" [7]He replied, "It is not for you to know the times or periods that the Father has set by his own authority. [8]But you will receive power when the Holy Spirit has come upon you; and you will be my witnesses in Jerusalem, in all Judea and Samaria, and to the ends of the earth." [9]When he had said this, as they were watching, he was lifted up, and a cloud took him out of their sight. [10]While he was going and they were gazing up toward heaven, suddenly two men in white robes stood by them. [11]They said, "Men of Galilee, why do you stand looking up toward heaven? This Jesus, who has been taken up from you into heaven, will come in the same way as you saw him go into heaven."

Psalm 47

[1]Clap your hands, all you peoples;
shout to God with loud songs of joy.
[2]For the LORD, the Most High, is awesome,
a great king over all the earth.
[3]He subdued peoples under us,
and nations under our feet.
[4]He chose our heritage for us,
the pride of Jacob whom he loves.
[5]God has gone up with a shout,
the LORD with the sound of a trumpet.
[6]Sing praises to God, sing praises;
sing praises to our King, sing praises.
[7]For God is the king of all the earth;
sing praises with a psalm.
[8]God is king over the nations;
God sits on his holy throne.
[9]The princes of the peoples gather
as the people of the God of Abraham.
For the shields of the earth belong to God;
he is highly exalted.

Ephesians 1:15-23

[15]I have heard of your faith in the Lord Jesus and your love toward all the saints, and for this reason [16]I do not cease to give thanks for you as I remember you in my prayers. [17]I pray that the God of our Lord Jesus Christ, the Father of glory, may give you a spirit of wisdom and revelation as you come to know him, [18]so that, with the eyes of your heart enlightened, you may know what is the hope to which he has called you, what are the riches of his glorious inheritance among the saints, [19]and what is the immeasurable greatness of his power for us who believe, according to the working of his great power. [20]God put this power to work in Christ when he raised him from the dead and seated him at his right hand in the heavenly places, [21]far above all rule and authority and power and dominion, and above every name that is named, not only in this age but also in the age to come. [22]And he has put all things under his feet and has made him the head over all things for the church, [23]which is his body, the fullness of him who fills all in all.

Luke 24:44-53

[44]Then he said to them, "These are my words that I spoke to you while I was still with you—that everything written about me in the law of Moses, the prophets, and the psalms must be fulfilled." [45]Then he opened their minds to understand the scriptures, [46]and he said to them, "Thus it is written, that the Messiah is to suffer and to rise from the dead on the third day, [47]and that repentance and forgiveness of sins is to be proclaimed in his name to all nations, beginning from Jerusalem. [48]You are witnesses of these things. [49]And see, I am sending upon you what my Father promised; so stay here in the city until you have been clothed with power from on high."

[50]Then he led them out as far as Bethany, and, lifting up his hands, he blessed them. [51]While he was blessing them, he withdrew from them and was carried up into heaven. [52]And they worshiped him, and returned to Jerusalem with great joy; [53]and they were continually in the temple blessing God.

Hymn and Keyboard Suggestions
O– "Come, Ye Faithful, Raise the Strain" (Acts, Luke)
    E199, P115, UM315 (PD)
        S-2   #161. Descant
        K-9   p. 27. Prelude/meditation/postlude
    E200, L132, P114 (PD), W456
        S-1   #29. Transposition to F major
"A Hymn of Glory Let Us Sing" (Acts)
    E218, P141
        S-1   #82-84. Various treatments
    L157, W469
        H-1   #96. Harmonization
        S-1   #198-204. Various treatments
        K-1(II) #46. Prelude/postlude
        K-8   p. 29. Harmonization
        K-9   p. 25. Prelude/postlude
        K-13   p. 3. Piano prelude/meditation
        K-15   p. 80. Piano prelude/postlude
"Hail the Day That Sees Him Rise" (Acts, Luke)
    E214, UM312, W471 (PD)
        S-1   #213-14. Transposition with descant
                 in F major
    B165
"Christ Jesus Lay in Death's Strong Bands" (Acts, Luke)
    E186, L134, P110, UM319 (PD)
"Hail Thee, Festival Day" (Acts, Luke)
    E216, L142, P120 UM324
        S-2   #164. Descant
"My Hope Is Built" (Eph.)
    B406, F92, L293, P379, UM368 (PD)
        S-2   #171. Trumpet descant
                 #172. Descant
    L294 (PD)
        H-1   #80. Harmonization
"All Hail the Power of Jesus' Name" (Eph., Luke)
    B200, F326, P143, UM155 (PD)
        S-2   #50. Descant
                 #51. Interlude
        K-6   p. 3. Prelude/postlude
        K-8   p. 27. Modulation, A-flat major to B-
                 flat major
    B201, E451, F327, L329 (PD)
        H-2   p. 21. Harmonization with descant
    B202, E450, F325, L328, P142, UM154 (PD),
    W494
        H-1   #56. Harmonization
        S-1   #66-70. Various treatments
        K-1(I)   #12. Prelude/postlude
        K-2   p. 6. Short prelude/postlude
        K-6   p. 3. Prelude/postlude
    W495

"Camina, Pueblo de Dios" ("Walk On, O People of God") (Eph., Luke)
    P296, UM305
C– "Thine Be the Glory" (Acts, Ps.)
    B163, F291, L145, P122, UM308
        S-1   #190. Arrangement for choir, hand-
                 bells, trumpets, organ
        S-2   #95. Brass/percussion arrangement,
                 descant and harmonization
C– "Hope of the World" (Eph.)
    UM178
        S-1   #343. Descant
        S-2   #189. Introduction
    E472, L493, P360, W565

Vocal Solos
"If God Be For Us" from *Messiah* (Acts, Luke)
V-2
"Rise Up, My Heart with Gladness" (Acts, Luke)
V-8   p. 36
"Jesus Christ Is Risen Today" (Ascension)
V-1   p. 50

Anthems
"All Hail the Power of Jesus' Name" (Acts)
arr. James Mulholland
National Music CH-25
SATB with organ and optional brass

"Clap Your Hands, Stamp Your Feet" (Ps.)
Ronald Nelson
Augsburg/Concordia 11-0649
Unison with keyboard

Hymn Anthem Suggestions
"Hail Thee, Festival Day" (Acts, Luke)
HA   p. 48
"Cristo Vive" ("Christ Is Risen") (Acts, Luke)
52IHA   #11

Other Suggestions
Hymn Idea: "All Hail the Power of Jesus' Name." If your congregation is familiar with the tunes CORONATION and DIADEM, you may wish to sing both. S-1, #69-70 gives interludes to use between the two. You might wish to have one side of the worship space sing CORONATION, and the other DIADEM, alternating sides as the hymn is sung. This gives the congregation an opportunity to enjoy hearing the singing of others. The use of a song leader is recommended!
Greeting: Acts 1:8. Receive power from the Holy Spirit.
Prayer: UM323. The Ascension (Acts, Luke, Eph.)

Acts 2:1-21

[1]When the day of Pentecost had come, they were all together in one place. [2]And suddenly from heaven there came a sound like the rush of a violent wind, and it filled the entire house where they were sitting. [3]Divided tongues, as of fire, appeared among them, and a tongue rested on each of them. [4]All of them were filled with the Holy Spirit and began to speak in other languages, as the Spirit gave them ability.

[5]Now there were devout Jews from every nation under heaven living in Jerusalem. [6]And at this sound the crowd gathered and was bewildered, because each one heard them speaking in the native language of each. [7]Amazed and astonished, they asked, "Are not all these who are speaking Galileans? [8]And how is it that we hear, each of us, in our own native language? [9]Parthians, Medes, Elamites, and residents of Mesopotamia, Judea and Cappadocia, Pontus and Asia, [10]Phrygia and Pamphylia, Egypt and the parts of Libya belonging to Cyrene, and visitors from Rome, both Jews and proselytes, [11]Cretans and Arabs—in our own languages we hear them speaking about God's deeds of power." [12]All were amazed and perplexed, saying to one another, "What does this mean?" [13]But others sneered and said, "They are filled with new wine."

[14]But Peter, standing with the eleven, raised his voice and addressed them, "Men of Judea and all who live in Jerusalem, let this be known to you, and listen to what I say. [15]Indeed, these are not drunk, as you suppose, for it is only nine o'clock in the morning. [16]No, this is what was spoken through the prophet Joel:

[17]'In the last days it will be, God declares,
   that I will pour out my Spirit upon all flesh,
      and your sons and your daughters shall prophesy,
   and your young men shall see visions,
      and your old men shall dream dreams.
[18]Even upon my slaves, both men and women,
   in those days I will pour out my Spirit;
      and they shall prophesy.
[19]And I will show portents in the heaven above
   and signs on the earth below,
      blood, and fire, and smoky mist.
[20]The sun shall be turned to darkness
   and the moon to blood,
      before the coming of the
         Lord's great and glorious day.
[21]Then everyone who calls on the
      name of the Lord shall be saved.'"

Psalm 104:24-34, 35b

[24]O LORD, how manifold are your works! In wisdom you have made them all; the earth is full of your creatures. [25]Yonder is the sea, great and wide, creeping things innumerable are there, living things both small and great. [26]There go the ships, and Leviathan that you formed to sport in it. [27]These all look to you to give them their food in due season; [28]when you give to them, they gather it up; when you open your hand, they are filled with good things. [29]When you hide your face, they are dismayed; when you take away their breath, they die and return to their dust. [30]When you send forth your spirit, they are created; and you renew the face of the ground. [31]May the glory of the LORD endure forever; may the LORD rejoice in his works—[32]who looks on the earth and it trembles, who touches the mountains and they smoke. [33]I will sing to the LORD as long as I live; I will sing praise to my God while I have being. [34]May my meditation be pleasing to him, for I rejoice in the LORD.

[35b]Bless the LORD, O my soul. Praise the LORD!

1 Corinthians 12:3b-13

[3b]No one can say "Jesus is Lord" except by the Holy Spirit. [4]Now there are varieties of gifts, but the same Spirit; [5]and there are varieties of services, but the same Lord; [6]and there are varieties of activities, but it is the same God who activates all of them in everyone. [7]To each is given the manifestation of the Spirit for the common good. [8]To one is given through the Spirit the utterance of wisdom, and to another the utterance of knowledge according to the same Spirit, [9]to another faith by the same Spirit, to another gifts of healing by the one Spirit, [10]to another the working of miracles, to another prophecy, to another the discernment of spirits, to another various kinds of tongues, to another the interpretation of tongues. [11]All these are activated by one and the same Spirit, who allots to each one individually just as the Spirit chooses.

[12]For just as the body is one and has many members, and all the members of the body, though many, are one body, so it is with Christ. [13]For in the one Spirit we were all baptized into one body—Jews or Greeks, slaves or free—and we were all made to drink of one Spirit.

John 7:37-39

[37]On the last day of the festival, the great day, while Jesus was standing there, he cried out, "Let anyone who is thirsty come to me, [38]and let the one who believes in me drink. As the scripture has said, 'Out of the believer's heart shall flow rivers of living water.' " [39]Now he said this about the Spirit, which believers in him were to receive; for as yet there was no Spirit, because Jesus was not yet glorified.

Hymn and Keyboard Suggestions

O– "O Worship the King" (Acts, Ps.)

    B16, F336, P476, UM73 (PD)

        H-1   #37. Harmonization

        S-1   #223-26. Various treatments

        K-8   p. 17. Introduction

    E388, L548 (PD)

        H-1   #45. Harmonization in G major

        S-2   #71. Introduction

                    #72-74. Harmonizations

        K-2   p. 10. Short prelude/postlude

        K-10   p. 13. Prelude/postlude

"Hail Thee, Festival Day" (Acts)

    E225, L142, UM324

        S-2   #164. Descant

"Of All the Spirit's Gifts to Me" (Acts)

    UM336

        S-2   #121. Descant

    B442

"Holy Spirit, Truth Divine" (Acts)

    L257, P321, UM465 (PD)

        S-1   #53. Descant

"Filled with the Spirit's Power" (Acts)

    L160, UM537

"Wind Who Makes All Winds That Blow" (Acts)

    P131

        S-1   #6. Descant

        K-9   p. 10. Prelude/postlude

    UM538

"Come, Holy Ghost, Our Souls Inspire" (Acts)

    E504, L472 and L473, P125, UM651 (PD)

        S-2   #186. Handbell arrangement

        K-4   p. 123. Prelude/postlude

    E503

"Like the Murmur of the Dove's Song" (Acts)

    E513, P314, UM544

        S-2   #30. Descant

"Many and Great, O God" (Ps.)

    B49, E385, P271 (PD), UM148, W503

        S-2   #104. Performance note

        K-11   p. 19. Prelude/meditation

"In Christ There Is No East or West" (1 Cor.)

    B385, F685, P439

        H-1   #73. Harmonization in E-flat major

        S-2   #162. Harmonization

        K-1(III) #77. Prelude/meditation (manuals only)

    E529, L359, P440, UM548, W659

        S-1   #231. Descant

                    #232. Brass quartet arrangement

                    #233. Harmonization

C– "Come Down, O Love Divine" (Acts)

    E516, L508, P313, UM475 (PD), W472

        S-1   #98-99. Descants

Vocal Solos

"Come Praise the Lord"

V-10   p. 8

"Spirit of Faith Come Down"

V-1   p. 43

"Spirit From on High" (alt. text)

V-4   p. 2

Anthems

"I'm Goin' to Sing" (Acts)

arr. Ronald Anderson

Choristers Guild A-217

Unison and SATB with keyboard

"The Spirit Leads On and On" (Acts)

John Ness Beck

Beckenhorst Press BP1270

SATB with keyboard, brass quartet, timpani, and

    congregation

"Hymn of Fire" (Acts)

Eugene Butler

SATB with keyboard

Richmond Music Press MI-140

Hymn Anthem Suggestions

"Come Down, O Love Divine" (Acts)

HA   p. 56

"Hail Thee, Festival Day" (Acts)

HA   p. 48

"Wind Who Makes All Winds That Blow" (Acts)

52IHA   #51

"Many and Great, O God" (Ps.)

52IHA   #33

Other Suggestions

Prayer: UM329. Prayer to the Holy Spirit (Acts)

Prayer: UM542. Day of Pentecost (Acts)

Genesis 1:1–2:4a

[1]In the beginning when God created the heavens and the earth, [2]the earth was a formless void and darkness covered the face of the deep, while a wind from God swept over the face of the waters. [3]Then God said, "Let there be light"; and there was light. [4]And God saw that the light was good; and God separated the light from the darkness. [5]God called the light Day, and the darkness he called Night. And there was evening and there was morning, the first day.

[6]And God said, "Let there be a dome in the midst of the waters, and let it separate the waters from the waters." [7]So God made the dome and separated the waters that were under the dome from the waters that were above the dome. And it was so. [8]God called the dome Sky. And there was evening and there was morning, the second day.

[9]And God said, "Let the waters under the sky be gathered together into one place, and let the dry land appear." And it was so. [10]God called the dry land Earth, and the waters that were gathered together he called Seas. And God saw that it was good. [11]Then God said, "Let the earth put forth vegetation: plants yielding seed, and fruit trees of every kind on earth that bear fruit with the seed in it." And it was so. [12]The earth brought forth vegetation: plants yielding seed of every kind, and trees of every kind bearing fruit with the seed in it. And God saw that it was good. [13]And there was evening and there was morning, the third day.

[14]And God said, "Let there be lights in the dome of the sky to separate the day from the night; and let them be for signs and for seasons and for days and years, [15]and let them be lights in the dome of the sky to give light upon the earth." And it was so. [16]God made the two great lights—the greater light to rule the day and the lesser light to rule the night—and the stars. [17]God set them in the dome of the sky to give light upon the earth, [18]to rule over the day and over the night, and to separate the light from the darkness. And God saw that it was good. [19]And there was evening and there was morning, the fourth day.

[20]And God said, "Let the waters bring forth swarms of living creatures, and let birds fly above the earth across the dome of the sky." [21]So God created the great sea monsters and every living creature that moves, of every kind, with which the waters swarm, and every winged bird of every kind. And God saw that it was good. [22]God blessed them, saying, "Be fruitful and multiply and fill the waters in the seas, and let birds multiply on the earth." [23]And there was evening and there was morning, the fifth day.

[24]And God said, "Let the earth bring forth living creatures of every kind: cattle and creeping things and wild animals of the earth of every kind." And it was so. [25]God made the wild animals of the earth of every kind, and the cattle of every kind, and everything that creeps upon the ground of every kind. And God saw that it was good.

[26]Then God said, "Let us make humankind in our image, according to our likeness; and let them have dominion over the fish of the sea, and over the birds of the air, and over the cattle, and over all the wild animals of the earth, and over every creeping thing that creeps upon the earth." [27]So God created humankind in his image, in the image of God he created them; male and female he created them. [28]God blessed them, and God said to them, "Be fruitful and multiply, and fill the earth and subdue it; and have dominion over the fish of the sea and over the birds of the air and over every living thing that moves upon the earth." [29]God said, "See, I have given you every plant yielding seed that is upon the face of all the earth, and every tree with seed in its fruit; you shall have them for food. [30]And to every beast of the earth, and to every bird of the air, and to everything that creeps on the earth, everything that has the breath of life, I have given every green plant for food." And it was so. [31]God saw everything that he had made, and indeed, it was very good. And there was evening and there was morning, the sixth day.

[1]Thus the heavens and the earth were finished, and all their multitude. [2]And on the seventh day God finished the work that he had done, and he rested on the seventh day from all the work that he had done. [3]So God blessed the seventh day and hallowed it, because on it God rested from all the work that he had done in creation.

[4]These are the generations of the heavens and the earth when they were created.

Psalm 8

[1]O LORD, our Sovereign, how majestic is your name in all the earth! You have set your glory above the heavens. [2]Out of the mouths of babes and infants you have founded a bulwark because of your foes, to silence the enemy and the avenger. [3]When I look at your heavens, the work of your fingers, the moon and the stars that you have established; [4]what are human beings that you are mindful of them, mortals that you care for them? [5]Yet you have made them a little lower than God, and crowned them with glory and honor. [6]You have given them dominion over the works of your hands; you have put all things under their feet, [7]all sheep and oxen, and also the beasts of the field, [8]the birds of the air, and the fish of the sea, whatever passes along the paths of the seas. [9]O LORD, our Sovereign, how majestic is your name in all the earth!

2 Corinthians 13:11-13

[11]Finally, brothers and sisters, farewell. Put things in order, listen to my appeal, agree with one another, live in peace; and the God of love and peace will be with you. [12]Greet one another with a holy kiss. All the saints greet you.

[13]The grace of the Lord Jesus Christ, the love of God, and the communion of the Holy Spirit be with all of you.

Matthew 28:16-20

[16]Now the eleven disciples went to Galilee, to the mountain to which Jesus had directed them. [17]When they saw him, they worshiped him; but some doubted. [18]And Jesus came and said to them, "All authority in heaven and on earth has been given to me. [19]Go therefore and make disciples of all nations, baptizing them in the name of the Father and of the Son and of the Holy Spirit, [20]and teaching them to obey everything that I have commanded you. And remember, I am with you always, to the end of the age."

Hymn and Keyboard Suggestions
O– "All Things Bright and Beautiful" (Gen.)
    E405, P267, UM147 (PD), W505
        S-2   #155-57. Various treatments
    B46 (PD)
"I Sing the Almighty Power of God" (Gen., Ps.)
    B42, E398, UM152 (PD)
        S-1   #131. Introduction
                   #132. Descant
        K-3   p. 25. Short prelude/postlude (man-
                   uals only)
        K-6   p. 10. Prelude/postlude
    P288 (PD)
        S-1   #115. Harmonization
    W502 (PD)
"Morning Has Broken" (Gen.)
    B48, E8, F5, P469, UM145, W674
        S-1   #50. Flute descant
                   #51. Descant
"Thanks to God Whose Word Was Written" (Gen.)
    E630, P331, W514
"God Created Heaven and Earth" (Gen.)
    P290, UM151
        S-1   #332. Arrangement for handbells,
                   Orff instruments
        S-2   #177. Orff instrument arrangement
"God, That Madest Earth and Heaven" (Gen.)
    F4, L281, UM688 (PD)
        S-2   #14. Descant
"When Love Is Found" (Gen., Communion)
    UM643, W745
"Lord, Our Lord, Thy Glorious Name" (Ps.)
    P163 (PD)
        K-1(I)   #26. Prelude/postlude
"How Great Thou Art" (Ps.)
    B10, F2, L532, P467, UM77
        S-1   #163. Harmonization
        K-15   p. 134. Piano prelude/meditation
"Freely, Freely" (Matt.)
    B273, UM389
        S-1   #135. Vocal descant idea
"Alleluia! Sing to Jesus!" (Matt.)
    E460, L158, P144 (PD), W737
        S-1   #168-71. Various treatments
        K-2   p. 12. Short prelude
        K-9   p. 7. Prelude/postlude
    E461

"Go, Make of All Disciples" (Matt.)
    UM571
        H-1   #87. Harmonization
        S-1   #195-96. Harmonization with descant
                   #197. Same harmonization in C
                   major
    W628
        S-1   #115. Harmonization
"Draw Us in the Spirit's Tether" (Matt., Communion)
    P504, UM632, W731
        S-1   #337. Performance note
C– "Lord, You Give the Great Commission" (Matt.,
    2 Cor.)
    P429, UM584, W470
        S-1   #4. Instrumental descant
                   #5. Vocal descant
    E528

Vocal Solos
"In the Beginning" (Gen.)
V-10   p. 11
"Morning Prayer" (Gen.)
V-7   p. 53

Anthems
"A New Benediction" (2 Cor.)
Deborah Govenor
Richmond Music MI-298
SATB with keyboard

"Go and Tell the People" in *A Season to Celebrate* (Matt.)
Allen Pote
Hinshaw Music HMB 144
SATB with keyboard, optional guitar, flute, and tam-
    bourine

Hymn Anthem Suggestions
"All Things Bright and Beautiful" (Gen.)
HA   p. 70
"God Created Heaven and Earth" (Gen.)
52IHA   #18
"Many and Great, O God" (Gen.)
52IHA   #33
"Freely, Freely" (Matt.)
52IHA   #16

Other Suggestions
Canticle: UM80. "Canticle of the Holy Trinity" (Trinity)
Sung Affirmation: UM85, P137. "We Believe in One True
    God" (Trinity)
Prayer: UM76. Trinity Sunday (Trinity)
Blessing: UM669. The Apostolic Blessing (2 Cor.)

Genesis 12:1-9

[1]Now the LORD said to Abram, "Go from your country and your kindred and your father's house to the land that I will show you. [2]I will make of you a great nation, and I will bless you, and make your name great, so that you will be a blessing. [3]I will bless those who bless you, and the one who curses you I will curse; and in you all the families of the earth shall be blessed."

[4]So Abram went, as the LORD had told him; and Lot went with him. Abram was seventy-five years old when he departed from Haran. [5]Abram took his wife Sarai and his brother's son Lot, and all the possessions that they had gathered, and the persons whom they had acquired in Haran; and they set forth to go to the land of Canaan. When they had come to the land of Canaan, [6]Abram passed through the land to the place at Shechem, to the oak of Moreh. At that time the Canaanites were in the land. [7]Then the LORD appeared to Abram, and said, "To your offspring I will give this land." So he built there an altar to the LORD, who had appeared to him. [8]From there he moved on to the hill country on the east of Bethel, and pitched his tent, with Bethel on the west and Ai on the east; and there he built an altar to the LORD and invoked the name of the LORD. [9]And Abram journeyed on by stages toward the Negeb.

Psalm 33:1-12

[1]Rejoice in the LORD, O you righteous. Praise befits the upright. [2]Praise the LORD with the lyre; make melody to him with the harp of ten strings. [3]Sing to him a new song; play skillfully on the strings, with loud shouts. [4]For the word of the LORD is upright, and all his work is done in faithfulness. [5]He loves righteousness and justice; the earth is full of the steadfast love of the LORD. [6]By the word of the LORD the heavens were made, and all their host by the breath of his mouth. [7]He gathered the waters of the sea as in a bottle; he put the deeps in storehouses. [8]Let all the earth fear the LORD; let all the inhabitants of the world stand in awe of him. [9]For he spoke, and it came to be; he commanded, and it stood firm. [10]The LORD brings the counsel of the nations to nothing; he frustrates the plans of the peoples. [11]The counsel of the LORD stands forever, the thoughts of his heart to all generations. [12]Happy is the nation whose God is the LORD, the people whom he has chosen as his heritage.

Romans 4:13-25

[13]For the promise that he would inherit the world did not come to Abraham or to his descendants through the law but through the righteousness of faith. [14]If it is the adherents of the law who are to be the heirs, faith is null and the promise is void. [15]For the law brings wrath; but where there is no law, neither is there violation.

[16]For this reason it depends on faith, in order that the promise may rest on grace and be guaranteed to all his descendants, not only to the adherents of the law but also to those who share the faith of Abraham (for he is the father of all of us, [17]as it is written, "I have made you the father of many nations")—in the presence of the God in whom he believed, who gives life to the dead and calls into existence the things that do not exist. [18]Hoping against hope, he believed that he would become "the father of many nations," according to what was said, "So numerous shall your descendants be." [19]He did not weaken in faith when he considered his own body, which was already as good as dead (for he was about a hundred years old), or when he considered the barrenness of Sarah's womb. [20]No distrust made him waver concerning the promise of God, but he grew strong in his faith as he gave glory to God, [21]being fully convinced that God was able to do what he had promised. [22]Therefore his faith "was reckoned to him as righteousness." [23]Now the words, "it was reckoned to him," were written not for his sake alone, [24]but for ours also. It will be reckoned to us who believe in him who raised Jesus our Lord from the dead, [25]who was handed over to death for our trespasses and was raised for our justification.

Matthew 9:9-13, 18-26

[9]As Jesus was walking along, he saw a man called Matthew sitting at the tax booth; and he said to him, "Follow me." And he got up and followed him.

[10]And as he sat at dinner in the house, many tax collectors and sinners came and were sitting with him and his disciples. [11]When the Pharisees saw this, they said to his disciples, "Why does your teacher eat with tax collectors and sinners?" [12]But when he heard this, he said, "Those who are well have no need of a physician, but those who are sick. [13]Go and learn what this means, 'I desire mercy, not sacrifice.' For I have come to call not the righteous but sinners."

[18]While he was saying these things to them, suddenly a leader of the synagogue came in and knelt before him, saying, "My daughter has just died; but come and lay your hand on her, and she will live." [19]And Jesus got up and followed him, with his disciples. [20]Then suddenly a woman who had been suffering from hemorrhages for twelve years came up behind him and touched the fringe of his cloak, [21]for she said to herself, "If I only touch his cloak, I will be made well." [22]Jesus turned, and seeing her he said, "Take heart, daughter; your faith has made you well." And instantly the woman was made well. [23]When Jesus came to the leader's house and saw the flute players and the crowd making a commotion, [24]he said, "Go away; for the girl is not dead but sleeping." And they laughed at him. [25]But when the crowd had been put outside, he went in and took her by the hand, and the girl got up. [26]And the report of this spread throughout that district.

Hymn and Keyboard Suggestions

O– "The God of Abraham Praise" (Gen.)

      B34, E401, L544, P488, UM116 (PD), W537

        H-1   #44. Harmonization

        S-1   #211. Harmonization

"If Thou But Suffer God to Guide Thee" (Gen.)

      B57, E635, L453, P282, UM142 (PD)

        K-5   p. 141. Harmonization in A minor

        K-1(IV) #94. Prelude/meditation

        K-5   p. 141. Various keyboard treatments,
                      through p. 152

"What Does the Lord Require" (Ps., Matt.)

      E605, P405, UM441, W624

        K-12   p. 31. Prelude

"Faith of Our Fathers" ("Faith of the Martyrs") (Rom.)

      B352, F526, L500, UM710 (PD), W571

        H-1   #60. Harmonization in G major

"O Christ, the Healer" (Rom., Matt.)

      P380, UM265, W747

        K-1(I)   #23. Short prelude (may be played
                      manuals only)

      L360

"Lord of the Dance" (Matt.)

      P302, UM261, W636

"Heal Us, Emmanuel, Hear Our Prayer" (Matt.)

      UM266 (PD)

        S-1   #149. Descant

        S-2   #67. Harmonization

        K-1(II) #55. Prelude/postlude (manuals
                      only)

"O For a Thousand Tongues to Sing" (Ps., Matt.)

      B216, E493, F349, L559, P466, UM57 (PD)

        S-1   #33-38. Various treatments

"O Jesus Christ, May Grateful Hymns Be Rising"
   (Matt.)

      E590, L427, P424, W646

"Draw Us in the Spirit's Tether" (Matt., Communion)

      P504, UM632, W731

        S-1   #337. Performance note

C– "My Hope Is Built" (Ps., Rom.)

      B406, F92, L293, P379, UM368 (PD)

        S-2   #171. Trumpet descant
                  #172. Descant

      L294 (PD)

        H-1   #80. Harmonization

Vocal Solos

"Assurance" (Gen., Rom., Matt.)

  V-7   p. 45

"We Walk with God" (Gen., Matt.)

  V-7   p. 42

Anthems

"Rock-a My Soul" (Gen.)
arr. Wallace Heaton
Theodore Presser 312-40566
SATB *a cappella*

"The God of Abraham Praise" (Gen.)
arr. Gerhard Krapf
Augsburg 11-1824
Two-part mixed chorus with keyboard

"A Festive Psalm" (Ps.)
Eugene Butler
Carl Fischer CM 8078
SATB with keyboard and optional children's choir

"What Does It Mean to Be a Christian?" (Matt.)
John Carter and Mary Kay Beall
Hope Publishing PP 127
Three-part mixed chorus, congregation, and keyboard

Hymn Anthem Suggestions

"He Leadeth Me: O Blessed Thought" (Gen.)
52IHA   #21
"Lord of the Dance" (Matt.)
52IHA   #31

Other Suggestions

A celebration of music ministry may be celebrated on this day in relationship to the psalm.

Hymn Idea: If your congregation is not familiar with "What Does the Lord Require" (E605, P405, UM441, W624), you may ask them to sing only on the final four measures ("Do justly, . . .") of each stanza.

Genesis 18:1-15

[1]The LORD appeared to Abraham by the oaks of Mamre, as he sat at the entrance of his tent in the heat of the day. [2]He looked up and saw three men standing near him. When he saw them, he ran from the tent entrance to meet them, and bowed down to the ground. [3]He said, "My lord, if I find favor with you, do not pass by your servant. [4]Let a little water be brought, and wash your feet, and rest yourselves under the tree. [5]Let me bring a little bread, that you may refresh yourselves, and after that you may pass on— since you have come to your servant." So they said, "Do as you have said." [6]And Abraham hastened into the tent to Sarah, and said, "Make ready quickly three measures of choice flour, knead it, and make cakes." [7]Abraham ran to the herd, and took a calf, tender and good, and gave it to the servant, who hastened to prepare it. [8]Then he took curds and milk and the calf that he had prepared, and set it before them; and he stood by them under the tree while they ate.

[9]They said to him, "Where is your wife Sarah?" And he said, "There, in the tent." [10]Then one said, "I will surely return to you in due season, and your wife Sarah shall have a son." And Sarah was listening at the tent entrance behind him. [11]Now Abraham and Sarah were old, advanced in age; it had ceased to be with Sarah after the manner of women. [12]So Sarah laughed to herself, saying, "After I have grown old, and my husband is old, shall I have pleasure?" [13]The LORD said to Abraham, "Why did Sarah laugh, and say, 'Shall I indeed bear a child, now that I am old?' [14]Is anything too wonderful for the LORD? At the set time I will return to you, in due season, and Sarah shall have a son." [15]But Sarah denied, saying, "I did not laugh"; for she was afraid. He said, "Oh yes, you did laugh."

Psalm 116:1-2, 12-19

[1]I love the LORD, because he has heard my voice and my supplications. [2]Because he inclined his ear to me, therefore I will call on him as long as I live.

[12]What shall I return to the LORD for all his bounty to me? [13]I will lift up the cup of salvation and call on the name of the LORD, [14]I will pay my vows to the LORD in the presence of all his people. [15]Precious in the sight of the LORD is the death of his faithful ones. [16]O LORD, I am your servant; I am your servant, the child of your serving girl. You have loosed my bonds. [17]I will offer to you a thanksgiving sacrifice and call on the name of the LORD. [18]I will pay my vows to the LORD in the presence of all his people, [19]in the courts of the house of the LORD, in your midst, O Jerusalem. Praise the LORD!

Romans 5:1-8

[1]Therefore, since we are justified by faith, we have peace with God through our Lord Jesus Christ, [2]through whom we have obtained access to this grace in which we stand; and we boast in our hope of sharing the glory of God. [3]And not only that, but we also boast in our sufferings, knowing that suffering produces endurance, [4]and endurance produces character, and character produces hope, [5]and hope does not disappoint us, because God's love has been poured into our hearts through the Holy Spirit that has been given to us.

[6]For while we were still weak, at the right time Christ died for the ungodly. [7]Indeed, rarely will anyone die for a righteous person—though perhaps for a good person someone might actually dare to die. [8]But God proves his love for us in that while we still were sinners Christ died for us.

Matthew 9:35–10:8 (9-23)

[35]Then Jesus went about all the cities and villages, teaching in their synagogues, and proclaiming the good news of the kingdom, and curing every disease and every sickness. [36]When he saw the crowds, he had compassion for them, because they were harassed and helpless, like sheep without a shepherd. [37]Then he said to his disciples, "The harvest is plentiful, but the laborers are few; [38]therefore ask the Lord of the harvest to send out laborers into his harvest."

[1]Then Jesus summoned his twelve disciples and gave them authority over unclean spirits, to cast them out, and to cure every disease and every sickness. [2]These are the names of the twelve apostles: first, Simon, also known as Peter, and his brother Andrew; James son of Zebedee, and his brother John; [3]Philip and Bartholomew; Thomas and Matthew the tax collector; James son of Alphaeus, and Thaddaeus; [4]Simon the Cananaean, and Judas Iscariot, the one who betrayed him.

[5]These twelve Jesus sent out with the following instructions: "Go nowhere among the Gentiles, and enter no town of the Samaritans, [6]but go rather to the lost sheep of the house of Israel. [7]As you go, proclaim the good news, 'The kingdom of heaven has come near.' [8]Cure the sick, raise the dead, cleanse the lepers, cast out demons. You received without payment; give without payment."

Hymn and Keyboard Suggestions

O– "Praise to the Lord, the Almighty" (Ps.)

B14 (PD), E390, F337, L543, P482, UM139, W547

H-1	#88. Harmonization in G major
H-2	p. 18. Harmonization with descant
S-1	#218-22. Various treatments
K-4	p. 140. Various keyboard treatments, through p. 146
K-8	p. 10. Interlude
K-14	p. 44. Piano prelude/postlude

"The God of Abraham Praise" (Gen.)

B34, E401, L544, P488, UM116 (PD), W537

H-1	#44. Harmonization
S-1	#211. Harmonization

"Come, My Way, My Truth, My Life" (Ps.)

E487, L513, UM164 (PD), W569

K-12	p. 35. Prelude/meditation

"O Thou, My Soul, Return in Peace" (Ps.)

P228 (PD)

S-2	#116-17. Harmonizations
K-6	p. 12. Prelude/meditation/postlude

"'Tis Finished! The Messiah Dies" (Rom.)

B148, UM282 (PD)

"In the Cross of Christ I Glory" (Rom.)

B554, E441, F251, L104, P84, UM295 (PD)

H-1	#51. Harmonization
S-1	#276-77. Harmonization with descant
K-2	p. 23. Short prelude/postlude

E442

"When I Survey the Wondrous Cross" (Rom.)

B144, F258, P101, UM298 (PD)

H-1	#36. Harmonization
S-1	#155. Descant
K-1 (II)	#31. Prelude/meditation
K-15	p. 73. Piano prelude/meditation

E474, L482, P100, UM299 (PD), W433

H-1	#19. Harmonization
S-1	#288. Transposition to E-flat major

"Blessed Assurance" (Rom.)

B334, F67, P341, UM369 (PD)

S-1	#24. Harmonization
K-15	p. 38. Piano prelude/postlude

"Standing on the Promises" (Rom.)

B335, UM374 (PD)

"O Love That Wilt Not Let Me Go" (Rom.)

B292, F404, L324, P384, UM480 (PD)

"Rescue the Perishing" (Matt., Rom.)

B559, F661, UM591 (PD)

K-8	p. 21. Introduction

"Freely, Freely" (Matt.)

B273, UM389

S-1	#135. Vocal descant idea

C– "Lord, You Give the Great Commission" (Matt.)

P429, UM584, W470

S-1	#4. Instrumental descant
	#5. Vocal descant

E528

C– "Here I Am, Lord" (Matt.)

P525, UM593

Vocal Solos

"O Love, That Wilt Not Let Me Go" (Rom.)

V-7   p. 49

"O For a Thousand Tongues to Sing" (Rom.)

V-1   p. 32

"Just As I Am" (Rom.)

V-3   p. 23

"Take My Life and Let It Be Consecrated" (Matt.)

V-3   p. 28

Anthems

"The Heavens Are Telling" from *The Creation* (Ps.)

F. J. Haydn

E. C. Schirmer 1188

SATB with STB trio and keyboard

"Alleluia" (Rom.)

Randall Thompson

E. C. Schirmer 1786

SATB *a cappella*

"Lord, Here Am I" (Matt.)

John Ness Beck

Beckenhorst Press BP1210

Two-part with keyboard (SATB available)

Hymn Anthem Suggestions

"Freely, Freely" (Rom., Matt.)

52IHA   #16

"How Like a Gentle Spirit" (Matt.)

52IHA   #24

Other Suggestions

Scripture response: B474, F488, UM418, stanza 3. "We Are Climbing Jacob's Ladder" (Rom.)

Response: B273, UM389. "Freely, Freely" (Matt.)

Genesis 21:8-21

[8]The child grew, and was weaned; and Abraham made a great feast on the day that Isaac was weaned. [9]But Sarah saw the son of Hagar the Egyptian, whom she had borne to Abraham, playing with her son Isaac. [10]So she said to Abraham, "Cast out this slave woman with her son; for the son of this slave woman shall not inherit along with my son Isaac." [11]The matter was very distressing to Abraham on account of his son. [12]But God said to Abraham, "Do not be distressed because of the boy and because of your slave woman; whatever Sarah says to you, do as she tells you, for it is through Isaac that offspring shall be named for you. [13]As for the son of the slave woman, I will make a nation of him also, because he is your offspring." [14]So Abraham rose early in the morning, and took bread and a skin of water, and gave it to Hagar, putting it on her shoulder, along with the child, and sent her away. And she departed, and wandered about in the wilderness of Beer-sheba.

[15]When the water in the skin was gone, she cast the child under one of the bushes. [16]Then she went and sat down opposite him a good way off, about the distance of a bowshot; for she said, "Do not let me look on the death of the child." And as she sat opposite him, she lifted up her voice and wept. [17]And God heard the voice of the boy; and the angel of God called to Hagar from heaven, and said to her, "What troubles you, Hagar? Do not be afraid; for God has heard the voice of the boy where he is. [18]Come, lift up the boy and hold him fast with your hand, for I will make a great nation of him." [19]Then God opened her eyes and she saw a well of water. She went, and filled the skin with water, and gave the boy a drink.

[20]God was with the boy, and he grew up; he lived in the wilderness, and became an expert with the bow. [21]He lived in the wilderness of Paran; and his mother got a wife for him from the land of Egypt.

Psalm 86:1-10, 16-17 (or Psalm 17)

[1]Incline your ear, O LORD, and answer me, for I am poor and needy. [2]Preserve my life, for I am devoted to you; save your servant who trusts in you. You are my God; [3]be gracious to me, O Lord, for to you do I cry all day long. [4]Gladden the soul of your servant, for to you, O Lord, I lift up my soul. [5]For you, O Lord, are good and forgiving, abounding in steadfast love to all who call on you. [6]Give ear, O LORD, to my prayer; listen to my cry of supplication. [7]In the day of my trouble I call on you, for you will answer me. [8]There is none like you among the gods, O Lord, nor are there any works like yours. [9]All the nations you have made shall come and bow down before you, O Lord, and shall glorify your name. [10]For you are great and do wondrous things; you alone are God.

[16]Turn to me and be gracious to me; give your strength to your servant; save the child of your serving girl. [17]Show me a sign of your favor, so that those who hate me may see it and be put to shame, because you, LORD, have helped me and comforted me.

Romans 6:1b-11

[1b]Should we continue in sin in order that grace may abound? [2]By no means! How can we who died to sin go on living in it? [3]Do you not know that all of us who have been baptized into Christ Jesus were baptized into his death? [4]Therefore we have been buried with him by baptism into death, so that, just as Christ was raised from the dead by the glory of the Father, so we too might walk in newness of life.

[5]For if we have been united with him in a death like his, we will certainly be united with him in a resurrection like his. [6]We know that our old self was crucified with him so that the body of sin might be destroyed, and we might no longer be enslaved to sin. [7]For whoever has died is freed from sin. [8]But if we have died with Christ, we believe that we will also live with him. [9]We know that Christ, being raised from the dead, will never die again; death no longer has dominion over him. [10]The death he died, he died to sin, once for all; but the life he lives, he lives to God. [11]So you also must consider yourselves dead to sin and alive to God in Christ Jesus.

Matthew 10:24-39

[24]"A disciple is not above the teacher, nor a slave above the master; [25]it is enough for the disciple to be like the teacher, and the slave like the master. If they have called the master of the house Beelzebul, how much more will they malign those of his household!

[26]"So have no fear of them; for nothing is covered up that will not be uncovered, and nothing secret that will not become known. [27]What I say to you in the dark, tell in the light; and what you hear whispered, proclaim from the housetops. [28]Do not fear those who kill the body but cannot kill the soul; rather fear him who can destroy both soul and body in hell. [29]Are not two sparrows sold for a penny? Yet not one of them will fall to the ground apart from your Father. [30]And even the hairs of your head are all counted. [31]So do not be afraid; you are of more value than many sparrows.

[32]"Everyone therefore who acknowledges me before others, I also will acknowledge before my Father in heaven; [33]but whoever denies me before others, I also will deny before my Father in heaven.

[34]"Do not think that I have come to bring peace to the earth; I have not come to bring peace, but a sword. [35]For I have come to set a man against his father, and a daughter against her mother, and a daughter-in-law against her mother-in-law; [36]and one's foes will be members of one's own household. [37]Whoever loves father or mother more than me is not worthy of me; and whoever loves son or daughter more than me is not worthy of me; [38]and whoever does not take up the cross and follow me is not worthy of me. [39]Those who find their life will lose it, and those who lose their life for my sake will find it."

Hymn and Keyboard Suggestions

O– "Sing with All the Saints in Glory" (Rom.)
      UM702 (PD), W467
          S-1   #173-76. Various treatments
          K-8   p. 23. Harmonization
          K-13   p. 16. Piano prelude/postlude
          K-15   p. 122. Piano prelude/postlude

O– "We Know That Christ Is Raised" (Rom.)
      E296, L189, P495, UM610, W721
          S-1   #118-27. Various treatments

"O Master, Let Me Walk with Thee" (Gen., Ps.)
      B279, E660, F442, L492, P357, UM430 (PD)
          S-2   #118. Descant
      E659

"I Need Thee Every Hour" (Gen., Ps.)
      B450, F443, UM397 (PD)

"Children of the Heavenly Father" (Gen., Matt.)
      B55, F89, L474, UM141
          S-2   #180-85. Various treatments
          K-8   p. 14. Short prelude/meditation

"Alleluia, Alleluia" (Rom.)
      B170, E178, P106, UM162, W441
          S-1   #14. Descant

"Baptized in Water" (Rom.)
      B362, P492, W720
          S-1   #50. Flute descant
                   #51. Descant
      E294

"Nearer, My God, to Thee" (Rom.)
      B458, UM528 (PD)
          H-1   #75. Harmonization

"This Is the Spirit's Entry Now" (Rom., Baptism)
      UM608
          S-1   #33-38. Various treatments
      L195, W722

"It Is Well with My Soul" (Matt., Rom.)
      B410, F495, L346, UM377 (PD)
          K-13   p. 21. Piano prelude/meditation
          K-15   p. 126. Piano prelude/meditation

"Take Up Thy Cross" (Matt.)
      UM415
          S-1   #141. Harmonization
                   #142-43. Descant and transposition
                        in A major
      B494, E675, L398, P393, W634

C– "Stand Up, Stand Up for Jesus" (Matt.)
      B485, E561, F616, L389, UM514 (PD)
          H-1   #90. Harmonization in A major
          S-2   #192-94. Various treatments
          K-1(IV) #92. Prelude/postlude
      B487

C– "Where He Leads Me" (Matt.)
      B288, F607, UM338 (PD)

Vocal Solos

"Lord, to Thee Do I Lift My Soul" (Ps.)
  V-8   p. 38
"Jesus, Lover of My Soul" (Gen., Ps.)
  V-1   p. 37
"It Is Well with My Soul" (Matt., Rom.)
  V-3   p. 3
"O Love, That Wilt Not Let Me Go" (Matt.)
  V-7   p. 49

Anthems

"His Eye Is on the Sparrow" (Gen.)
  in *Songs of Zion*
Abingdon Press
SATB *a cappella*

"Christ Is Risen!" (Rom.)
Jan Sanborn
Fred Bock B-G0368
SATB with organ

"Lord, Here Am I" (Matt.)
John Ness Beck
Beckenhorst Press BP1210
Two-part with keyboard (SATB available)

Hymn Anthem Suggestions

"Children of the Heavenly Father" (Gen., Matt.)
52IHA #7
"Alleluia, Alleluia" (Rom.)
52IHA #2

Other Suggestions

Prayer: UM531. For Overcoming Adversity (Gen.)
Response: B269 (PD), E676, F48, P394, UM375, W608,
  refrain. "There Is a Balm in Gilead" (Gen.)
Response: B71, UM143. "On Eagle's Wings" (Gen., Ps.)
Confession Response: B43, E651, F6, L554, P293, UM144,
  stanza 3. "This Is My Father's World"
Surround the scripture readings with the hymn "This Is My
  Father's World." Sing stanza 1 before the reading, stanza
  3 after Romans, and stanza 2 after Matthew.

Genesis 22:1-14

[1]After these things God tested Abraham. He said to him, "Abraham!" And he said, "Here I am." [2]He said, "Take your son, your only son Isaac, whom you love, and go to the land of Moriah, and offer him there as a burnt offering on one of the mountains that I shall show you." [3]So Abraham rose early in the morning, saddled his donkey, and took two of his young men with him, and his son Isaac; he cut the wood for the burnt offering, and set out and went to the place in the distance that God had shown him. [4]On the third day Abraham looked up and saw the place far away. [5]Then Abraham said to his young men, "Stay here with the donkey; the boy and I will go over there; we will worship, and then we will come back to you." [6]Abraham took the wood of the burnt offering and laid it on his son Isaac, and he himself carried the fire and the knife. So the two of them walked on together. [7]Isaac said to his father Abraham, "Father!" And he said, "Here I am, my son." He said, "The fire and the wood are here, but where is the lamb for a burnt offering?" [8]Abraham said, "God himself will provide the lamb for a burnt offering, my son." So the two of them walked on together.

[9]When they came to the place that God had shown him, Abraham built an altar there and laid the wood in order. He bound his son Isaac, and laid him on the altar, on top of the wood. [10]Then Abraham reached out his hand and took the knife to kill his son. [11]But the angel of the LORD called to him from heaven, and said, "Abraham, Abraham!" And he said, "Here I am." [12]He said, "Do not lay your hand on the boy or do anything to him; for now I know that you fear God, since you have not withheld your son, your only son, from me." [13]And Abraham looked up and saw a ram, caught in a thicket by its horns. Abraham went and took the ram and offered it up as a burnt offering instead of his son. [14]So Abraham called that place "The LORD will provide"; as it is said to this day, "On the mount of the LORD it shall be provided."

Psalm 13

[1]How long, O LORD? Will you forget me forever?
   How long will you hide your face from me?
[2]How long must I bear pain in my soul,
   and have sorrow in my heart all day long?
How long shall my enemy be exalted over me?
[3]Consider and answer me, O LORD my God!
Give light to my eyes, or I will sleep the sleep of death,
[4]and my enemy will say, "I have prevailed";
   my foes will rejoice because I am shaken.
[5]But I trusted in your steadfast love;
   my heart shall rejoice in your salvation.
[6]I will sing to the LORD,
   because he has dealt bountifully with me.

Romans 6:12-23

[12]Therefore, do not let sin exercise dominion in your mortal bodies, to make you obey their passions. [13]No longer present your members to sin as instruments of wickedness, but present yourselves to God as those who have been brought from death to life, and present your members to God as instruments of righteousness. [14]For sin will have no dominion over you, since you are not under law but under grace.

[15]What then? Should we sin because we are not under law but under grace? By no means! [16]Do you not know that if you present yourselves to anyone as obedient slaves, you are slaves of the one whom you obey, either of sin, which leads to death, or of obedience, which leads to righteousness? [17]But thanks be to God that you, having once been slaves of sin, have become obedient from the heart to the form of teaching to which you were entrusted, [18]and that you, having been set free from sin, have become slaves of righteousness. [19]I am speaking in human terms because of your natural limitations. For just as you once presented your members as slaves to impurity and to greater and greater iniquity, so now present your members as slaves to righteousness for sanctification.

[20]When you were slaves of sin, you were free in regard to righteousness. [21]So what advantage did you then get from the things of which you now are ashamed? The end of those things is death. [22]But now that you have been freed from sin and enslaved to God, the advantage you get is sanctification. The end is eternal life. [23]For the wages of sin is death, but the free gift of God is eternal life in Christ Jesus our Lord.

Matthew 10:40-42

[40]"Whoever welcomes you welcomes me, and whoever welcomes me welcomes the one who sent me. [41]Whoever welcomes a prophet in the name of a prophet will receive a prophet's reward; and whoever welcomes a righteous person in the name of a righteous person will receive the reward of the righteous; [42]and whoever gives even a cup of cold water to one of these little ones in the name of a disciple—truly I tell you, none of these will lose their reward."

Hymn and Keyboard Suggestions

O– "Lord God, Your Love Has Called Us Here" (Rom.)
    UM579
        S-1   #57-61. Various treatments
    P353

O– "Faith of Our Fathers" (Gen.)
    B352, F526, L500, UM710 (PD), W571
        H-1   #60. Harmonization in G major

"By Gracious Powers" (Gen., Ps.)
    E695 or E696, P342, UM517, W577

"If Thou But Suffer God to Guide Thee" (Ps.)
    B57, E635, L453, P282, UM142 (PD)
        K-5   p. 141. Harmonization in A minor
        K-1(IV)   #94. Prelude/meditation
        K-5   p. 141. Various keyboard treatments,
                          through p. 152

"Amazing Grace" (Rom.)
    B330, E671, F107, L448, P280, UM378 (PD),
    W583
        S-2   #5-7. Various treatments
        K-15   p. 146. Piano prelude/meditation

"Breathe on Me, Breath of God" (Rom.)
    W725
        S-1   #298. Harmonization
                  #299. Harmonization
        K-2   p. 27. Short prelude/postlude
        K-9   p. 47. Prelude/meditation
    E508, L488 (PD)
    B241, F161, P316, UM420 (PD)

"Creator of the Stars of Night" (Rom.)
    E60, L323, P4, UM692 (PD), W368
        S-2   #41. Handbell arrangement

"Make Me a Captive, Lord" (Rom.)
    UM421 (PD)
        H-1   #55. Harmonization in D major
        H-2   p. 6. Harmonization with descant in
                          D major
        S-1   #86-88. Various treatments
        K-2   p. 7. Short harmonization/pre-
                          lude/meditation/postlude
        K-13   p. 16. Piano prelude/postlude
    B278 (PD), P378

"O Jesus, I Have Promised" (Rom.)
    B276, F402, P388, UM396
        S-2   #9. Descant
    L503
        H-1   #64. Harmonization
        S-1   #243. Harmonization
        K-1(II)   #63. Prelude/meditation
    E655, P389

"Jesu, Jesu" (Matt., Rom.)
    B501, E602, P367, UM432, W431
        S-1   #63. Vocal part

"Cuando El Pobre" ("When the Poor Ones") (Matt.)
    P407, UM434

"There's a Spirit in the Air" (Matt.)
    UM192
        S-2   #144. Orff instrument arrangement
        K-1(III) #70. Prelude/postlude
        K-12   p. 6. Prelude/meditation
        K-12   p. 18. Postlude
    B393, P433, W531

C– "Where Cross the Crowded Ways of Life" (Matt.)
    E609, F665, L429, P408, UM427 (PD)
        S-1   #141. Harmonization
                  #142-43. Descant and transposition
                          in A major

Vocal Solos

"O Lord, Our God" (Ps.)
V-10   p. 24
"Amazing Grace" (Rom.)
V-3   p. 8
"When Mercy Seasons Justice" (Independence Day)
V-6   p. 50

Anthems

"A Psalm of David" (Ps.)
Robert Starer
Theodore Presser 312-40477
SATB with keyboard

"How Long Wilt Thou Forget Me, O Lord" (Ps.)
(A Psalm and a Proverb)
Ned Rorem
E. C. Schirmer 2674
SATB with piano or string quartet

Hymn Anthem Suggestions

"O Thou, in Whose Presence" (Ps.)
52IHA #38
"Cuando El Pobre" ("When the Poor Ones") (Matt.)
52IHA #12

Other Suggestions

Response: B501, E602, P367, UM432, W431, refrain. "Jesu,
  Jesu"
Response: B317, F629, UM337, refrain. "Only Trust Him"
Hymn Idea: "Amazing Grace." Vary the way each stanza is
  sung. Sing *a cappella*, led by a song leader. Allow one half
  of the congregation to listen to the other half sing.

Genesis 24:34-38, 42-49, 58-67

[34]So he said, "I am Abraham's servant. [35]The LORD has greatly blessed my master, and he has become wealthy; he has given him flocks and herds, silver and gold, male and female slaves, camels and donkeys. [36]And Sarah my master's wife bore a son to my master when she was old; and he has given him all that he has. [37]My master made me swear, saying, 'You shall not take a wife for my son from the daughters of the Canaanites, in whose land I live; [38]but you shall go to my father's house, to my kindred, and get a wife for my son.'

[42]"I came today to the spring, and said, 'O LORD, the God of my master Abraham, if now you will only make successful the way I am going! [43]I am standing here by the spring of water; let the young woman who comes out to draw, to whom I shall say, "Please give me a little water from your jar to drink," [44]and who will say to me, "Drink, and I will draw for your camels also"—let her be the woman whom the LORD has appointed for my master's son.'

[45]"Before I had finished speaking in my heart, there was Rebekah coming out with her water jar on her shoulder; and she went down to the spring, and drew. I said to her, 'Please let me drink.' [46]She quickly let down her jar from her shoulder, and said, 'Drink, and I will also water your camels.' So I drank, and she also watered the camels. [47]Then I asked her, 'Whose daughter are you?' She said, 'The daughter of Bethuel, Nahor's son, whom Milcah bore to him.' So I put the ring on her nose, and the bracelets on her arms. [48]Then I bowed my head and worshiped the LORD, and blessed the LORD, the God of my master Abraham, who had led me by the right way to obtain the daughter of my master's kinsman for his son. [49]Now then, if you will deal loyally and truly with my master, tell me; and if not, tell me, so that I may turn either to the right hand or to the left."

[58]And they called Rebekah, and said to her, "Will you go with this man?" She said, "I will." [59]So they sent away their sister Rebekah and her nurse along with Abraham's servant and his men. [60]And they blessed Rebekah and said to her, "May you, our sister, become thousands of myriads; may your offspring gain possession of the gates of their foes." [61]Then Rebekah and her maids rose up, mounted the camels, and followed the man; thus the servant took Rebekah, and went his way.

[62]Now Isaac had come from Beer-lahai-roi, and was settled in the Negeb. [63]Isaac went out in the evening to walk in the field; and looking up, he saw camels coming. [64]And Rebekah looked up, and when she saw Isaac, she slipped quickly from the camel, [65]and said to the servant, "Who is the man over there, walking in the field to meet us?" The servant said, "It is my master." So she took her veil and covered herself. [66]And the servant told Isaac all the things that he had done. [67]Then Isaac brought her into his mother Sarah's tent. He took Rebekah, and she became his wife; and he loved her. So Isaac was comforted after his mother's death.

Psalm 45:10-17

[10]Hear, O daughter, consider and incline your ear; forget your people and your father's house, [11]and the king will desire your beauty. Since he is your lord, bow to him; [12]the people of Tyre will seek your favor with gifts, the richest of the people [13]with all kinds of wealth. The princess is decked in her chamber with gold-woven robes; [14]in many-colored robes she is led to the king; behind her the virgins, her companions, follow. [15]With joy and gladness they are led along as they enter the palace of the king. [16]In the place of ancestors you, O king, shall have sons; you will make them princes in all the earth. [17]I will cause your name to be celebrated in all generations; therefore the peoples will praise you forever and ever.

Romans 7:15-25a

[15]I do not understand my own actions. For I do not do what I want, but I do the very thing I hate. [16]Now if I do what I do not want, I agree that the law is good. [17]But in fact it is no longer I that do it, but sin that dwells within me. [18]For I know that nothing good dwells within me, that is, in my flesh. I can will what is right, but I cannot do it. [19]For I do not do the good I want, but the evil I do not want is what I do. [20]Now if I do what I do not want, it is no longer I that do it, but sin that dwells within me.

[21]So I find it to be a law that when I want to do what is good, evil lies close at hand. [22]For I delight in the law of God in my inmost self, [23]but I see in my members another law at war with the law of my mind, making me captive to the law of sin that dwells in my members. [24]Wretched man that I am! Who will rescue me from this body of death? [25]Thanks be to God through Jesus Christ our Lord!

Matthew 11:16-19, 25-30

[16]"But to what will I compare this generation? It is like children sitting in the marketplaces and calling to one another, [17]'We played the flute for you, and you did not dance; we wailed, and you did not mourn.' [18]For John came neither eating nor drinking, and they say, 'He has a demon'; [19]the Son of Man came eating and drinking, and they say, 'Look, a glutton and a drunkard, a friend of tax collectors and sinners!' Yet wisdom is vindicated by her deeds."

[25]At that time Jesus said, "I thank you, Father, Lord of heaven and earth, because you have hidden these things from the wise and the intelligent and have revealed them to infants; [26]yes, Father, for such was your gracious will. [27]All things have been handed over to me by my Father; and no one knows the Son except the Father, and no one knows the Father except the Son and anyone to whom the Son chooses to reveal him.

[28]"Come to me, all you that are weary and are carrying heavy burdens, and I will give you rest. [29]Take my yoke upon you, and learn from me; for I am gentle and humble in heart, and you will find rest for your souls. [30]For my yoke is easy, and my burden is light."

Hymn and Keyboard Suggestions

O– "Come, Ye Sinners, Poor and Needy" (Matt.)
    B323 (PD), UM340, W756
      S-1   #283. Choral harmonization

O– "Your Love, O God, Has Called Us Here" (Gen., Ps.)
    B509
      H-1   #74. Harmonization
      S-1   #52. Descant
      K-8   p. 4. Prelude/meditation
    E353
      S-2   #191. Harmonization
    UM647
      S-2   #44. Descant

"When Love Is Found" (Gen., Ps., Communion)
    UM643, W745

"O Morning Star, How Fair and Bright" (Ps.)
    E497, L76, P69, UM247, W390
      K-1(IV) #97. Prelude
      K-3   p. 32. Short postlude
      K-5   p. 159. Various keyboard treatments, through p. 173

"Spirit of God, Descend upon My Heart" (Rom.)
    B245, F147, L486, P326, UM500 (PD)
      S-2   #125-28. Various treatments
      K-8   p. 24. Prelude/meditation

"Blessed Jesus, at Thy Word" (Rom.)
    E440, P454, UM596 (PD)
      S-2   #112-14. Various treatments
      K-1(II) #51. Prelude/postlude/meditation
      K-4   p. 135. Various keyboard treatments, through p. 139

"Lord, I Want to Be a Christian" (Rom.)
    B489, F421, P372 (PD), UM402
      K-7   p. 10. Prelude

"Love Divine, All Loves Excelling" (Rom.)
    B208, F21, UM384 (PD)
      H-1   #48. Harmonization in A major
      S-1   #41. Descant
            #42. Harmonization
    E657, L315, P376, W588 (PD)
      S-1   #168-71. Various treatments
      K-2   p. 12. Short prelude
      K-9   p. 7. Prelude/postlude

"Make Me a Captive, Lord" (Rom.)
    UM421 (PD)
      H-1   #55. Harmonization in D major
      H-2   p. 6. Harmonization with descant in D major
      S-1   #86-88. Various treatments
      K-2   p. 7. Short harmonization/prelude/meditation/postlude
      K-13 p. 16. Piano prelude/postlude
    B278 (PD), P378

"How Sweet the Name of Jesus Sounds" (Matt.)
    E644 (PD), F229, L345, W610
      H-1   #73. Harmonization in E-flat major
      S-2   #162. Harmonization
      K-1(III) #77. Prelude/meditation (manuals only)
    B453 (PD)

"I Heard the Voice of Jesus Say" (Matt.)
    W607
      S-2   #100-103. Various treatments
    B551 (PD), E692, F51, L497

C– "Jesus Loves Me" (Matt.)
    B344 (PD), F226, P304, UM191

C– "God Hath Spoken by the Prophets" (Gen., Matt.)
    UM108 (PD)
      H-1   #81. Harmonization
      S-1   #109. Descant
            #110. Harmonization
    L238, W516

Vocal Solos

"Come Unto Me" (Matt.)
V-10   p. 60
"He Shall Feed His Flock" from *Messiah* (Matt.)
V-2
"There Is a Balm in Gilead" (Matt.)
V-5   p. 111

Anthems

"A Hymn to God the Father" (Rom.)
John Ness Beck
Beckenhorst BP1335-2
SATB with keyboard

"Have Mercy, Lord" (Rom.)
Cristobal Morales
Concordia
SATB

Hymn Anthem Suggestions

"Come, Ye Sinners, Poor and Needy" (Matt.)
52IHA #10
"Jesus Loves Me" (Matt.)
52IHA #28

Other Suggestions

Response: B60, E488, F468, P339, UM451. "Be Thou My Vision" (Matt.)
Canticle: UM646. "Canticle of Love" (Gen., Ps.)
Prayer: UM602. Concerning the Scriptures (Rom.)
Prayer: UM423. Finding Rest in God (Matt.)
Poem: UM595. Whether the Word Be Preached or Read (Rom.)

Genesis 25:19-34

[19]These are the descendants of Isaac, Abraham's son: Abraham was the father of Isaac, [20]and Isaac was forty years old when he married Rebekah, daughter of Bethuel the Aramean of Paddan-aram, sister of Laban the Aramean. [21]Isaac prayed to the LORD for his wife, because she was barren; and the LORD granted his prayer, and his wife Rebekah conceived. [22]The children struggled together within her; and she said, "If it is to be this way, why do I live?" So she went to inquire of the LORD. [23]And the LORD said to her,

> "Two nations are in your womb,
> and two peoples born of you
> shall be divided;
> the one shall be stronger than the other,
> the elder shall serve the younger."

[24]When her time to give birth was at hand, there were twins in her womb. [25]The first came out red, all his body like a hairy mantle; so they named him Esau. [26]Afterward his brother came out, with his hand gripping Esau's heel; so he was named Jacob. Isaac was sixty years old when she bore them.

[27]When the boys grew up, Esau was a skillful hunter, a man of the field, while Jacob was a quiet man, living in tents. [28]Isaac loved Esau, because he was fond of game; but Rebekah loved Jacob.

[29]Once when Jacob was cooking a stew, Esau came in from the field, and he was famished. [30]Esau said to Jacob, "Let me eat some of that red stuff, for I am famished!" (Therefore he was called Edom.) [31]Jacob said, "First sell me your birthright." [32]Esau said, "I am about to die; of what use is a birthright to me?" [33]Jacob said, "Swear to me first." So he swore to him, and sold his birthright to Jacob. [34]Then Jacob gave Esau bread and lentil stew, and he ate and drank, and rose and went his way. Thus Esau despised his birthright.

Psalm 119:105-112

[105]Your word is a lamp to my feet and a light to my path. [106]I have sworn an oath and confirmed it, to observe your righteous ordinances. [107]I am severely afflicted; give me life, O LORD, according to your word. [108]Accept my offerings of praise, O LORD, and teach me your ordinances. [109]I hold my life in my hand continually, but I do not forget your law. [110]The wicked have laid a snare for me, but I do not stray from your precepts. [111]Your decrees are my heritage forever; they are the joy of my heart. [112]I incline my heart to perform your statutes forever, to the end.

Romans 8:1-11

[1]There is therefore now no condemnation for those who are in Christ Jesus. [2]For the law of the Spirit of life in Christ Jesus has set you free from the law of sin and of death. [3]For God has done what the law, weakened by the flesh, could not do: by sending his own Son in the likeness of sinful flesh, and to deal with sin, he condemned sin in the flesh, [4]so that the just requirement of the law might be fulfilled in us, who walk not according to the flesh but according to the Spirit. [5]For those who live according to the flesh set their minds on the things of the flesh, but those who live according to the Spirit set their minds on the things of the Spirit. [6]To set the mind on the flesh is death, but to set the mind on the Spirit is life and peace. [7]For this reason the mind that is set on the flesh is hostile to God; it does not submit to God's law—indeed it cannot, [8]and those who are in the flesh cannot please God.

[9]But you are not in the flesh; you are in the Spirit, since the Spirit of God dwells in you. Anyone who does not have the Spirit of Christ does not belong to him. [10]But if Christ is in you, though the body is dead because of sin, the Spirit is life because of righteousness. [11]If the Spirit of him who raised Jesus from the dead dwells in you, he who raised Christ from the dead will give life to your mortal bodies also through his Spirit that dwells in you.

Matthew 13:1-9, 18-23

[1]That same day Jesus went out of the house and sat beside the sea. [2]Such great crowds gathered around him that he got into a boat and sat there, while the whole crowd stood on the beach. [3]And he told them many things in parables, saying: "Listen! A sower went out to sow. [4]And as he sowed, some seeds fell on the path, and the birds came and ate them up. [5]Other seeds fell on rocky ground, where they did not have much soil, and they sprang up quickly, since they had no depth of soil. [6]But when the sun rose, they were scorched; and since they had no root, they withered away. [7]Other seeds fell among thorns, and the thorns grew up and choked them. [8]Other seeds fell on good soil and brought forth grain, some a hundredfold, some sixty, some thirty. [9]Let anyone with ears listen!"

[18]"Hear then the parable of the sower. [19]When anyone hears the word of the kingdom and does not understand it, the evil one comes and snatches away what is sown in the heart; this is what was sown on the path. [20]As for what was sown on rocky ground, this is the one who hears the word and immediately receives it with joy; [21]yet such a person has no root, but endures only for a while, and when trouble or persecution arises on account of the word, that person immediately falls away. [22]As for what was sown among thorns, this is the one who hears the word, but the cares of the world and the lure of wealth choke the word, and it yields nothing. [23]But as for what was sown on good soil, this is the one who hears the word and understands it, who indeed bears fruit and yields, in one case a hundredfold, in another sixty, and in another thirty."

Hymn and Keyboard Suggestions

O– "O Word of God Incarnate" (Ps., Matt.)
　　　E632, L231, P327, UM598 (PD)
　　　　　H-1　　#64. Harmonization in D major
　　　　　S-1　　#243. Harmonization
　　　　　K-1(II)　#63. Prelude/meditation
　"Dear Lord, Lead Me Day by Day" (Ps.)
　　　B459, UM411
　　　　　S-2　　#45. Flute descant
　"O Lord, May Church and Home Combine" (Ps., Matt.)
　　　B510, UM695
　　　　　S-2　　#105. Flute/violin descant
　　　　　　　　#106. Harmonization
　　　　　K-8　　p. 22. Prelude/meditation
　"Be Thou My Vision" (Rom.)
　　　B60, E488, F468, P339, UM451
　　　　　S-1　　#319. Arrangement for organ and
　　　　　　　　voices in canon
　　　　　K-12　p. 9. Prelude/meditation
　"Alas! and Did My Savior Bleed" (Rom.)
　　　B145, F274, L98, P78, UM294 (PD)
　　　　　S-2　　#116-17. Harmonizations
　　　　　K-6　　p. 12. Prelude/meditation/postlude
　　　B139, UM359 (PD)
　"Breathe on Me, Breath of God" (Rom.)
　　　W725
　　　　　S-1　　#298. Harmonization
　　　　　　　　#299. Harmonization
　　　　　K-2　　p. 27. Short prelude/postlude
　　　　　K-9　　p. 47. Prelude/meditation
　　　B241, F161, P316, UM420 (PD)
　　　E508, L488
　"Every Time I Feel the Spirit" (Rom.)
　　　P315, UM404
　"O Come and Dwell in Me" (Rom.)
　　　UM388 (PD)
　　　　　S-1　　#306-8. Various treatments
　　　　　K-1(III)　#64. Prelude/meditation
　"Come, Ye Thankful People, Come" (Matt.)
　　　B637, E290, F392, L407, P551, UM694 (PD),
　　　W759
　　　　　S-1　　#302. Harmonization with descant
　　　　　　　　#303. Harmonization
　　　　　K-1(III)　#76. Prelude/postlude (manuals
　　　　　　　　only)
　　　　　K-2　　p. 30. Short prelude/postlude
C– "O Jesus, I Have Promised" (Matt.)
　　　B276, F402, P388, UM396
　　　　　S-2　　#9. Descant
　　　L503
　　　　　H-1　　#64. Harmonization
　　　　　S-1　　#243. Harmonization
　　　　　K-1(II)　#63. Prelude/meditation
　　　E655, P389

Vocal Solos

"Every Time I Feel the Spirit" (Rom.)
V-5　　　　p. 5
"Spirit of Faith Come Down" (Rom.)
V-1　　　　p. 43
"Be Thou My Vision" (Rom.)
V-3　　　　p. 13

Anthems

"O Master, Let Me Walk with Thee" (Ps.)
Gilbert M. Martin
Hinshaw Music HMC-1031
SATB with keyboard

"Come Share the Spirit" (Rom.)
Kent Schneider (arr. John Wilson)
Agape AG 7236
SATB with keyboard and/or varied instruments

"Parable of the Sower" (Matt.)
Don McAfee
General Music, no #
SATB *a cappella*

Hymn Anthem Suggestions

"I Want to Walk as a Child of the Light" (Rom., Matt.)
52IHA　　#27
"Cantemos al Señor" ("Let's Sing unto the Lord")
52IHA　　#5

Other Suggestions

　This Matthean parable lends itself to a dramatic rendering, easily enacted by children or youth for an informal summer worship experience. The drama can be enacted by only one sower or as many as a dozen persons, acting as sower, seeds, birds, and thorns.
Introit: P315, UM404. "Every Time I Feel the Spirit" (Rom.)
Words of Assurance: Rom. 8:1
Prayer: UM146. At the Birth of a Child (Gen.)
Prayer: UM493. Three Things We Prayer (Ps.)
Response: UM473. "Lead Me Lord" (Ps. 25)

Genesis 28:10-19a

[10]Jacob left Beer-sheba and went toward Haran. [11]He came to a certain place and stayed there for the night, because the sun had set. Taking one of the stones of the place, he put it under his head and lay down in that place. [12]And he dreamed that there was a ladder set up on the earth, the top of it reaching to heaven; and the angels of God were ascending and descending on it. [13]And the LORD stood beside him and said, "I am the LORD, the God of Abraham your father and the God of Isaac; the land on which you lie I will give to you and to your offspring; [14]and your offspring shall be like the dust of the earth, and you shall spread abroad to the west and to the east and to the north and to the south; and all the families of the earth shall be blessed in you and in your offspring. [15]Know that I am with you and will keep you wherever you go, and will bring you back to this land; for I will not leave you until I have done what I have promised you." [16]Then Jacob woke from his sleep and said, "Surely the LORD is in this place—and I did not know it!" [17]And he was afraid, and said, "How awesome is this place! This is none other than the house of God, and this is the gate of heaven."

[18]So Jacob rose early in the morning, and he took the stone that he had put under his head and set it up for a pillar and poured oil on the top of it. [19a]He called that place Bethel.

Psalm 139:1-12, 23-24

[1]O LORD, you have searched me and known me. [2]You know when I sit down and when I rise up; you discern my thoughts from far away. [3]You search out my path and my lying down, and are acquainted with all my ways. [4]Even before a word is on my tongue, O LORD, you know it completely. [5]You hem me in, behind and before, and lay your hand upon me. [6]Such knowledge is too wonderful for me; it is so high that I cannot attain it. [7]Where can I go from your spirit? Or where can I flee from your presence? [8]If I ascend to heaven, you are there; if I make my bed in Sheol, you are there. [9]If I take the wings of the morning and settle at the farthest limits of the sea, [10]even there your hand shall lead me, and your right hand shall hold me fast. [11]If I say, "Surely the darkness shall cover me, and the light around me become night," [12]even the darkness is not dark to you; the night is as bright as the day, for darkness is as light to you.

[23]Search me, O God, and know my heart; test me and know my thoughts. [24]See if there is any wicked way in me, and lead me in the way everlasting.

Romans 8:12-25

[12]So then, brothers and sisters, we are debtors, not to the flesh, to live according to the flesh—[13]for if you live according to the flesh, you will die; but if by the Spirit you put to death the deeds of the body, you will live. [14]For all who are led by the Spirit of God are children of God. [15]For you did not receive a spirit of slavery to fall back into fear, but you have received a spirit of adoption. When we cry, "Abba! Father!" [16]it is that very Spirit bearing witness with our spirit that we are children of God, [17]and if children, then heirs, heirs of God and joint heirs with Christ—if, in fact, we suffer with him so that we may also be glorified with him.

[18]I consider that the sufferings of this present time are not worth comparing with the glory about to be revealed to us. [19]For the creation waits with eager longing for the revealing of the children of God; [20]for the creation was subjected to futility, not of its own will but by the will of the one who subjected it, in hope [21]that the creation itself will be set free from its bondage to decay and will obtain the freedom of the glory of the children of God. [22]We know that the whole creation has been groaning in labor pains until now; [23]and not only the creation, but we ourselves, who have the first fruits of the Spirit, groan inwardly while we wait for adoption, the redemption of our bodies. [24]For in hope we were saved. Now hope that is seen is not hope. For who hopes for what is seen? [25]But if we hope for what we do not see, we wait for it with patience.

Matthew 13:24-30, 36-43

[24]He put before them another parable: "The kingdom of heaven may be compared to someone who sowed good seed in his field; [25]but while everybody was asleep, an enemy came and sowed weeds among the wheat, and then went away. [26]So when the plants came up and bore grain, then the weeds appeared as well. [27]And the slaves of the householder came and said to him, 'Master, did you not sow good seed in your field? Where, then, did these weeds come from?' [28]He answered, 'An enemy has done this.' The slaves said to him, 'Then do you want us to go and gather them?' [29]But he replied, 'No; for in gathering the weeds you would uproot the wheat along with them. [30]Let both of them grow together until the harvest; and at harvest time I will tell the reapers, Collect the weeds first and bind them in bundles to be burned, but gather the wheat into my barn.'"

[36]Then he left the crowds and went into the house. And his disciples approached him, saying, "Explain to us the parable of the weeds of the field." [37]He answered, "The one who sows the good seed is the Son of Man; [38]the field is the world, and the good seed are the children of the kingdom; the weeds are the children of the evil one, [39]and the enemy who sowed them is the devil; the harvest is the end of the age, and the reapers are angels. [40]Just as the weeds are collected and burned up with fire, so will it be at the end of the age. [41]The Son of Man will send his angels, and they will collect out of his kingdom all causes of sin and all evildoers, [42]and they will throw them into the furnace of fire, where there will be weeping and gnashing of teeth. [43]Then the righteous will shine like the sun in the kingdom of their Father. Let anyone with ears listen!"

Hymn and Keyboard Suggestions

O– "Come, Ye Thankful People, Come" (Matt.)
B637, E290, F392, L407, P551, UM694 (PD),
W759
    S-1   #302. Harmonization with descant
            #303. Harmonization
    K-1(III) #76. Prelude/postlude (manuals only)
    K-2   p. 30. Short prelude/postlude

"The God of Abraham Praise" (Gen.)
B34, E401, L544, P488, UM116 (PD), W537
    H-1   #44. Harmonization
    S-1   #211. Harmonization

"We Are Climbing Jacob's Ladder" (Gen.)
B474, F488, UM418
    S-1   #187. Keyboard and/or choral arrangement

"Nearer, My God, to Thee" (Gen.)
B458, UM528 (PD)
    H-1   #75. Harmonization

"Creating God, Your Fingers Trace" (Ps.)
UM109
    S-2   #96. Descant
E394, P134

"Dear Lord, Lead Me Day by Day" (Ps.)
B459, UM411
    S-2   #45. Flute descant

"Immortal, Invisible, God Only Wise" (Ps.)
B6, E423, F319, L526, P263, UM103 (PD), W512
    H-2   p. 28. Harmonization with descant
    S-1   #300. Harmonization

"Thou Hidden Love of God" (Ps., Rom.)
UM414 (PD)
    K-1(III) #86. Prelude
    K-5   p. 73. Various keyboard treatments, through p. 87
    K-9   p. 42. Prelude/meditation

"Every Time I Feel the Spirit" (Rom.)
P315, UM404

"The Church's One Foundation" (Rom.)
B350, E525, F547, L369, P442, UM545 (PD) or UM546
    H-1   #62. Harmonization
    S-1   #25. Descant
            #26. Harmonization
    K-1(I) #8. Prelude/postlude

"We Plow the Fields and Scatter" (Matt.)
E291, F395, L362 (PD), P560

C– "Love Divine, All Loves Excelling" (Rom.)
B208, F21, UM384 (PD)
    H-1   #48. Harmonization in A major
    S-1   #41. Descant
            #42. Harmonization
E657, L315, P376, W588 (PD)
    S-1   #168-71. Various treatments
    K-2   p. 12. Short prelude
    K-9   p. 7. Prelude/postlude

Vocal Solos

"Spirit of Faith Come Down" (Rom.)
V-1   p. 43
"My Lord, What a Mornin'" (Rom., Matt.)
V-5   p. 30
"Then Shall the Righteous Shine Forth" (Matt.)
V-10   p. 13

Anthems

"Surely the Presence of the Lord Is in This Place" (Gen.)
Lanny Wolfe (arr. Charles F. Brown)
GlorySound A-5878
SATB with keyboard

"Wings of the Dawn" (Ps.)
Linda A. Spencer
GlorySound A-6183
SATB with keyboard

"Psalm 139" (Ps.)
Allen Pote
Choristers Guild CGA-610
SATB with piano

"Sing and Dance, Children of God" (Rom.)
Michael Bedford
Hinshaw HMC-379
Two-part with keyboard

Hymn Anthem Suggestions

"My Lord, What a Morning" (Rom., Matt.)
52IHA #34
"Jesus, Joy of Our Desiring" (Matt.)
52IHA #29

Other Suggestions

Introit: E302 or E303, UM563 or UM565, W558. "Father, We Thank You" (Matt.)
Canticle: UM205. "Canticle of Light and Darkness" (Ps.)
Response: B459, UM411, stanza 1. "Dear Lord, Lead Me Day by Day" (Ps.)

Genesis 29:15-28

[15]Then Laban said to Jacob, "Because you are my kinsman, should you therefore serve me for nothing? Tell me, what shall your wages be?" [16]Now Laban had two daughters; the name of the elder was Leah, and the name of the younger was Rachel. [17]Leah's eyes were lovely, and Rachel was graceful and beautiful. [18]Jacob loved Rachel; so he said, "I will serve you seven years for your younger daughter Rachel." [19]Laban said, "It is better that I give her to you than that I should give her to any other man; stay with me." [20]So Jacob served seven years for Rachel, and they seemed to him but a few days because of the love he had for her.

[21]Then Jacob said to Laban, "Give me my wife that I may go in to her, for my time is completed." [22]So Laban gathered together all the people of the place, and made a feast. [23]But in the evening he took his daughter Leah and brought her to Jacob; and he went in to her. [24](Laban gave his maid Zilpah to his daughter Leah to be her maid.) [25]When morning came, it was Leah! And Jacob said to Laban, "What is this you have done to me? Did I not serve with you for Rachel? Why then have you deceived me?" [26]Laban said, "This is not done in our country—giving the younger before the firstborn. [27]Complete the week of this one, and we will give you the other also in return for serving me another seven years." [28]Jacob did so, and completed her week; then Laban gave him his daughter Rachel as a wife.

Psalm 105:1-11, 45b

[1]O give thanks to the LORD, call on his name, make known his deeds among the peoples. [2]Sing to him, sing praises to him; tell of all his wonderful works. [3]Glory in his holy name; let the hearts of those who seek the LORD rejoice. [4]Seek the LORD and his strength; seek his presence continually. [5]Remember the wonderful works he has done, his miracles, and the judgments he uttered, [6]O offspring of his servant Abraham, children of Jacob, his chosen ones. [7]He is the LORD our God; his judgments are in all the earth. [8]He is mindful of his covenant forever, of the word that he commanded, for a thousand generations, [9]the covenant that he made with Abraham, his sworn promise to Isaac, [10]which he confirmed to Jacob as a statute, to Israel as an everlasting covenant, [11]saying, "To you I will give the land of Canaan as your portion for an inheritance."

[45b]Praise the LORD!

Romans 8:26-39

[26]Likewise the Spirit helps us in our weakness; for we do not know how to pray as we ought, but that very Spirit intercedes with sighs too deep for words. [27]And God, who searches the heart, knows what is the mind of the Spirit, because the Spirit intercedes for the saints according to the will of God.

[28]We know that all things work together for good for those who love God, who are called according to his purpose. [29]For those whom he foreknew he also predestined to be conformed to the image of his Son, in order that he might be the firstborn within a large family. [30]And those whom he predestined he also called; and those whom he called he also justified; and those whom he justified he also glorified.

[31]What then are we to say about these things? If God is for us, who is against us? [32]He who did not withhold his own Son, but gave him up for all of us, will he not with him also give us everything else? [33]Who will bring any charge against God's elect? It is God who justifies. [34]Who is to condemn? It is Christ Jesus, who died, yes, who was raised, who is at the right hand of God, who indeed intercedes for us. [35]Who will separate us from the love of Christ? Will hardship, or distress, or persecution, or famine, or nakedness, or peril, or sword? [36]As it is written,

"For your sake we are being
killed all day long;
we are accounted as sheep to
be slaughtered."

[37]No, in all these things we are more than conquerors through him who loved us. [38]For I am convinced that neither death, nor life, nor angels, nor rulers, nor things present, nor things to come, nor powers, [39]nor height, nor depth, nor anything else in all creation, will be able to separate us from the love of God in Christ Jesus our Lord.

Matthew 13:31-33, 44-52

[31]He put before them another parable: "The kingdom of heaven is like a mustard seed that someone took and sowed in his field; [32]it is the smallest of all the seeds, but when it has grown it is the greatest of shrubs and becomes a tree, so that the birds of the air come and make nests in its branches."

[33]He told them another parable: "The kingdom of heaven is like yeast that a woman took and mixed in with three measures of flour until all of it was leavened."

[44]"The kingdom of heaven is like treasure hidden in a field, which someone found and hid; then in his joy he goes and sells all that he has and buys that field.

[45]"Again, the kingdom of heaven is like a merchant in search of fine pearls; [46]on finding one pearl of great value, he went and sold all that he had and bought it.

[47]"Again, the kingdom of heaven is like a net that was thrown into the sea and caught fish of every kind; [48]when it was full, they drew it ashore, sat down, and put the good into baskets but threw out the bad. [49]So it will be at the end of the age. The angels will come out and separate the evil from the righteous [50]and throw them into the furnace of fire, where there will be weeping and gnashing of teeth.

[51]"Have you understood all this?" They answered, "Yes." [52]And he said to them, "Therefore every scribe who has been trained for the kingdom of heaven is like the master of a household who brings out of his treasure what is new and what is old."

Hymn and Keyboard Suggestions

O– "O Day of God, Draw Nigh" (Matt.)
      B623, E601, P452, UM730 (PD)
          S-1   #306-8. Various treatments
          K-1(III)   #64. Prelude/meditation

"When Love Is Found" (Gen.)
      UM643, W745

"Children of the Heavenly Father" (Rom.)
      B55, F89, L474, UM141
          S-2   #180-85. Various treatments
          K-8   p. 14. Short prelude/meditation

"In Thee Is Gladness" (Rom.)
      L552, UM169 (PD)
          K-4   p. 93. Various keyboard treatments,
                        through p. 96

"And Can It Be that I Should Gain" (Rom.)
      B147, F260, UM363 (PD)

"O Love That Wilt Not Let Me Go" (Rom.)
      B292, F404, L324, P384, UM480 (PD)

"By Gracious Powers" (Rom.)
      E695 or E696, P342, UM517, W577

"All Glory Be to God on High" (Rom.)
      E421 (PD), L166, P133, W527
          H-2   p. 4. Harmonization with descant
          K-1(I)   #1. Prelude/postlude

"Holy God, We Praise Thy Name" (Rom.)
      E366 (PD), F385, L535, P460, UM79, W524
          S-1   #151-52. Harmonization with des-
                        cant
                    #153. Descant
          K-1(I)   #28. Prelude or postlude (may be
                        played on manuals only)

"Like the Murmur of the Dove's Song" (Rom.)
      E513, P314, UM544
          S-2   #30. Descant

"I Love Thy Kingdom, Lord" (Matt.)
      B354, E524, F545, L368, UM540 (PD)
          H-1   #3*a*. Harmonization
          S-1   #311. Descant
                    #312. Harmonization
          K-1(III)   #78. Short prelude/postlude (may
                        be played manuals only)
          K-2   p. 29. Short prelude/postlude (man-
                        uals only)

"Jesus, Priceless Treasure" (Matt.)
      F277, L457, P365, UM532 (PD)
          K-4   p. 109. Variations, through p. 119
          K-9   p. 33. Prelude/meditation
          K-14   p. 48. Prelude/meditation/postlude
      L458 (PD)

"Seek Ye First" (Matt.)
      B478, E711, P333, UM405, W580
          K-15   p. 111. Piano prelude/meditation

C– "Hope of the World" (Rom.)
      UM178
          S-1   #343. Descant
          S-2   #189. Introduction
      E472, L493, P360, W565

Vocal Solos

"If God Be for Us" (Rom.)
V-2

"O Love, That Wilt Not Let Me Go" (Rom.)
V-7   p. 49

Anthems

"Who Shall Separate Us?" (Rom.)
John Ness Beck
Art Masters Studio 261
SATB with organ

"Where Your Treasure Is" (Matt.)
Mary McDonald
Purifoy Publishing 26044
SATB with keyboard

Hymn Anthem Suggestions

"Children of the Heavenly Father" (Rom.)
52IHA   #7
"Come, Ye Sinners, Poor and Needy" (Rom.)
52IHA   #10

Other Suggestions

Canticle: UM406. "Canticle of Prayer" (Rom.)
Response: B478, E711, P333, UM405, W580. "Seek Ye First"
   (Matt.)
Scripture Response: E695 or E696, P342, UM517, W577,
   stanza 1. "By Gracious Powers" (Rom.)
Benediction: E24, L274, P546, UM690 (PD), W678, stanza
   4. "The Day Thou Gavest, Lord, Is Ended" (Matt.)

Genesis 32:22-31

²²The same night he got up and took his two wives, his two maids, and his eleven children, and crossed the ford of the Jabbok. ²³He took them and sent them across the stream, and likewise everything that he had. ²⁴Jacob was left alone; and a man wrestled with him until daybreak. ²⁵When the man saw that he did not prevail against Jacob, he struck him on the hip socket; and Jacob's hip was put out of joint as he wrestled with him. ²⁶Then he said, "Let me go, for the day is breaking." But Jacob said, "I will not let you go, unless you bless me." ²⁷So he said to him, "What is your name?" And he said, "Jacob." ²⁸Then the man said, "You shall no longer be called Jacob, but Israel, for you have striven with God and with humans, and have prevailed." ²⁹Then Jacob asked him, "Please tell me your name." But he said, "Why is it that you ask my name?" And there he blessed him. ³⁰So Jacob called the place Peniel, saying, "For I have seen God face to face, and yet my life is preserved." ³¹The sun rose upon him as he passed Penuel, limping because of his hip.

Psalm 17:1-7, 15

¹Hear a just cause, O LORD; attend to my cry;
    give ear to my prayer from lips free of deceit.
²From you let my vindication come;
    let your eyes see the right.
³If you try my heart, if you visit me by night,
    if you test me, you will find no wickedness in me;
    my mouth does not transgress.
⁴As for what others do, by the word of your lips
    I have avoided the ways of the violent.
⁵My steps have held fast to your paths;
    my feet have not slipped.
⁶I call upon you, for you will answer me, O God;
    incline your ear to me, hear my words.
⁷Wondrously show your steadfast love,
    O savior of those who seek refuge
    from their adversaries at your right hand.

¹⁵As for me, I shall behold your
    face in righteousness;
    when I awake I shall be
    satisfied, beholding your likeness.

Romans 9:1-5

¹I am speaking the truth in Christ—I am not lying; my conscience confirms it by the Holy Spirit—²I have great sorrow and unceasing anguish in my heart. ³For I could wish that I myself were accursed and cut off from Christ for the sake of my own people, my kindred according to the flesh. ⁴They are Israelites, and to them belong the adoption, the glory, the covenants, the giving of the law, the worship, and the promises; ⁵to them belong the patriarchs, and from them, according to the flesh, comes the Messiah, who is over all, God blessed forever. Amen.

Matthew 14:13-21

¹³Now when Jesus heard this, he withdrew from there in a boat to a deserted place by himself. But when the crowds heard it, they followed him on foot from the towns. ¹⁴When he went ashore, he saw a great crowd; and he had compassion for them and cured their sick. ¹⁵When it was evening, the disciples came to him and said, "This is a deserted place, and the hour is now late; send the crowds away so that they may go into the villages and buy food for themselves." ¹⁶Jesus said to them, "They need not go away; you give them something to eat." ¹⁷They replied, "We have nothing here but five loaves and two fish." ¹⁸And he said, "Bring them here to me." ¹⁹Then he ordered the crowds to sit down on the grass. Taking the five loaves and the two fish, he looked up to heaven, and blessed and broke the loaves, and gave them to the disciples, and the disciples gave them to the crowds. ²⁰And all ate and were filled; and they took up what was left over of the broken pieces, twelve baskets full. ²¹And those who ate were about five thousand men, besides women and children.

Hymn and Keyboard Suggestions

O– "Come, O Thou Traveler Unknown" (Gen.)
    UM386
        S-2   #33-37. Various treatments
    E638 (PD) and E639

O– "Standing on the Promises" (Rom.)
    B335, F69, UM374 (PD)
    "Be Thou My Vision" (Gen.)
    B60, E488, F468, P339, UM451
        S-1   #319. Arrangement for organ and
                    voices in canon
        K-12   p. 9. Prelude/meditation
    "O Love That Wilt Not Let Me Go" (Gen.)
    B292, F404, L324, P384, UM480 (PD)
    "Sweet Hour of Prayer" (Gen., Matt.)
    B445, F439, UM496 (PD)
    "Pass Me Not, O Gentle Savior" (Ps.)
    B308, F416, UM351 (PD)
    "Holy Spirit, Truth Divine" (Rom.)
    L257, P321, UM465 (PD)
        S-1   #53. Descant
    "If Thou But Suffer God to Guide Thee" (Rom.)
    B57, E635, L453, P282, UM142 (PD)
        K-5   p. 141. Harmonization in A minor
        K-1(IV) #94. Prelude/meditation
        K-5   p. 141. Various keyboard treatments,
                    through p. 152
    "All My Hope Is Firmly Grounded" (Matt.)
    E665, UM132
    "Bread of the World" (Matt.)
    E301, P502, UM624
    "Break Thou the Bread of Life" (Matt., Communion)
    B263, F30, L235, P329, UM599 (PD)
        K-14   p. 46. Piano prelude/meditation
    "Let Us Break Bread Together" (Matt., Communion)
    B366, E325 (PD), F564, L212, P513, UM618,
    W727
        K-7   p. 17. Prelude/postlude/meditation
        K-11   p. 42. Prelude/meditation
    "O Food to Pilgrims Given" (Matt., Communion)
    E309, UM631
        K-1(III) #67. Prelude/postlude
        K-5   p. 51. Various keyboard treatments,
                    through p. 53
        K-10   p. 18. Variations
    E308
    "Now Let Us from This Table Rise" (Matt., Communion)
    UM634, W625
        S-2   #48. Descant
                #49. Harmonization

C– "God Be with You till We Meet Again" (Gen., Matt.)
    F523 and P540, UM672 (PD) and UM673 (PD)

Vocal Solos

"Come, O Thou Traveler Unknown" (Gen.)
V-1   p. 21
"O Love, That Wilt Not Let Me Go" (Gen.)
V-7   p. 49
"Of the Father's Love Begotten" (Rom.)
V-3   p. 17

Anthems

"Come, O Thou Traveler Unknown" (Gen.)
Erik Routley
Agape ER 1920
SATB with organ

"Give Ear Unto Me" (Ps.)
Benedetto Marcello
Novello 48.1067
Two-part

"Benedictus" (Rom.)
William Barnard
H. W. Gray
Unison

Hymn Anthem Suggestions

"Break Thou the Bread" (Matt.)
52IHA   #4
"This Is the Feast of Victory" (Communion)
52IHA   #44

Other Suggestions

Introit: E665, UM132, stanza 1. "All My Hope Is Firmly
    Grounded."
Prayer: UM477. For Illumination (Gen.)
Response: L257, P321, UM465, stanza 1. "Holy Spirit,
    Truth Divine" (Rom.)
Poem: UM387. Come, O Thou Traveler Unknown (Gen.)

Genesis 37:1-4, 12-28

[1]Jacob settled in the land where his father had lived as an alien, the land of Canaan. [2]This is the story of the family of Jacob.

Joseph, being seventeen years old, was shepherding the flock with his brothers; he was a helper to the sons of Bilhah and Zilpah, his father's wives; and Joseph brought a bad report of them to their father. [3]Now Israel loved Joseph more than any other of his children, because he was the son of his old age; and he had made him a long robe with sleeves. [4]But when his brothers saw that their father loved him more than all his brothers, they hated him, and could not speak peaceably to him.

[12]Now his brothers went to pasture their father's flock near Shechem. [13]And Israel said to Joseph, "Are not your brothers pasturing the flock at Shechem? Come, I will send you to them." He answered, "Here I am." [14]So he said to him, "Go now, see if it is well with your brothers and with the flock; and bring word back to me." So he sent him from the valley of Hebron.

He came to Shechem, [15]and a man found him wandering in the fields; the man asked him, "What are you seeking?" [16]"I am seeking my brothers," he said; "tell me, please, where they are pasturing the flock." [17]The man said, "They have gone away, for I heard them say, 'Let us go to Dothan.' " So Joseph went after his brothers, and found them at Dothan. [18]They saw him from a distance, and before he came near to them, they conspired to kill him. [19]They said to one another, "Here comes this dreamer. [20]Come now, let us kill him and throw him into one of the pits; then we shall say that a wild animal has devoured him, and we shall see what will become of his dreams." [21]But when Reuben heard it, he delivered him out of their hands, saying, "Let us not take his life." [22]Reuben said to them, "Shed no blood; throw him into this pit here in the wilderness, but lay no hand on him"—that he might rescue him out of their hand and restore him to his father. [23]So when Joseph came to his brothers, they stripped him of his robe, the long robe with sleeves that he wore; [24]and they took him and threw him into a pit. The pit was empty; there was no water in it.

[25]Then they sat down to eat; and looking up they saw a caravan of Ishmaelites coming from Gilead, with their camels carrying gum, balm, and resin, on their way to carry it down to Egypt. [26]Then Judah said to his brothers, "What profit is it if we kill our brother and conceal his blood? [27]Come, let us sell him to the Ishmaelites, and not lay our hands on him, for he is our brother, our own flesh." And his brothers agreed. [28]When some Midianite traders passed by, they drew Joseph up, lifting him out of the pit, and sold him to the Ishmaelites for twenty pieces of silver. And they took Joseph to Egypt.

Psalm 105:1-6, 16-22, 45b

[1]O give thanks to the LORD, call on his name, make known his deeds among the peoples. [2]Sing to him, sing praises to him; tell of all his wonderful works. [3]Glory in his holy name; let the hearts of those who seek the LORD rejoice. [4]Seek the LORD and his strength; seek his presence continually. [5]Remember the wonderful works he has done, his miracles, and the judgments he uttered, [6]O offspring of his servant Abraham, children of Jacob, his chosen ones.

[16]When he summoned famine against the land, and broke every staff of bread, [17]he had sent a man ahead of them, Joseph, who was sold as a slave. [18]His feet were hurt with fetters, his neck was put in a collar of iron; [19]until what he had said came to pass, the word of the LORD kept testing him. [20]The king sent and released him; the ruler of the peoples set him free. [21]He made him lord of his house, and ruler of all his possessions, [22]to instruct his officials at his pleasure, and to teach his elders wisdom.

[45b]Praise the LORD!

Romans 10:5-15

[5]Moses writes concerning the righteousness that comes from the law, that "the person who does these things will live by them." [6]But the righteousness that comes from faith says, "Do not say in your heart, 'Who will ascend into heaven?' " (that is, to bring Christ down) [7]"or 'Who will descend into the abyss?' " (that is, to bring Christ up from the dead). [8]But what does it say? "The word is near you, on your lips and in your heart" (that is, the word of faith that we proclaim); [9]because if you confess with your lips that Jesus is Lord and believe in your heart that God raised him from the dead, you will be saved. [10]For one believes with the heart and so is justified, and one confesses with the mouth and so is saved. [11]The scripture says, "No one who believes in him will be put to shame." [12]For there is no distinction between Jew and Greek; the same Lord is Lord of all and is generous to all who call on him. [13]For, "Everyone who calls on the name of the Lord shall be saved."

[14]But how are they to call on one in whom they have not believed? And how are they to believe in one of whom they have never heard? And how are they to hear without someone to proclaim him? [15]And how are they to proclaim him unless they are sent? As it is written, "How beautiful are the feet of those who bring good news!"

Matthew 14:22-33

[22]Immediately he made the disciples get into the boat and go on ahead to the other side, while he dismissed the crowds. [23]And after he had dismissed the crowds, he went up the mountain by himself to pray. When evening came, he was there alone, [24]but by this time the boat, battered by the waves, was far from the land, for the wind was against them. [25]And early in the morning he came walking toward them on the sea. [26]But when the disciples saw him walking on the sea, they were terrified, saying, "It is a ghost!" And they cried out in fear. [27]But immediately Jesus spoke to them and said, "Take heart, it is I; do not be afraid."

[28]Peter answered him, "Lord, if it is you, command me to come to you on the water." [29]He said, "Come." So Peter got out of the boat, started walking on the water, and came toward Jesus. [30]But when he noticed the strong wind, he became frightened, and beginning to sink, he cried out, "Lord, save me!" [31]Jesus immediately reached out his hand and caught him, saying to him, "You of little faith, why did you doubt?" [32]When they got into the boat, the wind ceased. [33]And those in the boat worshiped him, saying, "Truly you are the Son of God."

Hymn and Keyboard Suggestions
O– "Praise to the Lord, the Almighty" (Ps.)
        B14 (PD), E390, F337, L543, P482, UM139, W547
        H-1   #88. Harmonization in G major
        H-2   p. 18. Harmonization with descant
        S-1   #218-22. Various treatments
        K-4   p. 140. Various keyboard treatments, through p. 146
        K-8   p. 10. Interlude
"By Gracious Powers" (Gen.)
        E695 or E696, P342, UM517, W577
"Here I Am, Lord" (Gen., Matt., Rom.)
        P525, UM593
"Children of the Heavenly Father" (Gen., Ps.)
        B55, F89, L474, UM141
        S-2   #180-85. Various treatments
        K-8   p. 14. Short prelude/meditation
"At the Name of Jesus" (Rom.)
        E435, F351, L179, P148, UM168, W499
        S-2   #99. Descant
        B198 (PD)
        K-6   p. 7. Prelude
"Here, O Lord, Your Servants Gather" (Rom.)
        B179, P465, UM552
        S-1   #333. Orff arrangement
        S-2   #178. Flute descant
"How Shall They Hear the Word of God" (Rom.)
        UM649, W629
"I Love to Tell the Story" (Rom.)
        B572, F619, L390, UM156 (PD)
"O For a Heart to Praise My God" (Rom.)
        F357, UM417 (PD)
        S-1   #286. Descant
        K-2   p. 25. Short prelude/postlude
        W591
"I Know Whom I Have Believed" (Rom.)
        B337, F631, UM714 (PD)
"Dear Lord and Father of Mankind" (Matt.)
        B267, E652, F422, L506, P345, UM358 (PD)
        H-1   #70. Harmonization
        S-2   #151. Introduction
                #152. Violin descant
        E653
"Eternal Father, Strong to Save" (Matt.)
        B69, E608, F679, L467, P562 (PD)
        H-1   #80. Harmonization
"Give to the Winds Thy Fears" (Matt.)
        UM129 (PD)
        S-1   #129. Descant
        P286
"I Sought the Lord" (Matt.)
        E689, UM341 (PD), W593

"Lonely the Boat" (Matt.)
        P373, UM476
"Jesus, Savior, Pilot Me" (Matt.)
        L334, UM509 (PD)
C– "Jesus, Lover of My Soul" (Matt.)
        E699, F222, P303, UM479 (PD)
        S-1   #6. Descant
        K-9   p. 10. Prelude/postlude
        B180 (PD)
C– "We've a Story to Tell to the Nations" (Rom.)
        B586, F659, UM569 (PD)
        K-8   p. 26. Introduction

Vocal Solos
"How Beautiful Are the Feet" (Rom.)
V-2
"Jesus, Lover of My Soul" (Matt.)
V-1   p. 37

Anthems
"Praise Ye the Lord" (Ps.)
Alan Hovhaness
Associated Music Publishers A-208
SATB *a cappella*

"Jesus, Lover of My Soul" (Matt.)
Richard Moreland
Augsburg Fortress 11-10079
SATB with flute and keyboard

Hymn Anthem Suggestions
"He Leadeth Me: O Blessed Thought" (Gen.)
52IHA   #21
"Children of the Heavenly Father" (Gen., Ps.)
52IHA   #7
"How Shall They Hear the Word of God" (Rom.)
52IHA   #25
"Here, O Lord, Your Servants Gather" (Rom.)
52IHA   #22

Other Suggestions
Call to Confession: B317, F629, UM337 (PD), stanza 1. "Only Trust Him" (Rom.)
Response: B120, F208, P308, UM179 (PD), stanza 3. "O Sing a Song of Bethlehem" (Matt.)

Genesis 45:1-15

[1]Then Joseph could no longer control himself before all those who stood by him, and he cried out, "Send everyone away from me." So no one stayed with him when Joseph made himself known to his brothers. [2]And he wept so loudly that the Egyptians heard it, and the household of Pharaoh heard it. [3]Joseph said to his brothers, "I am Joseph. Is my father still alive?" But his brothers could not answer him, so dismayed were they at his presence.

[4]Then Joseph said to his brothers, "Come closer to me." And they came closer. He said, "I am your brother, Joseph, whom you sold into Egypt. [5]And now do not be distressed, or angry with yourselves, because you sold me here; for God sent me before you to preserve life. [6]For the famine has been in the land these two years; and there are five more years in which there will be neither plowing nor harvest. [7]God sent me before you to preserve for you a remnant on earth, and to keep alive for you many survivors. [8]So it was not you who sent me here, but God; he has made me a father to Pharaoh, and lord of all his house and ruler over all the land of Egypt. [9]Hurry and go up to my father and say to him, 'Thus says your son Joseph, God has made me lord of all Egypt; come down to me, do not delay. [10]You shall settle in the land of Goshen, and you shall be near me, you and your children and your children's children, as well as your flocks, your herds, and all that you have. [11]I will provide for you there—since there are five more years of famine to come—so that you and your household, and all that you have, will not come to poverty.' [12]And now your eyes and the eyes of my brother Benjamin see that it is my own mouth that speaks to you. [13]You must tell my father how greatly I am honored in Egypt, and all that you have seen. Hurry and bring my father down here." [14]Then he fell upon his brother Benjamin's neck and wept, while Benjamin wept upon his neck. [15]And he kissed all his brothers and wept upon them; and after that his brothers talked with him.

Psalm 133

[1]How very good and pleasant it is
   when kindred live together in unity!
[2]It is like the precious oil on the head,
   running down upon the beard,
on the beard of Aaron,
   running down over the collar of his robes.
[3]It is like the dew of Hermon,
   which falls on the mountains of Zion.
For there the LORD ordained his blessing,
   life forevermore.

Romans 11:1-2a, 29-32

[1]I ask, then, has God rejected his people? By no means! I myself am an Israelite, a descendant of Abraham, a member of the tribe of Benjamin. [2a]God has not rejected his people whom he foreknew.

[29]For the gifts and the calling of God are irrevocable. [30]Just as you were once disobedient to God but have now received mercy because of their disobedience, [31]so they have now been disobedient in order that, by the mercy shown to you, they too may now receive mercy. [32]For God has imprisoned all in disobedience so that he may be merciful to all.

Matthew 15:(10-20) 21-28

[10]Then he called the crowd to him and said to them, "Listen and understand: [11]it is not what goes into the mouth that defiles a person, but it is what comes out of the mouth that defiles." [12]Then the disciples approached and said to him, "Do you know that the Pharisees took offense when they heard what you said?" [13]He answered, "Every plant that my heavenly Father has not planted will be uprooted. [14]Let them alone; they are blind guides of the blind. And if one blind person guides another, both will fall into a pit." [15]But Peter said to him, "Explain this parable to us." [16]Then he said, "Are you also still without understanding? [17]Do you not see that whatever goes into the mouth enters the stomach, and goes out into the sewer? [18]But what comes out of the mouth proceeds from the heart, and this is what defiles. [19]For out of the heart come evil intentions, murder, adultery, fornication, theft, false witness, slander. [20]These are what defile a person, but to eat with unwashed hands does not defile."

[21]Jesus left that place and went away to the district of Tyre and Sidon. [22]Just then a Canaanite woman from that region came out and started shouting, "Have mercy on me, Lord, Son of David; my daughter is tormented by a demon." [23]But he did not answer her at all. And his disciples came and urged him, saying, "Send her away, for she keeps shouting after us." [24]He answered, "I was sent only to the lost sheep of the house of Israel." [25]But she came and knelt before him, saying, "Lord, help me." [26]He answered, "It is not fair to take the children's food and throw it to the dogs." [27]She said, "Yes, Lord, yet even the dogs eat the crumbs that fall from their masters' table." [28]Then Jesus answered her, "Woman, great is your faith! Let it be done for you as you wish." And her daughter was healed instantly.

Hymn and Keyboard Suggestions

O– "Where Charity and Love Prevail" (Gen., Ps.)
    UM549
        H-1   #73. Harmonization in E-flat major
        S-2   #162. Harmonization
        K-1(III)   #77. Prelude/meditation (manuals only)
    E581, L126

O– "In Christ There Is No East or West" (Ps., Rom.)
    B385, F685, P439
        H-1   #73. Harmonization in E-flat major
        S-2   #162. Harmonization
        K-1(III)   #77. Prelude/meditation (manuals only)
    E529, L359, P440, UM548, W659
        S-1   #231. Descant
                     #232. Brass quartet arrangement
                     #233. Harmonization

"And Are We Yet Alive" (Gen., Ps.)
    UM553 (PD)
        H-1   #78. Harmonization

"Help Us Accept Each Other" (Gen., Ps.)
    UM560
        S-2   #1. Descant
    P358, W656

"This Is a Day of New Beginnings" (Gen., Rom., Matt.)
    B370, UM383, W661

"Behold the Goodness of Our Lord" (Ps.)
    P241

"Depth of Mercy" (Rom.)
    UM355 (PD)
        S-1   #53. Descant
    B306

"O Christ, the Healer" (Rom., Matt.)
    P380, UM265, W747
        K-1(I)   #23. Short prelude (may be played manuals only)
    L360

"Silence, Frenzied, Unclean Spirit" (Matt.)
    UM264, W751

C– "There's a Wideness in God's Mercy" (Rom.)
    B25 (PD), F115, UM121
        K-8   p. 30. Prelude/meditation
    E470 (PD)
        H-1   #48. Harmonization in A major
        S-1   #41. Descant
                     #42. Harmonization
    P298, W595 (PD)
        H-1   #25. Harmonization
        S-1   #178. Harmonization
                     #179. Harmonization
    E469, L290, W596

C– "My Faith Looks Up to Thee" (Matt.)
    B416, E691, F84, L479, P383, UM452 (PD)
        H-1   #72. Harmonization in D major
        S-2   #142. Flute/violin descant
        K-1(III)   #69. Prelude/meditation
        K-14   p. 12. Piano prelude/meditation

Vocal Solos

"I Will Sing of Thy Great Mercies" (Rom., Matt.)
V-4   p. 43
"Just As I Am"
V-3   p. 23

Anthems

"O Jesu, Fili David" (Matt.)
("O Jesus, Son of David")
Josquin Des Pres
Tetra AB 169
SA(T)B with organ

"My Jesus, I Love Thee" (Matt.)
arr. Robert Sterling
GlorySound A-6144
SATB with keyboard

Hymn Anthem Suggestions

"Children of the Heavenly Father" (Gen.)
52IHA   #7
"This Is a Day of New Beginnings" (Gen., Rom., Matt.)
52IHA   #43

Other Suggestions

Response: UM264, W751, stanza 4. "Silence, Frenzied, Unclean Spirit" (Matt.)
Response: UM263, stanzas 1 & 7. "When Jesus the Healer Passed Through Galilee" (Matt.)
Benediction Response: P358, UM560, W656, stanza 4. "Help Us Accept Each Other"
Benediction Response: B387, F560, L370, P438, UM557 (PD). "Bless Be the Tie That Binds"

Exodus 1:8–2:10

[8]Now a new king arose over Egypt, who did not know Joseph. [9]He said to his people, "Look, the Israelite people are more numerous and more powerful than we. [10]Come, let us deal shrewdly with them, or they will increase and, in the event of war, join our enemies and fight against us and escape from the land." [11]Therefore they set taskmasters over them to oppress them with forced labor. They built supply cities, Pithom and Rameses, for Pharaoh. [12]But the more they were oppressed, the more they multiplied and spread, so that the Egyptians came to dread the Israelites. [13]The Egyptians became ruthless in imposing tasks on the Israelites, [14]and made their lives bitter with hard service in mortar and brick and in every kind of field labor. They were ruthless in all the tasks that they imposed on them.

[15]The king of Egypt said to the Hebrew midwives, one of whom was named Shiphrah and the other Puah, [16]"When you act as midwives to the Hebrew women, and see them on the birthstool, if it is a boy, kill him; but if it is a girl, she shall live." [17]But the midwives feared God; they did not do as the king of Egypt commanded them, but they let the boys live. [18]So the king of Egypt summoned the midwives and said to them, "Why have you done this, and allowed the boys to live?" [19]The midwives said to Pharaoh, "Because the Hebrew women are not like the Egyptian women; for they are vigorous and give birth before the midwife comes to them." [20]So God dealt well with the midwives; and the people multiplied and became very strong. [21]And because the midwives feared God, he gave them families. [22]Then Pharaoh commanded all his people, "Every boy that is born to the Hebrews you shall throw into the Nile, but you shall let every girl live."

[1]Now a man from the house of Levi went and married a Levite woman. [2]The woman conceived and bore a son; and when she saw that he was a fine baby, she hid him three months. [3]When she could hide him no longer she got a papyrus basket for him, and plastered it with bitumen and pitch; she put the child in it and placed it among the reeds on the bank of the river. [4]His sister stood at a distance, to see what would happen to him.

[5]The daughter of Pharaoh came down to bathe at the river, while her attendants walked beside the river. She saw the basket among the reeds and sent her maid to bring it. [6]When she opened it, she saw the child. He was crying, and she took pity on him, "This must be one of the Hebrews' children," she said. [7]Then his sister said to Pharaoh's daughter, "Shall I go and get you a nurse from the Hebrew women to nurse the child for you?" [8]Pharaoh's daughter said to her, "Yes." So the girl went and called the child's mother. [9]Pharaoh's daughter said to her, "Take this child and nurse it for me, and I will give you your wages." So the woman took the child and nursed it. [10]When the child grew up, she brought him to Pharaoh's daughter, and she took him as her son. She named him Moses, "because," she said, "I drew him out of the water."

Psalm 124

[1]If it had not been the LORD who was on our side—let Israel now say—[2]if it had not been the LORD who was on our side, when our enemies attacked us, [3]then they would have swallowed us up alive, when their anger was kindled against us; [4]then the flood would have swept us away, the torrent would have gone over us; [5]then over us would have gone the raging waters. [6]Blessed be the LORD, who has not given us as prey to their teeth. [7]We have escaped like a bird from the snare of the fowlers; the snare is broken, and we have escaped. [8]Our help is in the name of the LORD, who made heaven and earth.

Romans 12:1-8

[1]I appeal to you therefore, brothers and sisters, by the mercies of God, to present your bodies as a living sacrifice, holy and acceptable to God, which is your spiritual worship. [2]Do not be conformed to this world, but be transformed by the renewing of your minds, so that you may discern what is the will of God—what is good and acceptable and perfect.

[3]For by the grace given to me I say to everyone among you not to think of yourself more highly than you ought to think, but to think with sober judgment, each according to the measure of faith that God has assigned. [4]For as in one body we have many members, and not all the members have the same function, [5]so we, who are many, are one body in Christ, and individually we are members one of another. [6]We have gifts that differ according to the grace given to us: prophecy, in proportion to faith; [7]ministry, in ministering; the teacher, in teaching; [8]the exhorter, in exhortation; the giver, in generosity; the leader, in diligence; the compassionate, in cheerfulness.

Matthew 16:13-20

[13]Now when Jesus came into the district of Caesarea Philippi, he asked his disciples, "Who do people say that the Son of Man is?" [14]And they said, "Some say John the Baptist, but others Elijah, and still others Jeremiah or one of the prophets." [15]He said to them, "But who do you say that I am?" [16]Simon Peter answered, "You are the Messiah, the Son of the living God." [17]And Jesus answered him, "Blessed are you, Simon son of Jonah! For flesh and blood has not revealed this to you, but my Father in heaven. [18]And I tell you, you are Peter, and on this rock I will build my church, and the gates of Hades will not prevail against it. [19]I will give you the keys of the kingdom of heaven, and whatever you bind on earth will be bound in heaven, and whatever you loose on earth will be loosed in heaven." [20]Then he sternly ordered the disciples not to tell anyone that he was the Messiah.

Hymn and Keyboard Suggestions

O– "Guide Me, O Thou Great Jehovah" (Exod.)
　　　　B56, E690, F608, L343, P281, UM127 (PD)
　　　　S-1　　#76. Descant
　　　　　　　#77. Harmonization
　　　　K-6　　p. 30. Prelude/postlude
"God Will Take Care of You" (Exod.)
　　　　B64, F56, UM130 (PD)
"Now Israel May Say" (Ps.)
　　　　P236 (PD)
　　　　H-1　　#85. Harmonization
　　　　K-1(II)　#68. Prelude/meditation/postlude
　　　　K-2　　p. 22. Short prelude/meditation/
　　　　　　　　postlude
"As Those of Old Their First Fruits Brought" (Rom.)
　　　　B639, E705, P414
　　　　S-1　　#131. Introduction
　　　　　　　#132. Descant
　　　　K-3　　p. 25. Short prelude/postlude (man-
　　　　　　　　uals only)
　　　　K-6　　p. 10. Prelude/postlude
"Take My Life, and Let It Be" (Rom.)
　　　　B277 (PD), P391
　　　　S-2　　#78. Descant
　　　　　　　#79. Harmonization
　　　　　　　#80. Introduction
　　　　E707
　　　　H-1　　#66. Harmonization
　　　　L406 (PD)
　　　　K-1(II)　#71. Prelude/meditation
　　　　B283 (PD), UM399 (PD)
"Jesus, the Very Thought of Thee" (Matt.)
　　　　B225, F465, L316, P310, UM175 (PD)
　　　　H-1　　#15. Harmonization
　　　　S-1　　#291. Descant
　　　　　　　#292. Harmonization
　　　　K-2　　p. 26. Short prelude/meditation
　　　　K-6　　p. 22. Prelude/meditation
　　　　K-15　　p. 63. Piano prelude/meditation
　　　　E642
　　　　H-1　　#42. Harmonization
"The Church of Christ, in Every Age" (Matt.)
　　　　B402
　　　　S-1　　#141. Harmonization
　　　　　　　#142-43. Descant and transposition
　　　　　　　　in A major
　　　　L433, P421
　　　　S-2　　#191. Harmonization
　　　　UM589
　　　　K-12　　p. 14. Prelude/meditation
　　　　W626
　　　　S-2　　#53. Descant

C– "Christ for the World We Sing" (Matt.)
　　　　E537, F686, UM568 (PD)
　　　　S-1　　#185. Harmonization
　　　　　　　#186. Descant
　　　　K-1(II)　#37. Prelude/postlude
　　　　K-2　　p. 20. Short prelude/meditation
　　　　K-14　　p. 8. Piano prelude/postlude
C– "Go Forth for God" (Ps.)
　　　　UM670
　　　　S-1　　#138-39. Harmonization with des-
　　　　　　　　cant
　　　　　　　#140. Harmonization
　　　　E347

Vocal Solos
"Take My Life" (Rom.)
V-3　　p. 28
"The Master's Touch" (Rom.)
V-6　　p. 5
"Praise"
V-6　　p. 36

Anthems
"The Birth of Moses" (Exod.)
Normand Lockwood
Merrymount (Mercury) MC 140
SSA with piano and flute

"Upon This Rock" (Matt.)
John Ness Beck
G. Schirmer 11467
SATB with organ and optional brass sextet

Hymn Anthem Suggestions
"Children of the Heavenly Father" (Exod.)
52IHA　#7
"Father, We Thank You" (Exod., Rom.)
52IHA　#15

Other Suggestions
Prayer: UM146. At the Birth of a Child (Exod.)
Prayer: UM607. A Covenant Prayer in the Wesleyan Tradi-
　　tion (Rom.)
Scripture Response: UM188, W543. "Christ Is the World's
　　Light" (Matt.)
Benediction Response: E347, UM670. "Go Forth for God"
　　(Ps., Matt.)

INDEX OF SCRIPTURES REFERENCED

INDEX OF SCRIPTURES REFERENCED

INDEX OF PSALMS REFERENCED

REVISED COMMON LECTIONARY

September 3, 1995
13th Sunday After Pentecost
Proper 17 [22]
Jeremiah 2:4-13 or
  Sirach 10:12-18 or
  Proverbs 25:6-7
Psalm 81:1, 10-16 or *Psalm 112*
Hebrews 13:1-8, 15-16
Luke 14:1, 7-14

September 10, 1995
14th Sunday After Pentecost
Proper 18 [23]
Jeremiah 18:1-11 or
  Deuteronomy 30:15-20
Psalm 139:1-6, 13-18 or *Psalm 1*
Philemon 1-21
Luke 14:25-33

September 17, 1995
15th Sunday After Pentecost
Proper 19 [24]
Jeremiah 4:11-12, 22-28 or
  Exodus 32:7-14
Psalm 14 or *Psalm 51:1-10*
1 Timothy 1:12-17
Luke 15:1-10

September 24, 1995
16th Sunday After Pentecost
Proper 20 [25]
Jeremiah 8:18–9:1 or *Amos 8:4-7*
Psalm 79:1-9 or *Psalm 113*
1 Timothy 2:1-7
Luke 16:1-13

October 1, 1995
17th Sunday After Pentecost
Proper 21 [26]
Jeremiah 32:1-3*a*, 6-15 or
  Amos 6:1a, 4-7
Psalm 91:1-6, 14-16 or
  Psalm 146
1 Timothy 6:6-19
Luke 16:19-31.

October 8, 1995
18th Sunday After Pentecost
Proper 22 [27]
Lamentations 1:1-6 or
  Habakkuk 1:1-4; 2:1-4
Psalm 137 or *Psalm 37:1-9*
2 Timothy 1:1-14
Luke 17:5-10

October 15, 1995
19th Sunday After Pentecost
Proper 23 [28]
Jeremiah 29:1, 4-7 or
  2 Kings 5:1-3, 7-15c

Psalm 66:1-12 or *Psalm 111*
2 Timothy 2:8-15
Luke 17:11-19

October 22, 1995
20th Sunday After Pentecost
Proper 24 [29]
Jeremiah 31:27-34 or
  Genesis 32:22-31
Psalm 119:97-104 or *Psalm 121*
2 Timothy 3:14–4:5
Luke 18:1-8

October 29, 1995
21st Sunday After Pentecost
Proper 25 [30]
Joel 2:23-32 or *Sirach 35:12-17*
  or *Jeremiah 14:7-10, 19-22*
Psalm 65 or *Psalm 84:1-7*
2 Timothy 4:6-8, 16-18
Luke 18:9-14

November 1, 1995
All Saints
Daniel 7:1-3, 15-18
Psalm 149
Ephesians 1:11-23
Luke 6:20-31

November 5, 1995
22nd Sunday After Pentecost
Proper 26 [31]
Habakkuk 1:1-4; 2:1-4 or
  Isaiah 1:10-18
Psalm 119:137-144 or
  Psalm 32:1-7
2 Thessalonians 1:1-4, 11-12
Luke 19:1-10

November 12, 1995
23rd Sunday After Pentecost
Proper 27 [32]
Haggai 2:1–9 or
  Job 19:23-27a
Psalm 145:1-5, 17-21 or
  Psalm 98 or Psalm 17:1-9
2 Thessalonians 2:1-5, 13-17
Luke 20:27-38

November 19, 1995
24th Sunday After Pentecost
Proper 28 [33]
Isaiah 65:17-25 or *Malachi 4:1-2a*
Isaiah 12 or *Psalm 98*
2 Thessalonians 3:6-13
Luke 21:5-19

November 23, 1995
Thanksgiving Day
Deuteronomy 26:1-11

Psalm 100
Philippians 4:4-9
John 6:25-35

November 26, 1995
Christ the King Sunday
Proper 29 [34]
Jeremiah 23:1-6 or
  Jeremiah 23:1-6
Luke 1:68-79 or *Psalm 46*
Colossians 1:11-20
Luke 23:33-43

December 3, 1995
1st Sunday of Advent
Isaiah 2:1-5
Psalm 122
Romans 13:11-14
Matthew 24:36-44

December 10, 1995
2nd Sunday of Advent
Isaiah 11:1-10
Psalm 72:1-7, 18-19
Romans 15:4-13
Matthew 3:1-12

December 17, 1995
3rd Sunday of Advent
Isaiah 35:1-10
Psalm 146:5-10 or *Luke 1:47-55*
James 5:7-10
Matthew 11:2-11

December 24, 1995
4th Sunday of Advent
Isaiah 7:10-16
Psalm 80:1-7, 17-19
Romans 1:1-7
Matthew 1:18-25

December 24/25, 1995
Christmas Eve/Day
Isaiah 9:2-7
Psalm 96
Titus 2:11-14
Luke 2:1-20

December 31, 1995
1st Sunday After Christmas Day
Isaiah 63:7-9
Psalm 148
Hebrews 2:10-18
Matthew 2:13-23

January 1, 1996
Watch Night/New Year
Ecclesiastes 3:1-13
Psalm 8
Revelation 21:1-6*a*

Matthew 25:31-46

January 6, 1996
Epiphany of the Lord
Isaiah 60:1-6
Psalm 72:1-7, 10-14
Ephesians 3:1-12
Matthew 2:1-12

January 7, 1996
Baptism of the Lord
Isaiah 42:1-9
Psalm 29
Acts 10:34-43
Matthew 3:13-17

January 14, 1996
2nd Sunday After the
  Epiphany
Isaiah 49:1-7
Psalm 40:1-11
1 Corinthians 1:1-9
John 1:29-42

January 21, 1996
3rd Sunday After the Epiphany
Isaiah 9:1-4
Psalm 27:1, 4-9
1 Corinthians 1:10-18
Matthew 4:12-23

January 28, 1996
4th Sunday After the Epiphany
Micah 6:1-8
Psalm 15
1 Corinthians 1:18-31
Matthew 5:1-12

February 4, 1996
5th Sunday After the Epiphany
Isaiah 58:1-9*a* (9*b*-12)
Psalm 112:1-9 (10)
1 Corinthians 2:1-12 (13-16)
Matthew 5:13-20

February 11, 1996
6th Sunday After the Epiphany
Deuteronomy 30:15-20 or
  Sirach 15:15-20
Psalm 119:1-8
1 Corinthians 3:1-9
Matthew 5:21-37

February 18, 1996
Transfiguration Sunday
Exodus 24:12-18
Psalm 2 or *Psalm 99*
2 Peter 1:16-21
Matthew 17:1-9

February 21, 1996
Ash Wednesday
Joel 2:1-2, 12-17 or *Isaiah 58:1-12*
Psalm 51:1-17
2 Corinthians 5:20*b*–6:10
Matthew 6:1-6, 16-21

February 25, 1996
1st Sunday in Lent
Genesis 2:15-17; 3:1-7
Psalm 32
Romans 5:12-19
Matthew 4:1-11

March 3, 1996
2nd Sunday in Lent
Genesis 12:1-4*a*
Psalm 121
Romans 4:1-5, 13-17
John 3:1-17 or *Matthew 17:1-9*

March 10, 1996
3rd Sunday in Lent
Exodus 17:1-7
Psalm 95
Romans 5:1-11
John 4:5-42

March 17, 1996
4th Sunday in Lent
1 Samuel 16:1-13
Psalm 23
Ephesians 5:8-14
John 9:1-41

March 24, 1996
5th Sunday in Lent
Ezekiel 37:1-14
Psalm 130
Romans 8:6-11
John 11:1-45

March 31, 1996
Passion/Palm Sunday
Liturgy of the Palms
Matthew 21:1-11
Psalm 118:1-2, 19-29
Liturgy of the Passion
Isaiah 50:4-9*a*
Psalm 31:9-16
Philippians 2:5-11
Matthew 26:14–27:66 or
    Matthew 27:11-54

April 4, 1996
Holy Thursday
Exodus 12:1-4 (5-10), 11-14
Psalm 116:1-2, 12-19
1 Corinthians 11:23-26
John 13:1-17, 31*b*-35

April 5, 1996
Good Friday

Isaiah 52:13–53:12
Psalm 22
Hebrews 10:16-25 or
    Hebrews 4:14-16; 5:7-9
John 18:1–19:42

April 7, 1996
Easter Day
Acts 10:34-43 or *Jeremiah 31:1-6*
Psalm 118:1-2, 14-24
Colossians 3:1-4 or *Acts 10:34-43*
John 20:1-18 or *Matthew 28:1-10*

April 14, 1996
2nd Sunday of Easter
Acts 2:14*a*, 22-32
Psalm 16
1 Peter 1:3-9
John 20:19-31

April 21, 1996
3rd Sunday of Easter
Acts 2:14*a*, 36-41
Psalm 116:1-4, 12-19
1 Peter 1:17-23
Luke 24:13-35

April 28, 1996
4th Sunday of Easter
Acts 2:42-47
Psalm 23
1 Peter 2:19-25
John 10:1-10

May 5, 1996
5th Sunday of Easter
Acts 7:55-60
Psalm 31:1-5, 15-16
1 Peter 2:2-10
John 14:1-14

May 12, 1996
6th Sunday of Easter
Acts 17:22-31
Psalm 66:8-20
1 Peter 3:13-22
John 14:15-21

May 19, 1996
Ascension Sunday
Acts 1:1-11
Psalm 47 or *Psalm 93*
Ephesians 1:15-23
Luke 24:44-53

May 26, 1996
Pentecost Sunday
Acts 2:1-21 or *Numbers 11:24-30*
Psalm 104:24-34, 35*b*
1 Corinthians 12:3*b*-13 or
    Acts 2:1-21
John 20:19-23 or *John 7:37-39*

June 2, 1996
Trinity Sunday
Genesis 1:1–2:4*a*
Psalm 8
2 Corinthians 13:11-13
Matthew 28:16-20

June 9, 1996
2nd Sunday After Pentecost
Proper 5 [10]
Genesis 12:1-9 or
    Hosea 5:15–6:6
Psalm 33:1-12 or *Psalm 50:7-15*
Romans 4:13-25
Matthew 9:9-13, 18-26

June 16, 1996
3rd Sunday After Pentecost
Proper 6 [11]
Genesis 18:1-15 (21:1-7) or
    Exodus 19:2-8a
Psalm 116:1-2, 12-19 or
    Psalm 100
Romans 5:1-8
Matthew 9:35–10:8 (9-23)

June 23, 1996
4th Sunday After Pentecost
Proper 7 [12]
Genesis 21:8-21 or
    Jeremiah 20:7-13
Psalm 86:1-10, 16-17 or *Psalm
    69:7-10 (11-15), 16-18*
Romans 6:1*b*-11
Matthew 10:24-39

June 30, 1996
5th Sunday After Pentecost
Proper 8 [13]
Genesis 22:1-14 or
    Jeremiah 28:5-9
Psalm 13 or *Psalm 89:1-4, 15-18*
Romans 6:12-23
Matthew 10:40-42

July 7, 1996
6th Sunday After Pentecost
Proper 9 [14]
Genesis 24:34-38, 42-49, 58-67
    or *Zechariah 9:9-12*
Psalm 45:10-17 or *Song of
    Solomon 2:8-13 or Psalm
    145:8-14*
Romans 7:15-25*a*
Matthew 11:16-19, 25-30

July 14, 1996
7th Sunday After Pentecost
Proper 10 [15]
Genesis 25:19-34 or
    Isaiah 55:10-13
Psalm 119:105-112 or
    Psalm 65:(1-8) 9-13

Romans 8:1-11
Matthew 13:1-9, 18-23

July 21, 1996
8th Sunday After Pentecost
Proper 11 [16]
Genesis 28:10-19*a* or *Wisdom of
    Solomon 12:13, 16-19
    or Isaiah 44:6-8*
Psalm 139:1-12, 23-24 or
    Psalm 86:11-17
Romans 8:12-25
Matthew 13:24-30, 36-43

July 28, 1996
9th Sunday After Pentecost
Proper 12 [17]
Genesis 29:15-28 or
    1 Kings 3:5-12
Psalm 105:1-11, 45*b* or *Psalm 128
    or Psalm 119:129-136*
Romans 8:26-39
Matthew 13:31-33, 44-52

August 4, 1996
10th Sunday After Pentecost
Proper 13 [18]
Genesis 32:22-31 or *Isaiah 55:1-5*
Psalm 17:1-7, 15 or *Psalm
    145:8-9, 14-21*
Romans 9:1-5
Matthew 14:13-21

August 11, 1996
11th Sunday After Pentecost
Proper 14 [19]
Genesis 37:1-4, 12-28 or
    1 Kings 19:9-18
Psalm 105:1-6, 16-22, 45*b* or
    Psalm 85:8-13
Romans 10:5-15
Matthew 14:22-33

August 18, 1996
12th Sunday After Pentecost
Proper 15 [20]
Genesis 45:1-15 or
    Isaiah 56:1, 6-8
Psalm 133 or *Psalm 67*
Romans 11:1-2*a*, 29-32
Matthew 15:(10-20) 21-28

August 25, 1996
13th Sunday After Pentecost
Proper 16 [21]
Exodus 1:8–2:10 or *Isaiah 51:1-6*
Psalm 124 or *Psalm 138*
Romans 12:1-8
Matthew 16:13-20

WORSHIP PLANNING SHEET #1

Date_____   Color:_____

Preacher: _____

Liturgist: _____

Selected Scripture:_____

Selected Hymns	No.	Placement

Psalter #_____

Keyboard Selections

Title	Composer	Placement

Anthems

Title	Choir	Composer	Placement

Vocal Solos

Title	Singer	Composer	Placement

Other Ideas:

Acolytes: _____

Head Usher:_____

Altar Guild contact:_____

Other participants:

_____

WORSHIP PLANNING SHEET #2

Date:_____   Sunday:_____   Color:_____

Preacher: _____

Liturgist:_____

Opening Voluntary   Composer

_____

Hymn   Tune name   No.

_____

Opening Prayer: _____

Prayer for Illumination: _____

First Lesson:_____

Psalter: _____

Second Lesson: _____

Gospel Lesson: _____

Hymn   Tune name   No.

_____

Response to the Word:_____

_____

Prayers of the People:_____

Offertory   Composer

_____

Communion Setting: _____

Communion Hymns   Tune name   No.

_____

_____

_____

Closing Hymn   Tune name   No.

_____

Benediction: _____

Closing Voluntary   Composer

_____

RESOURCE FEEDBACK

Please complete the following questionnaire about this new resource. Suggestions will be used to develop future editions of *The United Methodist Music and Worship Planner*.

The Planner Format

I found the printed format of the Planner to be

_____of little help.

_____of moderate help.

_____of great help.

Suggestions _____

_____

_____

Hymn Suggestions

I found the hymn suggestions to be

_____of little help.

_____of moderate help.

_____of great help.

Suggestions _____

_____

_____

Psalter Reference

I found the psalter reference to be

_____of little help.

_____of moderate help.

_____of great help.

Suggestions _____

_____

_____

Keyboard Suggestions

I found the keyboard suggestions to be

_____of little help.

_____of moderate help.

_____of great help.

Suggestions _____

_____

Suggested collections for inclusion in the Planner _____

_____

_____

Vocal Solos

I found the solo suggestions to be

_____of little help.

_____of moderate help.

_____of great help.

Suggestions _____

_____

Suggested collections for inclusion in the Planner _____

_____

_____

_____

Anthem Suggestions

I found the anthem suggestions to be

_____ of little help.
_____ of moderate help.
_____ of great help.

Suggestions _____

_____

_____

Hymn Anthem Suggestions

I found the hymn anthem suggestions to be

_____ of little help.
_____ of moderate help.
_____ of great help.

Suggestions _____

_____

_____

Other Suggestions

I found the other suggestions to be

_____ of little help.
_____ of moderate help.
_____ of great help.

Suggestions _____

_____

_____

Indexes

I found the indexes to be

_____ of little help.
_____ of moderate help.
_____ of great help.

Suggestions _____

_____

_____

Church Size   _____ 0-100 members
_____ 100-500 members
_____ 500-1000 members
_____ Over 1000 members

Lectionary Use

My church _____ does use the *Revised Common Lectionary* on a regular basis.
_____ does not

Further Comments _____

_____

_____

_____

Send your completed questionnaire to: ***The Music and Worship Planner,*** The United Methodist Publishing House, 201 Eighth Ave., South, Nashville, TN 37203.